D1439031

The Silver Lining

First Limited Edition of 1,000 copies:
April 2003

By: John Haughton (01) 832 5415
email: jjhaughton@hotmail.com

Book design, layout and reproduction:
EGM Design (01) 835 3470
and John Haughton

Cover design:
Ray O'Brien, Ken Kirwan, Conor Walsh and John Haughton

Credits include Gary Casserly and Aidan Kelly both for proof reading and editing.

All maps (except those listed below) are based on Ordnance Survey by permission of the Government (Permit no. 5454).

Published in Ireland by the Finglas Environmental Heritage Project. As in the case of the publications 'Finglas Through the Ages' and 'Finglas - A Celebration', part of the proceeds from 'The Silver Lining' will go towards a further publication in the series.

Set in Adobe Garamond Regular 9.5pt

This book is from a Limited First Edition of 1,000 copies only which is signed and numbered by the author.

This book is no. 452/1000

John Haughton

Acknowledgments

I wish to thank Aidan Kelly, editor of The Northside People, and Gary Casserly of the Finglas Environmental Heritage Project for their support, encouragement and painstaking proof reading of various drafts which was invaluable to me in bringing the project to fruition. Sincere thanks to Pearse Cahill for making photographs available and for the many hours he spent familiarising me with Kildonan and Iona National Airways.

To all the staff of EGM Design, particularly Ray O'Brien, Ken Kirwan, Conor Walsh, Ann Mulvaney, Julie O' Brien and Mark Hanrahan for their very professional approach and personal interest in the book.

Gratitude is due also to the Heritage Council who part funded our previous publication 'Finglas-A Celeberation', thus indirectly helping to make this publication a reality.

Finally, thanks to Pascal Conrey of Albion Properties, Finglas Credit Union, EGM Design and Graham & Heslip for their generous sponsorship. Thanks also Sr. Katherine, Richard O Sullivan, Captain John Duggan, Chris Bruton, Brendan and Gerry Ellis, Oonagh Hammond, Siobhán Mulcahy and Eddie Kinane, The Aviation Museum, Castlemoate House, Collinstown, Dublin Airport: The Foynes Aviation Museum, Limerick: The Military Archives, Dublin.

By Richard O' Sullivan, De Soutter Mark II EI-AAD and Kildonan Aerodrome

Dedication

This book is dedicated to my wife Ann, my daughters Tanya and Neasa, my sons John and Ronan, and my grandson Cameron, my mother, father, brothers and sisters. It is also dedicated to the memory of Lady Heath; her relations and friends; and the people associated with Kildonan, especially Pearse Cahill and the Cahill family without whom the wonder and inspiration of Kildonan would not have existed.

About the Author

John Haughton is a town planner and sociologist and worked for years in the Public Service in Ireland until he retired in 2001. His interest in aviation developed in the 1980s when he pioneered with colleague Dara Larkin a Community Planning Project in Finglas Co.Dublin called The Finglas Enlivenment Project which included the Finglas Environmental Heritage Project. Two publications; Finglas through the Ages and "Finglas - A Celebration" followed. Out of the research John developed a great interest in the aircraft and the people who flew at Kildonan, and the great aviation achievements of the period, particularly the unique achievements of Sophie Pierce better known as Lady Heath. The book represents twelve years of research & dedication. John has travelled widely including Scotland, England, Wales, Spain, Madeira, France, Holland, Hawaii, Poland, USA, Mexico, Former Yugoslavia, Dubrovnic, Montinegro.

Foreword

The writing of this book has taken 12 years and the inspiration was Sophie Pierce whose incredible achievements have not been sufficiently well publicised to date.

If there are any inaccuracies or omissions in this book I sincerely apologise and hope that they can be made good at some future time.

The book is written by one who is not an expert in the field of aviation but who developed a great interest in all aspects of Kildonan Aerodrome, its people and aircraft.

The names of Sophie (Mary) Pierce, Sophie Elliott-Lynn and Lady (Mary) Heath are used interchangably throughout this publication. Also, Marjorie Bayley-Butler became Sister Katherine and the names are also used interchangably throughout the publication.

This book is published by the Finglas Environmental Heritage Project which is a not-for-profit group. The group has published several books about Finglas including "Finglas through the Ages" and "Finglas - A Celebration".

The story of Kildonan is a story of which Finglas can be justly proud.

Contents

Introduction

Chapter One

23 Flying clubs and flying craft

Chapter Two

29 The Flying Flea - Pou de Ciel

Chapter Three

35 James Fitzmaurice and the Flight of the Bremen, 1928

Chapter Four

47 Paddy Saul and the Southern Cross transatlantic flight, 1930

Chapter Five

56 Irish Army Air Corps

Chapter Six

63 The Irish Aero Club

Chapter Seven

69 Pearse Cahill

Chapter Eight

75 Iona National Airways

Chapter Nine

110 Hugh Cahill's role in aviation history

Chapter Ten

117 Ireland's first commercial aircraft

Chapter Eleven

125 Sir Alan Cobham's first Irish air display

Chapter Twelve

138 Everson Flying Services

Chapter Thirteen

159 Dublin Air Ferries

Chapter Fourteen

175 Kildonan - The Aer Lingus connection

Chapter Fifteen

195 Kildonan - 1933-1936 A memory by Sr. Katherine Bayley-Butler

Chapter Sixteen

215 Kildonan - brief reminiscences by Chris Bruton

Chapter Seventeen

219 Kildonan people - by Captain John Duggan

Chapter Eighteen

243 Lady Heath - The Silver Lining - A Tribute by the Author

Chapter Nineteen

255 Lady Heath Ireland's greatest aviator/aviatrix

278 Forgotten Herione - Lady Mary Heath by Siobhán Mulcahy

Appendix 1

302 Kindonan Roll Call - Supplementary

Pioneers Poem by Oliver St. John Gogarty

There are Death Valleys in the air,
Niagaras in the atmosphere,
Vaster than all, and deadlier than
The fields and seas that yield to man.
Deep is the surge no coast confines
Whose landmarks are the heavenly signs,
The sea that makes its mariners
Kinsmen to sun and beaconing stars,
Lords of the world-surrounding blue,
Dauntless, determined to undo
Old Time's conspiracy with Space
Till the Antipodes embrace;
And heaven itself sets side by side
All that the gulfs of the world divide.

O. G.

Aviation, Vol. 1 No. 2, February 1935

Introduction

This book is about the people associated with Kildonan Aerodrome, Finglas, Co. Dublin, Ireland, and about the aircraft which flew there. It is about a special time, the 1930s and the late twenties with a unique atmosphere and ambiance. It is about a place called Finglas. It is about the inter-relationship of people, aircraft, time and place resulting in a unique blend - Kildonan. The unique atmosphere of the time is partly captured by the poems of Oliver St. John Gogarty. Some of his verses are included.

The book is a celebration of what was a golden age of flying, when during a time of peace between two World Wars, the general public, for the first time, discovered the joys of flying.

More than anyone else, this book is about Ireland's greatest aviator/aviatrix, Lady Heath (Sophie Mary Pierce), born in Newcastle West in Limerick. She spent her later years at Kildonan, an aerodrome built by Hugh Cahill. This book celebrates her great adventures.

It sets out to record the contributions of Hugh Cahill, founder of Kildonan; Lady Heath, Ireland's greatest pioneering aviator; J.R. Currie, joint inventor of the 'Currie-Wot' aircraft; Sir Alan Cobham, the greatest proponent of air displays in the 1930s; and the Mayor of Sempill, who played a major role in the development of world-wide civil aviation and paid a special visit to Kildonan. It is also about the multitude of other Kildonan people, from the first flying priest, Fr. Furlong, and his flying dog Bruno; to Sr. Katherine, who left Kildonan to pursue a life in religion and makes the comparison in a unique way between two lives - religion and aviation.

It is about Mick Brady, who serviced the aircraft; and Chris Bruton, prominent member of the National Irish Junior Aviation Club, who for so many years played such an important role in the development of aviation clubs and councils.

It is about Pearse Cahill, son of Hugh, who some 20 years after the flying ceased at Kildonan, re-established Iona National Airways Ltd. The company which Hugh had originally founded, and set up the Irish Aero Club which commemorated the club of the same name which operated at Baldonnel Aerodrome through most of the 1930s side by side with the Kildonan flying clubs.

The book is about Captain J.N. Duggan, whose extraordinary memory for detail of events at Kildonan and aviation in the 1930s helped to verify much of the detail; George Weston, photographer, who left a unique set of photographs taken at the aerodrome; and Oonagh Hammond and her late husband Ivan, both of whom learned to fly at Kildonan. Oonagh talks about the Aer Lingus connection and remembers Ivan, later to become chief pilot with Aer Lingus.

The book is about O.E. Armstrong, chief pilot at Kildonan for several years, who pioneered many demonstration flights in the promotion of civil aviation in Ireland and who became the first chief pilot of Aer Lingus, the national airline.

In many of the chapters, the story of Kildonan is told directly by those who flew at Kildonan or who were actively involved at the aerodrome, including Oonagh Hammond, Chris Bruton, Sr. Katherine and Captain John N. Duggan. Not least of all was George Morris, caretaker and cook at Kildonan, who was a Finglas man and later joined Aer Lingus.

John Roque's 'Environs of Dublin' with improvements and additions by Bernard Scales, 1773

Introduction

For the aircraft enthusiast, details, including photographic coverage, are provided of the many aircraft which flew at Kildonan or visited the aerodrome. A detailed history is provided of the first air charter aircraft which was operated by Iona National Airways Ltd., although it flew from Baldonnel and not Kildonan in 1930. This aircraft was the Desoutter Mark II EI-AAD, which after a long and busy flying history was restored and is now preserved at the terminal building at Launceston Airport, Tasmania, Australia.

The name Finglas is from the Irish 'Fionn Glais', meaning 'bright stream', and takes its name from the small stream which meandered through the village of Finglas. In the 1930s, Finglas, born of Ireland's first 'Golden Age', was rustic and quaint. The bright stream is today buried in culvert under the dual-carriageway which now divides it east and west. The green pastures of the surrounding countryside are now a suburb designed in haste to accommodate the inhabitants of the over-crowded tenements of Dublin's inner city. Green fields, mature trees, history and heritage were all casualties.

Year after year, the inhabitants of Dublin's inner city were forced to sever close kinship ties and to set down shallow roots in an area which was alien to them. They would never fully identify with their new environment and this latter fact, coupled with the retreat of the native villagers and the insensitivity of private and public enterprise, left the entire heritage of the area unprotected.

Today, a new identity and pride of place is being created and heritage has taken on a real meaning for the community. The rich association with history and the arts has been re-discovered. A new identity is emerging - a kind of second Golden Age. How many areas can boast the historical treasures which bedeck Finglas: an early monastic settlement, St. Canice's; a Celtic Cross, the Nethercross; a Norman castle, Dunsoghly; a holy well, St. Patrick's; and an observatory, Dunsink.

It was not just in the sphere of aviation that Finglas was a leader in the 1930s. Merville Dairies, later to become Premier Dairies, was a leader in the development of industrial enterprise in the Irish Free State. Merville Dairies was established at the beginning of the century. Hugh Cahill, founder of Kildonan Aerodrome, serviced the lorries which Merville used to collect the milk for the dairy.

Besides the whine and drone of the little craft flying to and from Kildonan Aerodrome on long never-ending summer evenings during the 1930s, other sounds wafted along the distilled air of sweet summer breezes and vied for attention. It was not the intricate melodies of blackbird and song-thrush, but the piping created by deft hands, whose pitch and timing was so perfect that one wondered if the eerie sounds emanated from earth or ether. These tunes heard over aircraft and bird-song were the creation of the young Finglas born Seamus Ennis and his father who lived at Jamestown Road. Seamus was later to be crowned 'Ard Ri of the uilleann pipes'.

As the sound of aircraft engines soared and fell in seemingly never ending cadences, so did the little 'king' reach the dizzy heights of musical creativity. The result was a unique blend of sound known only to Finglas. Whine and drone alternated between aircraft and musician, each soaring, gliding, falling, like a giant bird of prey, with the grace and blithe spirit of a golden eagle. Each tune from the pipes was a filagree woven in heaven and never to be repeated, full of versatility and virtuosity. Soon the whole country would relish the sounds and Seamus Ennis would make a unique contribution to the musical folklore of these islands.

The cradle of Finglas rocked 'The Child' of commercial aviation in Ireland and the little 'High King' of the uilleann pipes.

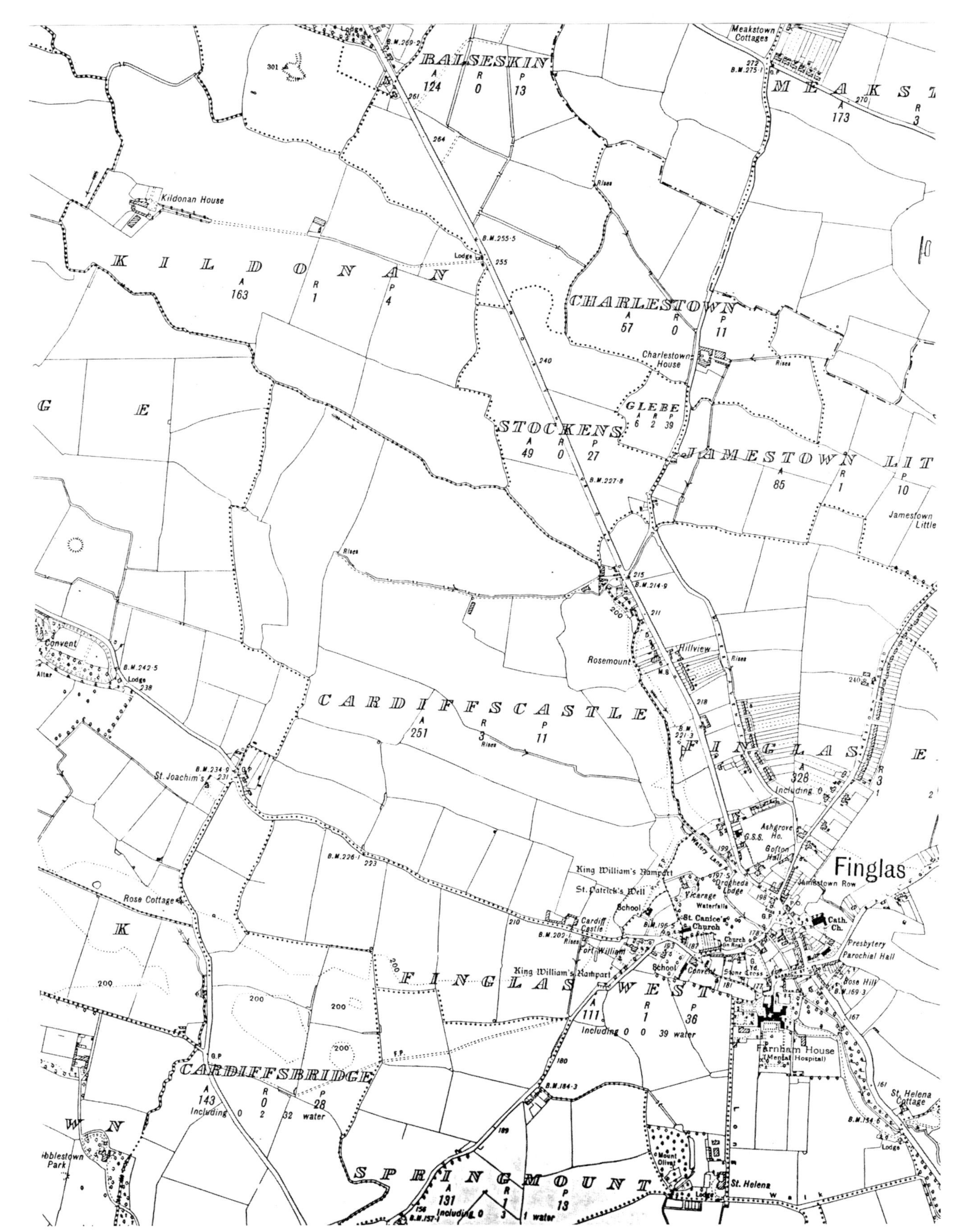

Finglas in the 1930s map

What does the name 'Kildonan' mean to the reader of this book?

Perhaps it is just a pleasant sounding name which, however benign to the ear, has no association with any known place. Yet in the context of the marvel of the infancy of commercial flying in this country, the name Kildonan should be on the lips of every school child. It is not the purpose of this book to ask the why or the wherefore, vis a vis this lack of knowledge, but to put the magical record of a decade of wonderful flying at Kildonan in writing for the first time in a comprehensive way for you, the reader, to experience for yourself.

Kildonan Aerodrome was located about a mile northwest of the village of Finglas, Co. Dublin, adjacent to the Derry Road - a national primary route connecting Dublin with Derry City. Kildonan House, which was located on the Kildonan lands on which the aerodrome existed, is still there and at the time of writing in good repair. Kildonan House is located more than one quarter of a mile directly west of the Derry Road. The aerodrome was located between the above road and Kildonan House. Both the aerodrome and the house were served by the same laneway. Today, the entrance gates to the laneway leading to Kildonan House, not visible from the main road, can be easily located because they are situated immediately south of the ESB electrical power station. A large quarry, Huntstown Quarry, operated by the company Roadstone, has its entrance just north of the ESB station. The fields which were used for the aerodrome remain but the existence of the power station means that there is no possibility of even having a minor commemorative air display there.

Kildonan had a fine big purpose built hangar which could accommodate 20 aircraft, with a larger storage area for parts at first floor level. Attached to the hangar was a very comfortable and spacious club house for staff and visitors. The airfield itself could accommodate the aircraft of the day as witnessed by the fact that it was able to accommodate the largest aircraft of Sir Alan Cobham's Circus. Until Kildonan Aerodrome was approved for use by civil aircraft and customs facilities in June 1932, all aircraft coming from abroad to the Irish Free State had to land at Baldonnel, a military aerodrome, in order to clear customs.

Three different companies operated consecutively at Kildonan between 1931 and 1938. The first was Iona National Airways Ltd., founded by Hugh Cahill. It operated there from 1931 to 1933. This company had been set up a year earlier by Hugh at Baldonnel military aerodrome. Everson Flying Services followed from 1933 to 1935. The name was derived from the two people who operated the company, namely Lady C. Nelson and Mr. George Everett. The name Iona on the other hand originated from the name of Hugh Cahill's automobile garage which was located at Cross Guns Bridge, Glasnevin, Dublin. The third and last company was Dublin Air Ferries, 1935-1938, with Lady Heath and Jack Williams at the helm. The association of Lady Heath with Kildonan goes back several years before the setting up of Dublin Air Ferries and is one which gives a special stamp of achievement to the Kildonan operations. Her achievements in pioneering aviation cannot be over-emphasised.

Kildonan provided a comprehensive range of flying services, varying from time to time in emphasis and intensity. It carried out a multitude of air charter flights, pilot training, emergency ambulance flights, pioneering mail flights, photographic assignments, air displays, novelty flying and joy-riding flights, usually associated with air pageants and displays. One of Hugh Cahill's most ambitious undertakings was a demonstration air mail and passenger flight from Baldonnel to Berlin, via London and Amsterdam, having linked up with a first leg which was flown from Oranmore in Galway by Captain O.E. Armstrong, chief pilot with Iona National Airways Ltd. Colonel Charles Russell, the main proponent of the concept of a national airline in the Irish Free State, was part of the crew of the giant Fokker aircraft which flew the main part of the flight from Baldonnel to Berlin. Through the operations of Kildonan, newspapers could have important photographs of big events in time to meet early editions of their papers. Mercy and ambulance flights were

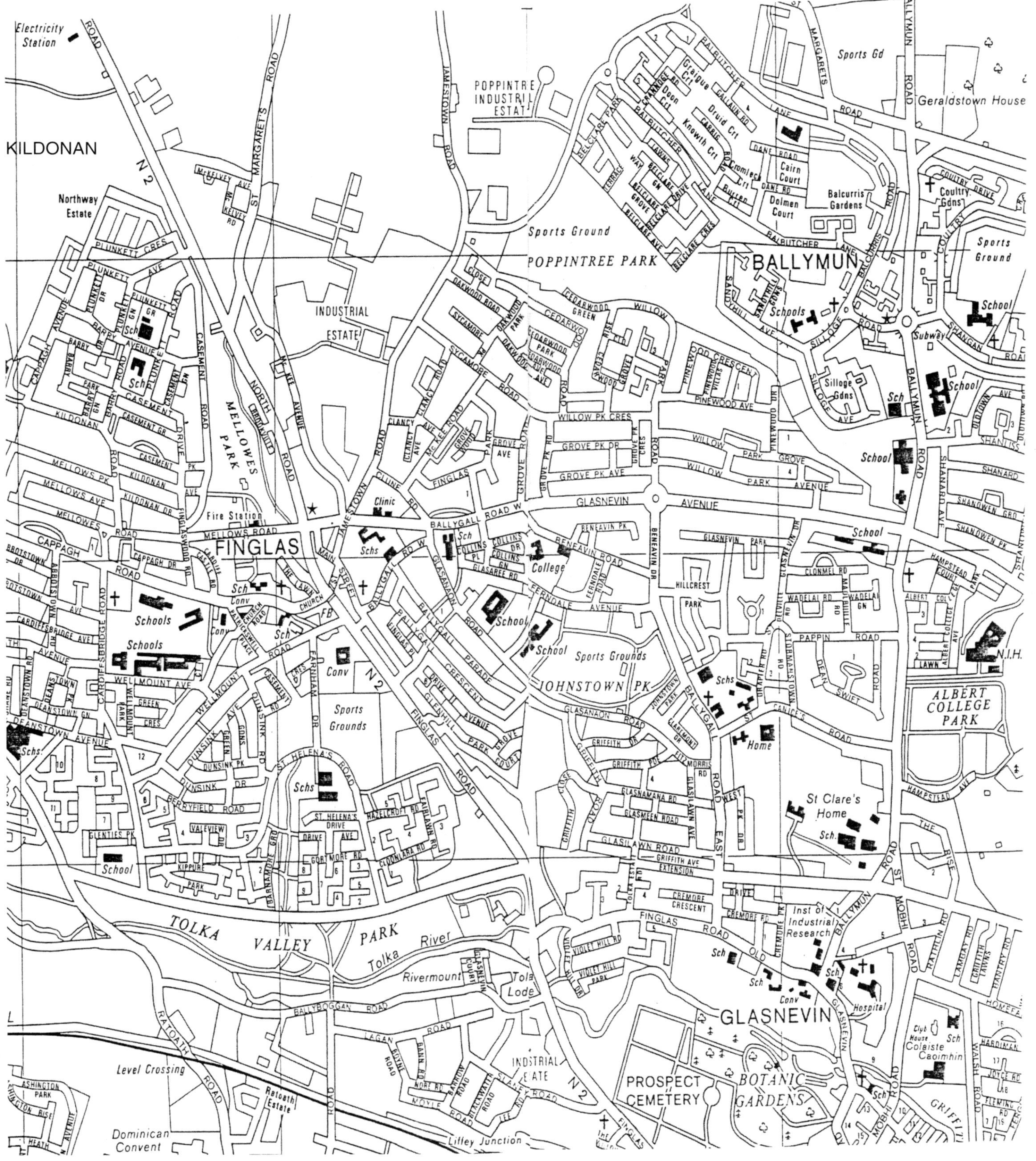

Finglas in the 1990s

In its seven years of business, Kildonan Aerodrome had no fatalities. This was an outstanding record by any standards

now possible and when a massive snow-fall cut off all services and isolated Meath from the rest of the country, Hugh Cahill and Iona National Airways were on hand to bring food and medicine to the affected areas. The food was supplied by the Dublin firm, Findlater's.

In its seven years of business, Kildonan Aerodrome had no fatalities. This was an outstanding record by any standards. It is difficult to access to what extent it was due to the very high levels of maintenance of the Kildonan fleet of aircraft or the supervision of flying operations. In any case, safety first was the motto which was strictly adhered to. In contrast, there were fatalities unfortunately associated with flying operations at Baldonnel Aerodrome, involving both aircraft and personnel of the Irish Aero Club and the Irish Army Air Corps.

During 1933, which also marked the high point in flying activities in the Irish Free State, there were seven fatalities. On May 24th, Major S.W. Dunckley and Mr. Christopher Clayton perished in the sea off Dalkey. Captain W. R. Elliott, chief instructor of the Irish Aero Club, and his passenger, Mr. William Ower, crashed and died in Limerick on July 7th at Sir Alan Cobham's Air Circus. On August 3rd, Lieutenant J.P. Twohig of the Irish Army Air Corps was killed at Clondalkin. Captain Oscar Heron and Private R. Tobin crashed and died at an air display in the Phoenix Park on August 5th.

The 1930s were the golden age of flying in Ireland. Never again would aircraft be so primitive and so dependent on the skill level of the pilot. The pilot was exposed to the elements in an open cockpit, listening to the music of the wires which, together with the struts, kept wings and aircraft together. It was a sound whose pitch depended on the speed of the aircraft like music played by the wind. The pilot was in a way part of the very aircraft which he flew. Its reactions to the nuances of terrain and elements were also his. The relationship was a kind of symbiosis, giving rise to the phrase: "He flew by the seat of his pants." Technology had not yet come between man and machine, insulating him from the excitement and trauma of flight, the agony and the ecstasy.

The primitive aircraft of the 1930s were little more than an open-roof motor car in flight. There was no communication between the pilot and the airfield. Flying was a personal and personalised experience. The pilot's equipment was basic and unsophisticated in the extreme, compared with the luxury of today. Automation has now cushioned the pilot from the essential flying experience. The thrill, the elation, the terror are gone. Flying has become sanitised. Imagine on the one hand flying high in a blue-domed sky with the occasional high-cirrus tail of cloud, as near to heaven as one can get, and on the other hand being pounded on your soft leather helmeted head by hailstones as big as stones, the plaything of the angry elements threatening to hurl you to earth, with the fear of being dashed to pieces on the jagged rocks below, alone, helpless, paralysed with deep shock, unable to communicate with a soul.

Though Hugh Cahill's motivation in setting up Kildonan Aerodrome (and the first company to operate the aerodrome, namely, Iona National Airways Ltd.) was to make it a commercial success, the pervading new-found spirit of the times was about enjoying the freedom of flying in the skies. This feeling was common to the pioneering aviators such as Lady Heath, and to the ordinary citizens who visited Sir Alan Cobham's first Irish air pageant at Kildonan. And apart from Cobham's Circus, as it was called, there were many air displays organised by Iona National Airways Ltd. and the companies which followed, when the public travelled in droves to experience what was advertised as 'joy-riding' over Dublin City and the surrounding areas. Kildonan organised many public displays throughout the country, as did the Irish Aero Club which operated a flying school at Baldonnel Military Aerodrome.

The Barnstorming era:

In the 1920s. and the 1930s. aviation was brought to the masses by the barnstormers. In the United States and Great Britain they traveled around like Elizabethan troupes of players, moving from town to town, landing on any suitable open space, and giving daring air displays. The impetus came in Great Britain from the number of war-surplus aeroplanes. Many young men bought an old Avro 504K or D.H.9, then traveled and flew and put on sensational shows for the spectators. Wing walking, inverted flying, loop the loop, slow roles, "joy-riding"were all included in their routines.

The relatively new phenomenon of personalised aircraft and the spectacle of aircraft flying, unrelated to military life, was something to get very excited about. Barriers were being broken down and flying was no longer the sole preserve of the elite. For the first time, the masses were to enjoy the new experience. They were encouraged to visit Kildonan to view the aircraft and sample the joys of riding high over town and country. There was an open door situation, with no need for security such as one experiences in a modern airport. People were drawn in huge numbers to experience the joy of flying and to savour the sounds, be it whine, dirge or throb, and there were the smells of burnt aviation fuel and the dope painted on the wings, the smell of which often pervaded the hangar. Then there was the leather helmet, the tube which the pilots used to communicate, the gloves and the goggles, which made every pilot look like a flying ace.

John J. Dunne, aviation historian, commenting on the birth of Irish civil aviation, concluded that if any one year can be said to have given flying its major decisive lift, that year can only be 1933 when it really got off the ground in Ireland.

"It would seem that Pegasus, or some other airborne god, had decreed that the Irish people were ready to attack the skies. It was a summer of air shows, or air pageants, or displays, depending on the publicity men involved, when the hitherto earthbound citizenry could flirt with death in the skies above Dublin in gallant little Gypsy Moths or Puss Moths, and all for half a crown a go. The air displays...featured little aircraft in a variety of contortions, like loops, spins, rolls or 'falling leaf' lunacy, that thumbed a nose (or propeller) at all the primary rules of aerodynamics. They walked on canvas wings high above the gasping crowd, hung precariously out of struts and made dramatic parachute descents, while the packed field below held its breath...It was in that year of 1933 that Sir Alan Cobham lectured to a group of would-be aviators in the unlikely surroundings of the gallery of Clery's store in O'Connell Street on his numerous adventures as one of the great pioneers of flying...1933 deserves to be re-called as the year that Ireland got its wings."

Besides Sir Alan Cobham's air circus/pageant, which was held at Kildonan and hosted by Hugh Cahill of Iona National Airways Ltd., there was a multitude of other air displays held at different aerodromes, including Baldonnel. But it was Cobham's Circus at Kildonan which stole the show, where pageantry of the air reached its zenith in an atmosphere which was never to be repeated. The people of Ireland had never seen anything like the flying wizardry of Cobham's Circus. Fifteen thousand people are reported to have seen this never to be forgotten display. The dare-devil flying, loop-the-loop, inverted flying, bombing the crowd, wing spotting, scared, thrilled and satiated the crowd. The hosting of this brilliant spectacle was a first for Kildonan, Hugh Cahill and Finglas. The breathtaking flying wizardry by the world's greatest exponents of these skills took place with the finest collection of the best and most colourful aircraft of the day.

DH9J - close up view (Richard O' Sullivan)

Avro 504K - "Taking off at Tallaght" (Richard O' Sullivan)

Lady Heath

Lady Heath

Hugh Cahill was the first entrepreneur and father of civil aviation in Ireland. Consequently, he has a special place in aviation history. In the late 1920s and 1930s, almost daily new frontiers were being established. Not least of these were the remarkable achievements of Lady Heath (Sophie Pierce), arguably the only home-grown pioneering aviator/aviatrix who can rank amongst the greats. After her amazing feats in aviation, she chose to spend her last active years from 1931 at Kildonan and later on as managing director of the third and last company, Dublin Air Ferries, which operated from Kildonan from 1935-1938.

She, like so many other great aviators had, in the late 1920s, accepted the challenge, risking life and limb, testing the machines to their limit in the furtherance of aviation and for the love of flying. The air routes which we take for granted today were painfully and meticulously worked out the hard way by the pioneers of the day with very often the minimum of equipment and maps. Lady Heath paid the ultimate price for her pioneering efforts when she had an aviation accident in the United States which almost cost her her life. She never recovered from this accident. A mere glance at the record of her achievements is sufficient to realise that she occupies a niche which is unique in Irish and world aviation history. If this book does nothing else but illustrate this clearly, it would be sufficient reward for writing it. Lady Heath is truly the queen of Irish and world aviation, a star among stars.

Lady Heath recieves a bouquet of flowers on her arrival at Croydon aerodrome, following her epic flight from Capetown, South Africa May 17th. 1928

Lady Heath was born Mary Pierce Evans in Newcastle West, Limerick in 1896. She flew the first solo flight from Cape Town, South Africa via Cairo, to Croydon, London and was holder of the world's altitude record. She was the first woman to hold a commercial licence in Great Britain, was the first woman to win an open air race in these islands and was a winner of the coveted Grosvenor Cup. Apart from her personal achievements, not least of all in breaking into the male preserve of commercial flying, she encouraged other women to participate in flying and set up a special scholarship which was administered by the Irish Aero Club. She also helped to gain access for women into other careers from which they were traditionally barred. A keen athlete herself, Lady Heath was a co-founder of the British Women's Amateur Athletic Association and was largely responsible for securing the right for women athletes to participate in the Olympic Games.

Tragically, a near fatal accident, while she was participating in the Ohio State Races, Cleveland, U.S.A., cut short a brilliant flying career and left her with a silver plate inserted in her skull. But she had already achieved more in about five years than any other aviator in Ireland would ever achieve in a lifetime. Some people believed that Lady Heath's aircraft had been tampered with before the race began in Cleveland but this was not proven at the subsequent enquiries.

Lady Heath devoted her final years in developing air-mindedness and participation in flying among many groups of people. Immediately after her great achievements, she gave many lecture tours. After her air crash in the United States, she spent a short time flying with the Irish Aero Club out of Baldonnel but soon moved to Kildonan, where she set up The National Irish Junior Aviation Club, The Tramway Club and the Dublin Aero Club. The present day Aviation Council, the governing body for aviation, can be traced directly from the National Irish Junior Aviation Club. She was also the first president of the Irish Gliding Association.

Together with her husband Jack Williams, she set up the last of the three companies which operated out of Kildonan, namely Dublin Air Ferries.

Lady Heath

One may ask how the great individual achievements of Lady Heath can be compared with the achievements of the Bremen crew, of which James Fitzmaurice was a member. Indeed, one might go further and suggest that the achievements of some of our great airline pilots should also be mentioned in the same league as pioneers such as Sophie Pierce, James Fitzmaurice and Paddy Saul of Southern Cross fame. The steady, dependable, sterling performances of these great pilots do not grab the headlines but taken together, the myriad flights day after day surely add up to greatness. One such pilot learned to fly at Kildonan and went on to become chief pilot of the Irish Free State's first national airline. His dedication to flying and his allegiance to the national airline was nothing short of heroic. His name was Ivan Hammond. And to single out Ivan is not in any way to belittle the achievements of other Irish pilots and airmen, and others who dedicated their lives to flying in this country or abroad. Other names often mentioned in this context are Kelly Rogers and Darby Kennedy.

Also eligible for the Hall of Aviation Fame are the entrepreneurs, such as Hugh Cahill and the men of vision with great insight into what was needed, often far ahead of their times, including men like Col. Charles Russell and Sean O'hUadhaigh. The former sowed the seeds for the great national airline, Aer Lingus. The latter became the first chairman of Aer Lingus. And there were the other two pioneers of Aer Lingus, the first chief engineer Johnny Maher, and their first pilot, Captain Oliver Eric Armstrong, who had flown for years previously at Kildonan Aerodrome.

Tragically, a near fatal accident, while she was participating in the Ohio State Races, Cleveland, U.S.A., cut short a brilliant flying career

Apart from Sophie Pierce, there were other great women aviators, including Lily Dillon, who with E.J. Dease piloted the first aircraft to land on the Aran Islands at Inishmore. The aircraft was a Klemm Swallow, which landed there on March 27th, 1935.

When it is a question of selecting Ireland's greatest aviator/aviatrix, Sophie Pierce stands out in my opinion like a beacon. But it is for the reader of aviation history to form his or her own opinion. In any case, the name James Fitzmaurice is also a main contender for the highest accolade.

Col. James Fitmaurice stamp

Mr. E.J. Dease

Lily Dillon

Oliver St. John Gogarty - pilots' poet

Throughout the history of Kildonan, although the main thrust is one of optimism and great achievement and atmosphere, there are tinges of sadness. Sadness that Kildonan did not last forever; that Lady Heath's ill health cut short such a brilliant aviation career, full of unique achievements. Sadness that historical records are so incomplete.

Oliver St. John Gogarty, himself a pilot and friend of Lady Heath, has written several poems following the deaths of members of the Irish Aero Club (which operated at Baldonnel Aerodrome). These deaths were mourned by all those associated with flying in Ireland. Kildonan had a unique record of no fatalities.

Nothing demonstrates the close association of Finglas and Kildonan Aerodrome more than the fact that the local Roman Catholic curate of Finglas parish, Fr. Furlong, was also a pilot at Kildonan. Fr. Furlong not only flew at Kildonan, but also travelled extensively throughout the country promoting aviation. He was Ireland's first flying priest. Kildonan also had a flying dog because Fr. Furlong brought his red setter 'Bruno' flying with him wherever he went. Kildonan also boasts of a flying nun, Sr. Katherine (Marjory Bayley Butler). Although she did not fly as a nun at Kildonan, Sr. Katherine trained and took out a pilot's licence at the aerodrome, and entered a convent only days after getting her wings. Sr. Katherine's chapter, 'Kildonan - A Memory', is included in this book, together with her comparison between the life of a pilot and the life of religion.

Kildonan, Hugh Cahill and Iona National Airways Ltd. represented the first spring of civil aviation in the Irish Free State. Aer Lingus, which began its operations in 1936 towards the end of the Kildonan enterprise, heralded the second spring. Aer Lingus set up operations, first temporarily at Baldonnel, and then at the disused RAF airfield at Collinstown, now Dublin Airport. This fledgling company of the late 1930s, interrupted for a time by the Second World War, came of age in a very short time. It blossomed into an autumn of plenty, achieving the highest standards in every facet of the aviation business and in time became a symbol of quality and excellence in aviation enterprise.

The opening of a national subsidised airline in 1936, on the doorstep of Kildonan Aerodrome, resulted in both companies competing for what was at the time a very limited market and heralded the death knell for Kildonan. But Kildonan had paved the way for the onward march of civil aviation in the Irish Free State and, as it were, passed the baton on to the national airline. Kildonan had run a very strong first leg of the commercial aviation relay.

De Havilland D.H 84 Dragon in flight

Aer Lingus was formed in 1936, and its first chairman was Sean O'hUadhaigh. The 'Iolar' (the Eagle), a De Havilland 84 Dragon 2 EI-ABI, flew from Dublin to Bristol on its inaugural flight in May 1936. The first Aer Lingus chief pilot was O. E. Armstrong of Kildonan Aerodrome. Ivan Hammond of Kildonan was also one of the first pilots of the new airline.

A second aircraft, a DH 86A, was acquired by Aer Lingus on September 14th, 1936 and registered EI-ABK. This aircraft was named the 'Eire'.

The Iolar was sold in February 1938. A new aircraft, a DH89 Dragon Rapide, was then acquired. This aircraft was named Iolar 11, and registered EI-ABP. The 'Sasana', a DH 86B, registered EI-ABT, was soon added to the fleet.

At the beginning, Aer Lingus Teoranta operated in conjunction with West Coast Air Services Ltd., running regular services between Dublin, Bristol and London, and between Dublin, the Isle of Man and Liverpool, with its registered address at 39 Upper O'Connell Street, Dublin.

Sean O'hUadhaigh was the first chairman not only of Aer Lingus, but also of Aer Rianta Teoranta, which was formed in April 1937.

This book is intended for everyone interested in the birth and golden years of flying in Ireland. It is intended for the aviation enthusiast, for the historian, for all the friends and relations of those who were associated with Kildonan Aerodrome. It is also intended for the people of Finglas. Kildonan was part of Finglas and the aerodrome and its history must be seen in its historical context. The book is also intended for the general reader. Women readers will be particularly interested in the unique achievements of one of Ireland's most remarkable women, Lady Heath.

This book is intended to be a tribute to the many people associated with Kildonan and others who promoted civil aviation in a special way during the lifetime of the aerodrome.

Although the 1930s and the late 20s can be called the golden age of flying, right through this decade the storm clouds of war were gathering on the European mainland. Kildonan and its people were oblivious, or at least unconcerned, by Hitler's meteoric rise to power with all its forebodings. Not so far away were the sounds and rumblings of The Second World War. There were no storm clouds at Kildonan. There were blue skies, the occasional high cirrus and the green fertile pastures of the never ending plain of Moynalta, stretching as far as the eye could see.

The Second World War broke out on September 1st, 1939, when Hitler invaded Poland. All private aircraft were grounded and impounded in the Irish Free State. The civil airfields, including Kildonan, Collinstown and Weston, were staked in order to prevent aircraft landings. Kildonan had already ceased operations in August 1938. Aer Lingus, the national airline, had begun its operations in 1936.

Contents description

A separate chapter is devoted to each of the three companies which operated at Kildonan, namely Iona National Airways Ltd., Everson Flying Services and Dublin Air Ferries. Hugh Cahill was the father of commercial aviation in Ireland, so a separate chapter is devoted to his role.

This is followed by a detailed account of the Desoutter Mark II EI-AAD, which operated for a brief spell at Baldonnel in 1930 before Iona National Airways Ltd. moved to Kildonan. The Desoutter Mark II was in effect Ireland's first commercial aircraft used for charter flights. The highlight of the golden age of the 1930s was 1933, when Sir Alan Cobham held the first and biggest air display at Kildonan and a chapter is devoted to this.

Oonagh Hammond, whose husband Ivan was to become chief pilot of Aer Lingus, has written a chapter entitled 'Kildonan, the Aer Lingus Connection', which highlights important links between personnel of Kildonan and Aer Lingus. Both Oonagh Hammond (Scannell), her husband Ivan and O. E. Armstrong, the first chief pilot of Aer Lingus, did their training (and in the case of Armstrong, his flying) during the 1930s at Kildonan.

Sr. Katherine (Marjory Bayley-Butler) has added to her first account of flying at Kildonan, 'Kildonan - A Memory'.

Chris Bruton was a prominent and enthusiastic member of the National Irish Junior Aviation Club, founded by Lady Heath at Kildonan in order to encourage air-mindedness among young people of the day.

Harry Ferguson, who made the first successful aeroplane flight in Ireland on New Year's Eve, 1909, pictured with Ireland's first aeroplane passenger, Rita Marr

Chris went on to play an important role in the development of the clubs which succeeded the Junior Club, right on to the Aviation Council, the governing body for aviation in the Republic of Ireland. Chris has written the chapter, 'Kildonan - Brief Reminiscences'. The Aviation Council can be traced back directly to its source, The National Irish Junior Aviation Club, founded by Lady Heath.

Captain J. N. Duggan, who learned to fly at Kildonan, has provided the information for the chapter entitled 'Kildonan People'. His recollections are supplemented by this author's research. The chapter for the most part is related in the first person (Captain Duggan's own recollections).

There are two chapters about Lady Heath. Kildonan had many great people but Lady Heath has given it a special stamp of approval not least because of the sustained efforts she made to develop the clubs which she fostered there. 'Lady Heath - Ireland's Greatest Aviator/Aviatrix' details her many achievements. 'The Silver Lining' is a tribute by the author to Lady Heath, an effort to demonstrate her efforts and aspirations as she promoted flying at Kildonan. It is presented as a day in the life of Lady Heath as she journeyed to Finglas and related to the place and the aerodrome, and then taking her aircraft, which she had named 'The Silver Lining', for a flight over the surrounding countryside. Her likely thoughts, reminiscences, fears and aspirations are related, based on the information and facts which some of her friends and acquaintances have related to this author. This chapter is descriptive of Lady Heath, the Finglas area, Kildonan and the flying experience. It is different in style and delivery from the other chapters. This is by design, in order to suit the mood of the occasion. While this book is primarily and substantially about the history of Kildonan Aerodrome, its people and aircraft and the great pioneering aviation achievements of its most famous personality, Lady Heath, the author felt that it was appropriate at the outset to include a number of short chapters as follows:

- Flying clubs and flying craft, as narrated by Captain J.N. Duggan
- The phenomenon of the Flying Flea (Pou du Ciel)
- James Fitzmaurice and the Flight of the Bremen, 1928
- Paddy Saul and the Southern Cross transatlantic (east to west) flight, 1930
- The Irish Army Air Corps
- The Irish Aero Club
- Pearse Cahill, son of Hugh

These represent many of the relevant achievements of the period.

At the beginning of the Century Irishman Harry Ferguson was at the cutting edge of pioneering aviation. He was born in Dromore, County Down. Six years and fourteen days after the Wright brothers' world's first aeroplane flight, he made the first aeroplane flight in Ireland close to his home at Hillsborough, County Down. He built and flew his own aircraft. A replica of Ferguson's original aircraft was constructed by Captain J.C. Kelly Rogers in the 1950's and is at present on display in the Ulster Folk Museum, outside Belfast. This book does not purport to be a complete history of Irish aviation in the late 1920s and 1930s. It is difficult to single out individual achievers for special mentioning when there are so many. Yet in the sphere of the administration of civil aviation, Richard Whitelegge O'Sullivan appears to the author to deserve such a mention.

Richard O'Sullivan, aviator

Richard Whitelegge O'Sullivan

Richard Whitelegge O'Sullivan, who died on June 23rd, 2000, aged 95, belonged to the generation which was at the birth of the age of air travel in Ireland. His life spanned the history of powered flight from the Wright brothers to the Concorde and Jumbo jet. As aeronautical engineer to the Air Corps, he was among a small key group who selected the site at Rineanna, which is now Shannon International Airport. It became the refuelling link for the development of transatlantic air travel and for many years virtually all aircraft flying between the two continents stopped off at Shannon. He selected Rineanna and his decision was backed by Charles Lindberg, who was brought in by Pan American Airways to assist them in building up a route structure linking Europe and North America. Richard O'Sullivan was born in Dublin on May 9th, 1905. He graduated from Trinity College with B.A. and B.E. degrees, in 1927. He went to London and worked with the Fairey Aviation Company as a technical assistant in the design office from 1928 to 1934. During this time he joined the reserve of air force officers' general duties flying branch and was awarded his wings in 1929. In 1934, he was appointed assistant aeronautical engineer to the Air Corps in the Department of Defence at Baldonnel. A year later he was promoted chief aeronautical engineer. In 1945, he transferred to the Department of Industry and Commerce as chief aeronautical officer. He retired from this post in 1970 but was retained as adviser on aeronautics until 1973 when he retired from the Civil Service. In his capacity as chief aeronautical officer, Richard O'Sullivan was responsible for the licensing of aircraft. He had responsibility for the investigation of accidents involving Irish aircraft. He helped to set up the International Civil Aviation Organisation in Montreal which monitored air safety throughout the world. He chaired the governmental investigation into the 1968 Aer Lingus Tuskar Rock crash. A member of the Royal Aeronautical Society since 1933, he was elected Fellow in 1969, served as chairman of the Dublin branch from 1973 to 1976 and as president in 1978.

The Wright Brothers visit the Short Brothers, Wilbur and Orville are seated centre front. The three Short Brothers are in the back (low left) 1909

Short Brothers

No account of Aviation in Ireland in the 1930s would be complete without reference to the Short Brothers. Oswald and Eustace Short first set up a business as manufacturers of Aerial balloons at Hove, Sussex in April 1901. Shorts came to Ireland in 1937. In conjunction with shipbuilders Harland and Wolff, it established an aircraft at Belfast Lough. In 1948 Shorts transferred its Rochester design and manufacturing activities to Belfast. As a result Ireland was the birthplace of world famous aircraft including the Sterling, Sunderland, Sandringham, Sealand, Belfast, Skyvan, Shorts 330, Shorts 360, Sherpa and Tucano. In 1909 Shorts No.2 biplane was the first British aircraft to fly a circular mile. In 1957 the world's first fixed-wing vertical take-off and landing aircraft, the Shorts SC.1 made its maiden flight.

The Silver Streak. The first experimental all-metal biplane built by Shorts.

The Hon. C.S. rolls in his Short-Wright flyer in 1909. The aeroplane was one of the six contracted to Shorts by the Wright Brothers

Chapter One

Flying clubs and flying craft

Chapter 1

Flying clubs and flying craft

Geoffrey De Havilland

The two main aircraft contenders for the flying clubs

The London Aero Club was the first to come into being under the Government subsidised scheme for light aeroplane clubs. Geoffrey de Havilland, with his Moth which had a Cirrus engine originally with about 60 h.p.(rather low), gained a lead on Avro because Avro, while it had machines ready, had intended putting in Armstrong Siddley Gennet engines and for some reason the Gennet engine was not coming up to expectations. The fact that the Gennet engine was not available resulted in the Avros being held up. As a result, it had not got machines available when the clubs wanted them. Geoffrey de Havilland had captured the early market and his machines went into the first clubs to be formed in Britain.

Many pilots favoured the Avro Avian as a far superior aircraft and for very good reason

The clubs had been waiting eagerly for a suitable light aircraft and Geoffrey De Havilland was able to supply it at the right time. Another consequence of the opportune timing by de Havilland was that once some early owners bought their own Moths and started to embark on long distance record flying, that established the de Havilland Moth. Eventually, the Avro Avian came on the market, having rejected the Armstrong Siddley Gennet engine, settling instead for the Cirrus II but it had lost out considerably to de Havilland, who had also put a lot of money into advertising. Geoffrey de Havilland also leased Stag Lane Aerodrome to the London Aero Club, which became its own airfield. He leased it at very reasonable terms to the London Aero Club and that was another very clever move or marketing strategy.

However, many pilots favoured the Avro Avian as a far superior aircraft and for very good reason. In the case of the Moth, the centre section struts appeared structurally weak for the machine and if the pilot made a heavy landing, he would see the struts bow out or flex excessively. It may have been a safety factor but it was very off-putting. Sometimes when attempting a loop, when one came over the top and the pressure on the wing changed from the lower wing to the upper wing, these struts would flex violently, unnerving the pilot. You never got that in the Avro, which was altogether a more robust machine with a far better undercarriage as well, with certain modifications invented by that superb pilot, Bert Hinkler. So much for the two main contenders for the flying club market for light aircraft.

A.V. Roe

The Armstrong Siddley Gennet was a seven cylinder, air cooled radial engine, the cylinders being splayed out in the radius of a circle. It was regarded as a good engine when the manufacturers overcame the initial faults. It did hold back the Avros because the company had intended, and had built, its machines to take a radial engine rather than an in-line engine. Consequently, it had to re-design the forward part of the fuselage in order to accommodate an in-line engine.

The Cirrus engine was developed by a firm called A.D.C. (Aircraft Disposal Company) which was formed after the First World War to sell off surplus aircraft from the Royal Air Force. You would buy Avro 504Ks., which had been the basic trainer and a very good one throughout the war years and for many years to come with the R.A.F., but you could still buy from A.D.C. an engine which it had developed and came to be known as the Cirrus I. It developed through Cirrus II, Cirrus III and Cirrus Hermes and each engine was certainly better than its predecessor. By the time it got to Cirrus III, the engine was, in the opinion of many experts, far superior to what de Havilland developed later as the Gypsy engine.

Avro 504

Captain Kennedy getting ready to take off in his Tiger Moth

The Gypsy engine

De Havilland, having flown in the war, was aware that the French firm of Renault had a V.8 engine which was well known for its reliability in one of the early wartime aircraft called a de Havilland Six, a machine which was really a forerunner of the Moth. It looked like a big moth aircraft in layout. This Renault engine was known throughout the Royal Flying Corps and R.A.F. as a thoroughly reliable engine, a real old work-horse. It had no outstanding performance in other regards. Geoffrey De Havilland focused on this engine and thought that if he split the crank-case to take just four cylinders, he would have his engine. In effect, he made two engines out of one. Instead of having two banks of cylinders as you had in the Renault V.8, you now had one bank of four.

The Moth was developed in 1924 and came on the market in 1925. De Havilland had decided to manufacture an engine of his own rather than rely on the Cirrus I which was not a sufficiently reliable engine. He had started off at first with the Cirrus I engine because there was nothing else available at the time for that type of aircraft.

Tiger Moth

Probably the most famous training aircraft of all, the Tiger Moth first flew in 1931. When production ended, more than 7,000 had been built in Britain, Canada, Australia and New Zealand. Relatively few are still airworthy. Its distinctive de Havilland-style tail and swept-back wings make the Tiger Moth fairly easy to recognise. Powered by a 130hp Gypsy Major engine, the Tiger Moth cruises at about 90 mph (145km/hr).

D.H. Tiger Moth. Maker: De Havilland, UK

EI-AHM. Owned, flown and here photgraphed by George Flood, Dublin, this immaculate DH82A Tiger Moth is any pilot's dream

Captain P.W. (Darby) Kennedy

Darby Kennedy learned to fly with the Irish Aero Club in 1932. He went on to qualify as a pilot with the Air Service Training School at Hamble in England. While there he qualified also in engineering and telegraphy. In 1935 he joined Imperial Airways and flew their long routes and skippered their flying boats. He set up Weston Aerodrome and Flying School in 1938. Weston is located near Leixlip on the Dublin Kildare border. His first aircraft there was a BA Swallow, a low-wing monoplane with a Pobjoy radial engine, and a development of the Klemm Swallow. In the same year he joined Aer Lingus as a First Officer. O.E. Armstrong, Ivan Hammond (both from Kildonan Aerodrome) and B. Blythe were Captains at that time. Between 1945 and 1947 he was Chief Pilot at Aer Lingus after which he left to develop his air charter and flying school at Weston Aerodrome. In 1960 he rejoined Aer Lingus. He retired from Aer Lingus in 1971. Apart from the air charter and flying school, Weston was also used as a base for films such as the Blue Max and Darling Lili. At the time of writing, Darby Kennedy is retired and living in Spain.

The late Arthur Wignell DD (EI-BKA), Pitts Special

A section of the housing available for privately-owned machines at Stag lane, the home of the Moth. A lock-up may be rented at less than the cost of similar facilities for a car in London. Below is a corner of the Moth Garage. The folding wings enable at least three times as many mchines to be housed in a given space

Chapter Two

Chapter

The Flying Flea - Pou du Ciel

Chapter Two

The Flying Flea - Pou du Ciel

The Flying Flea

(A machine christened 'The Flying Flea' is now being manufactured in England at a cost of £75)

I've had a flip in a Monospar,
I've held the stick of a Moth:
I've looped the loop in an Avro Swoop,
And with Angels plighted troth.
But these are rather expensive things,
Too dear for a chap like me;
And I itch to fly through the azure sky,
On the wings of a Flying Flea.
I've flown to Berlin in the Dutchman's 'Dove',
And that was a hearty trip;
And once I crashed and a hedgerow smashed,
At the end of a joyous flip.
But that was several years ago,
And now I am glad to see;
That for 'Seventy Five' I'll zoom and dive,
On the wings of the Flying Flea.

P.O.P.

The first 'Pou du Ciel' (Flying Flea) home made aeroplane constructed in England made a flight to Heston, Middlesex, recently. Less than 10ft. in length, it can be built for about £75. It has a 10h.p. Ford engine, converted for use in the 'Pou' by Sir John Carden. The machine was constructed by Mr. S. V. Appleby. Photo shows Mr. S. V. Appleby seated in his 'Pou du Ciel' ready for flight. Topical Press photograph

The idea that the man in the street, the amateur constructor, could build and fly his own aircraft was banned for all times

M. Henri Mignet of France had been working for a long time on the idea of a really low-powered aeroplane. When he had built the Pou du Ciel, Flying Flea No. 4, in August 1933, it became an established class. It had a simple 20 h.p. inverted twin Aubier-et-Dunne two stroke engine. Mignet crossed the Channel in his aircraft and gave the first public demonstration in England at Shoreham Aerodrome in Sussex. Thousands of spectators watched the little aircraft, with its peculiar tandem wing arrangement.

For a time in France and in England, it became a craze among many enthusiasts to send for the assembly kit and instructions and to build the Flying Flea at home and attempt to fly it. But the little aircraft was inherently unstable and it was soon banned. The idea that the man in the street, the amateur constructor, could build and fly his own aircraft was banned for all times. Flying could not be brought to the masses in this way. The dream of personalising aircraft just as you would a motor car, which was conceived by many in the wave of hysteria which accompanied the great displays of the golden age of the 1930s, was heavily dented by the danger perceived in putting an aircraft in the hands of an amateur.

So gradually, the shutters went up. Licensing rules and regulations became more debilitating and the idea of the ordinary man in the street flying his own aircraft, just as he might drive his car, became more and more a pipe dream. The many Flying Fleas which had been constructed in the sheds and garages of Britain were never to fly once the ban had been imposed. An exception was G-AEBB, built in Southampton by Kenneth W. Owen, which first flew in Eastleigh in early 1936. It was one of the few Fleas to receive a renewed authorisation to fly after the general ban. In 1941, this aircraft was passed to the 424 Squadron of the Air Training Corps at Southampton for ground handling and instructional purposes and remained with the squadron until it was donated to the Schuttleworth Collection at Old Warden, where it was restored to taxiing condition. The engine in this model was originally a 1,300 c.c. Henderson and as restored, a 25 h.p. Scott Squirrel.

The Mignet-designed Pou du Ciel craze did not hit the Irish Free State and only three or four machines were built in total, one of which was built by J.C. Malone, who had in 1930 accompanied Hugh Cahill to England to collect his very first aircraft for his new Iona National Airways venture, the Desoutter Mark II.

Some observers might think that even the mention of this tiny aircraft, the Flying Flea, is totally irrelevant to a discussion on aviation in the Irish Free State and particularly so in the case of Kildonan. But not so, because this machine was thought for a time to be capable of bringing flying right down to the grassroots. The Flying Flea could be built at home at a cost of £80 and was marketed at £150.

Mignet Pou du Ciel G-AEBB

The Auto Giro

Juan de la Cierva, inventor of the Autogiro

The "Autogiro"

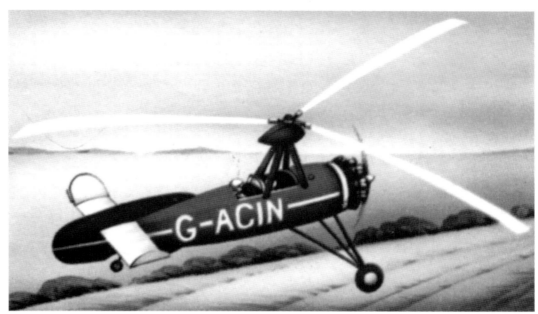

Cierva Autogiro

The autogiro was a plane with no wings and the precursor of the helicopter. Juan de la Cierva invented it. On the 18th. of September 1928 the Cierva C.8. 11 Autogiro with a 200 h.p. Lynx engine piloted by its inventor crossed the English Channel for the first time. There were teething problems associated with the initial design. Unlike the helicopter, which was to supercede it, the engine did not propel the rotor blades and a long take-off run was required. The Autogiro got its lift from a free windmill one free to rotate not driven by an engine. The engine drove an airscrew, which pulled the machine along, and the forward movement then caused the lifting windmill to rotate and to produce lift. On bumpy take-off ground the rotor blades could collide with the tail.

The Autogiro was a combination between a plane and a helicopter

One of Cierva's Autogiro, 5 blade propeller

With the ban on any further flying of the Flying Flea, it was back to the aero clubs to popularise flying

Also in this category, that is, the 'flying scooter' class, was a new 'Drone' which could be built at home with parts supplied by the makers for £175. There were several other rivals of the Flying Flea. Following two fatal accidents in France, General Delain, the Minister for Air, ordered a thorough inspection of the Midget design by experts. The Flying Flea had no aileron control and although its design made this unnecessary, the fact remains that the machine responded in a different manner to the pilot's handling than the ordinary machine. When a pilot flying a Flea attempted to correct a lateral tilt by instinctive movement of the joystick, the effect was the opposite to that which he was accustomed and this could be fatal.

Although J. C. Malone built a Pou du Ciel at his home in Malahide Co. Dublin, he never flew the aircraft. Pearse Cahill, son of Hugh Cahill, recalls building one. Scott's Flying Circus, successor to Sir Alan Cobham's air pageants, included a Pou du Ciel in his display in the Phoenix Park in 1936. This aircraft was registered G-AEFK.

In January 1937, one of the very few Flying Fleas built in the Irish Free State, the handiwork of Messrs. William Benson, Grace and Gallagher, was at Kildonan undergoing final adjustments prior to being test flown.

With the ban on any further flying of the Flying Flea, it was back to the aero clubs to popularise flying. In the case of England, it was the subsidised flying clubs, starting with the London Aero Club and the Lancashire Aero Club which popularised flying. And it was the coming of the Gypsy Moth and the Avro Avian which operated in these clubs and were the popular aircraft of the day. There were many good aircraft between times but the Gypsy and the Avian more than held their own, dominating the scene. Some like the Bluebird disappeared. The Robinson Redwing carried on, right up to the last war. That was an excellent aircraft too.

It was left to the clubs and the club atmosphere to popularise flying and keep the idea of personalised flying alive. In the case of The Irish Free State, the relevant clubs were The Irish Aero Club, situated at Baldonnel; the Dublin Aero Club; The National Irish Junior Aviation Club; and The Tramways Aero Club, which began at Kildonan.

The clubs in Britain supplied the nucleus of pilots for the Royal Air Force, both men and women. The women went to the A.T.A. and the men went directly into the service.

Aviation, June 1935

THE IRISH TIMES, WEDNESDAY, JULY 4, 1928.

BLIN'S WELCOME TO THE BREMEN CREW.

Dublin's welcome to The Bremen crew

Chapter Three

James Fitzmaurice and the Flight of the Bremen, 1928

Professor Hugo Junkers

Chapter 3

James Fitzmaurice and the Flight of the Bremen, 1928

Professor Hugo Junkers

The Bremen was the brainchild of Professor Hugo Junkers. He had started business as a manufacturer of water heating appliances at Dessau. Due to his interest in aviation, he built an aviation research centre in 1910. In 1915, he built his first aircraft, a Junkers JU-1. During the war, in association with Anthony Fokker, he produced some 400 military aircraft. After the war, Professor Junkers constructed the first all metal low wing monoplane. But it was his W-33 which was particularly successful, establishing several long distance endurance records. This aircraft had the characteristic corrugated sheet metal skin.

The Atlantic east to west - an impossible task

Different theories have been put forward to explain the very frightening number of fatalities which wiped out so many experienced pilots

Up to the time of the successful Bremen flight, an east-west crossing of the Atlantic was regarded as still virtually impossible. American flyers, Charles Lindberg among them, refused huge sums of money to take up the challenge. Such was the fear of attempting an east-west crossing that two American companies had offered the princely sum of $50,000 ($2 million in today's terms) for the American who would make the first east-west crossing. Less than a year before, two gallant Frenchmen, Nungesser and Coli, had left the Paris Velodrome for America - never to return. Their aircraft was a Lavasseur landplane. This was early 1927, while later the same year a seasoned Imperial Airways airman, Colonel Minchin, with Princess Lowenstein Wertheim and Leslie Hamilton, flew the east-west route. It is believed that they got as far as Newfoundland, only to die in the surrounding waters. Doomed also was Captain Hinchliffe, who was also an Imperial Airways pilot, and Miss Elsie Mackay, who met the same fate in a Stinson monoplane.

Different theories have been put forward to explain the very frightening number of fatalities which wiped out so many experienced pilots. Weather conditions alone are not a sufficient explanation. One theory which deserves serious consideration is that put forward by Fred W. Hotson in his excellent book, 'The Bremen', namely the 'spiral dive' or the 'death spiral' as it was called. This phenomenon was experienced and commented on by Alcock and Brown in relation to their west to east crossing of the Atlantic in 1919 and was also experienced and analysed by Captain Koehl vis a vis his attempted east to west crossing in 1927. Fitzmaurice's experience in flying the 'Camel' aircraft, which with its rotary engine tended to go into a vicious spin, could have been invaluable in overcoming the death spiral, which the Bremen crew may have encountered during their historic flight. Fitzmaurice and Koehl were probably equally competent in the face of such an eventuality.

The Princess Xenia. A single-engined Bristol Jupiter Fokker 7 monoplane. It was painted brown and blue

In 1927 an Imperial Airways pilot Captain Robert Henry (all weather mac) Mcintosh persuaded an American millionaire, William B. Leeds to finance his attempt at an east-west crossing of the Atlantic. He chose "The Princess Xenia" a fokker single engine monoplane as his aircraft and Commandant James Christopher Fitzmaurice of the Irish Army Air Corps as his co-pilot. With the help of Count John McCormack and Senator Oliver St. John Gogarty £11,000 was raised for the pioneering effort of Fitmaurice. They aborted the flight because of fierce weather conditions. They landed on Beale strand near Ballybunnion, Co.Kerry. A month before two German Junkers W.33 aircraft, the "Bremen" and the "Europa" had set from Dessau airfield for the east to west crossing of the Atlantic. Both flights were abandoned, the first due to bad weather and the latter because of engine trouble.

The 70 radio station hook-up meant that every American was in tune with the momentous happenings

James Fitzmaurice was everyone's idea of a dashing airman. He looked the part as well as fulfilling all aspects of the role. Koehl was a burly little man, wearing a felt hat. He did not look like an airman at all. Yet he held the Blue Max, the decoration 'pour la merite'. He was a 'superb' airman nevertheless and this was the highest honour a German pilot could receive.

The Baron Gunther von Heunefeld was a formidable sight. He had only one eye and wore a monocle. He was quite tall and thin.

Commandant James C. Fitzmaurice was, at the time of the Bremen flight, Officer Commanding the Irish Army Air Corps, whose headquarters were at Baldonnel Aerodrome, now Casement Aerodrome. He was born on January 6th, 1898 in Dublin. Like Captain Koehl, he had also made an unsuccessful attempt to cross the Atlantic in 1927, when he was co-pilot of the 'Princess Xenia' with Captain R.H. McIntosh.

A Royal welcome in the U.S.A.

As already stated, the story of the Bremen has been best told by Fred Hotson in a book of the same name, i.e.'The Bremen'. He recalls in his account that for 19 days, the New York Times carried headlines relating to this epic flight on its front page. A special act had to be passed by Congress to allow the first decoration of non-Americans. The pitch of excitement in the United States was unprecedented. The three airmen were mega stars. The New York Times recorded 11,663 phone calls about the Bremen.

New York's welcome to the Bremen crew was broadcast through a network of 70 radio stations, accounting for practically every wavelength. The crowds grew bigger and bigger, choking the arteries of the city. There was no more room on the sidewalks. Planes flew overhead in salute. Thousands more looked in admiration out of every building along the victory route, waving and throwing streamers which formed a vast carpet for the victors as they paraded along Broadway towards the City Hall. Mayor Walker stood up to address the crowd when the crew had joined the welcoming party. When the speeches were over, a woman, in wavering falsetto, sang the 'Star Spangled Banner' as the crowd grew silent and stood to attention.

When these formalities were over, the victors continued their parade up Fifth Avenue to Central Park. They passed Madison Square, packed to capacity, and the Statue of the Eternal Light. The 70 radio station hook-up meant that every American was in tune with the momentous happenings. All three of the Bremen pilots addressed the U.S. Congress with Fitzmaurice wearing the uniform of the Irish Army Corps.

Junkers F-13 in flight.
The Junkers F-13 was one of the most significant aeroplanes ever built - with the 1st practicable cantilver, low-wing, all metal passenger machine

The Bremen

East-west transatlantic flights

1) Goose Bay 2) Greenly Island, where the Bremen landed 3) Gander stop off for E-W flights until the jets, even now used at times of very bad conditions by the Jumbos 4) Tim Severin and perhaps St. Brendan landed 5) Harbour Grace, where Kingsford Smith on his way from Portmarnock to New York was forced to stop-off in 1930. Paddy Saul of Sutton was navigator (almost forgotten also). Mollison (solo) was also forced to stop-off here on his flight from Portmarnock to New York in 1932

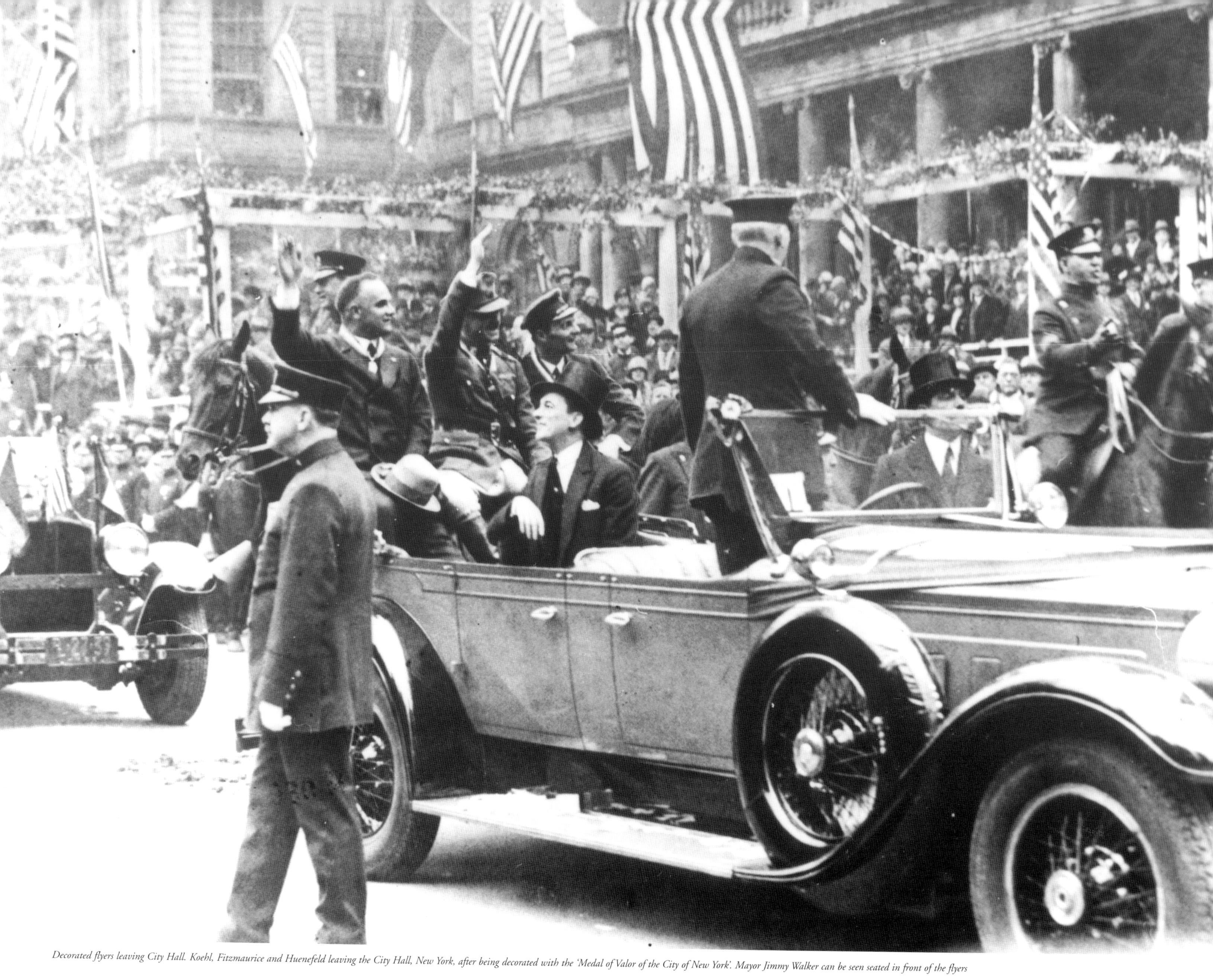

Decorated flyers leaving City Hall. Koehl, Fitzmaurice and Huenefeld leaving the City Hall, New York, after being decorated with the 'Medal of Valor of the City of New York'. Mayor Jimmy Walker can be seen seated in front of the flyers

New York welcome for the Bremen crew, Broadway. Topical Press Agency

Heart of Homage! Multitude merges in one beat

Chicago Herald and Examiner - Sunday May 13, 1928

Gripping scene at Soldier Field Stadium, where 100,000 persons gathered and gave flyers their just tribute. School children, patriotic societies and civic organisations formed a great heart through which coursed the colours of the flags of America.

Germany and Ireland while packed grandstands roared their approval of the gorgeous tribute. The picture shows the size of the immense crowd that poacked the stadium to pay tribute to the flyers

The Atlantic flyers are welcomed in New York. The daring crew of the Bremen-Baron von Huenefeld, Major Fitzmaurice and Capt. Koehl-parade up Broadway amidst a virtual shower of torn paper and ticker tape and New York's millions hail their heroic feat. Topical Press Agency

The Bremen Crew:
The Metropole, Dublin, The Graphic Studios, 114 St. Stephen's Green West, Dublin

Commdt. James Fitmaurice (hands on hips) with a group of pilot Officers at Baldonnel in 1927

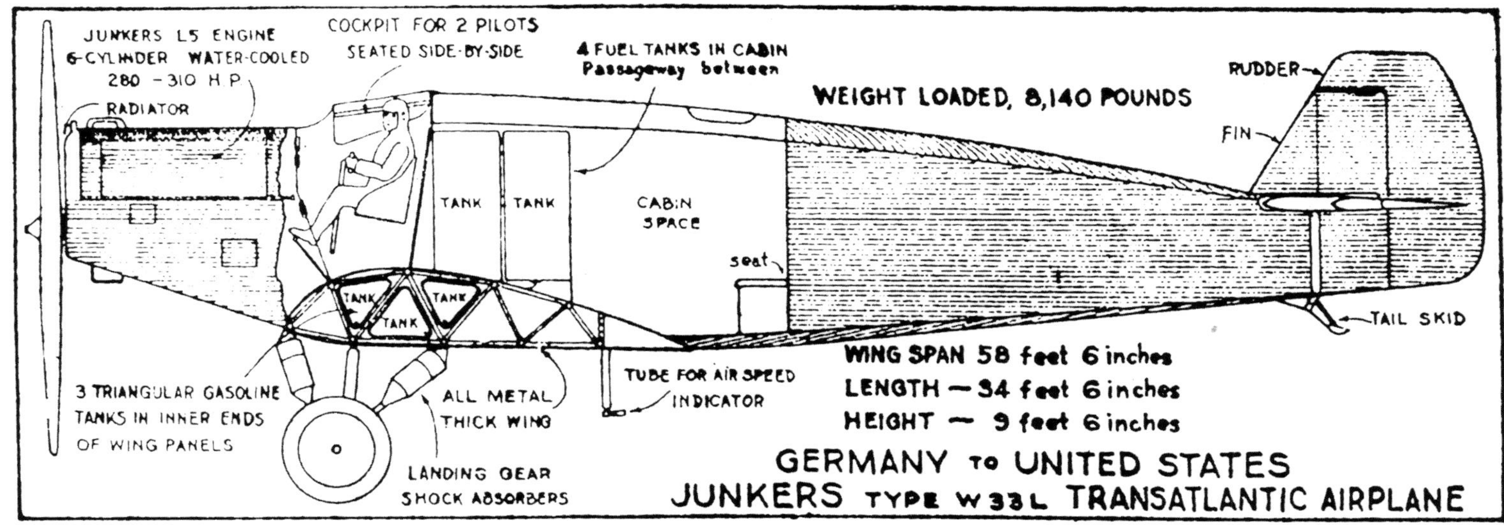

The plan of the "Bremen"

'Fitz' and 'All-weather Mac' dauntless pilots of Princess Xenia, were to meet many years after their transatlantic adventure as guests on 'This is Your Life'

Bremen: A Junkers W33 Freighter. Wingspan 70.75m, length 10.5m, speed 180km/h, range 1000km. The type served with Lufthansa from 1928 to 1942.

Unfortunate. the Vimy damaged by landing in a bog

The Vickers Vimy at Newfoundland, before its epic flight.

Artist impression of Vickers vimy in flight

The Bremen and Dunsink Observatory

Charles Martin of Dunsink Observatory, Finglas, played a vital role in the Flight of the Bremen. He was assistant astronomer at Dunsink Observatory from 1893 until 1921 when he became acting director - a post he held until his death in June 1936. In recognition of his ability, he was awarded an M.A. degree by Trinity College in 1921. His total service of 43 years at Dunsink exceeds that of any other person except Charles Thompson, assistant from 1817 to 1874. Charles Martin was keenly interested in long distant aviation and was instrumental in planning the course taken by the first successful E-W Atlantic flight by Baron von Huemefeld, Captain Koehl and Major Fitzmaurice in the Junkers aircraft, 'Bremen', in April 1928. This piece of navigational work was clearly of great importance and successful.

Source: ' Dunsink Observatory, 1785-1985, A Bicentennial History ' by Patrick A. Wayman

Arthur Whitten Brown

John Alcock

James Fitzmaurice (1898-1963)

RECORD ATLANTIC FLIGHTS

Date	Pilot	Distance	Time	Machine
June, 1919	Sir John Alcock and Sir Arthur Whitten Brown	1,890 miles—First non-stop Atlantic aeroplane flight. From St. John's, Newfoundland, to Ireland, winning *Daily Mail* £10,000 prize.	16 hours, 12 minutes ..	Twin-engined Vickers biplane.
1924	U.S. Army airmen ..	27,000 miles—In stages round the world	336 flying hours	Douglas biplanes
1926	Commandante Franco	6,259 miles in stages from Spain to South America, including non-stop ocean flight of 1,500 miles.	59½ hours	Dornier flying-boat
May 20-21, 1927	Capt. Lindbergh ..	3,639 miles—New York to Paris non-stop. (First solo flight across Atlantic.)	33½ hours	220-h.p. Ryan monoplane
April, 1928	Capt. Kohl, Baron von Huenfeld, Commander Fitzmaurice.	2,300 miles—Ireland to Labrador. (First non-stop North Atlantic aeroplane flight from east to west.)	36 hours	German Bremen monoplane.
June, 1930	Squad.-Ldr. Kingsford-Smith.	1,900 miles—Ireland to Newfoundland. (Second non-stop North Atlantic flight from east to west.)	32 hours, 17 minutes ..	"Southern Cross" monoplane.
Sept., 1930	Capt. Costes and M. Bellonte.	3,700 miles—Paris to New York. (First non-stop flight from Europe to New York.)	37 hours 17 minutes ..	Breguet biplane 750 h.p. engine.
June-July, 1931 ..	Messrs. Post and Gatty	16,500 miles—Round-the-world flight in stages	8 days, 15 hours, 51 minutes.	Lockhead Vega mon., 590 h.p. "Wasp" engine.
July, 1931	Messrs. Boardman and Polando.	4,984 miles—Non-stop flight from New York to Constantinople	49 hours	Bellanca monoplane, Wright engine.
Nov., 1931	Bert Hinkler	2,000 miles—From Port Natal, Brazil, to Bathurst on African coast. (First west-to-east South Atlantic flight, and first light aeroplane Atlantic crossing.)	22 hours	Puss Moth monoplane
May 20-21, 1932 ..	Miss Amelia Earhart (Mrs. G. P. Putnam.)	2,026 miles—Newfoundland to Ireland. (First solo Atlantic flight by woman aviator.)	13½ hours	Lockhead Vega mon., 420 h.p. "Wasp" engine.
Aug. 18-19, 1932 ..	Mr. J. A. Mollison ..	2,600 miles—Portmarnock, Ireland, to Pennfield Ridge, New Brunswick. (First solo flight across North Atlantic from east to west.)	30½ hours	D.H. Puss Moth, 120 h.p. Gipsy engine.
July, 1933	Mr. Wiley Post	16,500 miles—Round the world in stages—New York back to New York, via Germany, Russia, and Alaska.	7 days, 18 hours, 49 minutes.	Lockhead "Vega" monoplane "Wasp" engine.
July, 1933	Mr. and Mrs. J. A. Mollison.	3,300 miles—Trans-Atlantic flight from Pendine Sands, Carmarthenshire, to Bridgeport, 60 miles from New York.	39 hours	D.H. Dragon, two Gipsy Major engines.
July-Aug., 1933 ..	Marshal Italo Balbo and 100 Italian airmen.	11,770 miles—Return squadron flight across Atlantic—the first of its kind—from Rome to Chicago and back.	42 days from start to finish including halts *en route*.	25 Savoia-Marchetti flying-boats started, 23 returned.
Aug., 1933	Mr. Paul Codos and M. Maurice Rossi.	5,657 miles (non-stop)—New York across Atlantic to Kayak, Syria.	54 hours, 44 minutes ..	Bleriot long-range monoplane (Hispano-Suiza motor.)
Sept. 22-23, 1935 ..	Lieut. Vaitkus	New York—Ireland	25 hours	Lockhead "Vega."

Captain James Fitzmaurice's grave at Glasnevin Cemetery (no. 158 1/2 i.e. half grave). Photo taken on April 14th, 1989

Chapter Four

Paddy Saul and the Southern Cross transatlantic flight, 1930

The New York Times.

Copyright, 1930, by The New York Times Company.

• • • • NEW YORK, TUESDAY, JUNE 24, 1930. TWO CENTS

KINGSFORD-SMITH HOPS FROM IRELAND WITH 3 AIDES FOR NON-STOP FLIGHT HERE; BAD WEATHER FACES THEM ON THIS SIDE

Associated Press Photo

FLYING HERE ACROSS THE ATLANTIC
Major Charles Kingsford-Smith, Who Started From Ireland at Dawn on the Perilous Trip Westward

34 HOURS IN AIR ESTIMATED

Skies Clear After Heavy Rain and Thousands See the Start.

HOPE TO REACH NEW YORK

Course Will Lie Over Great Circle to Newfoundland and Then Down the Coast.

LIGHT PROVISIONS TAKEN

Fliers Carrying Four Flasks of Coffee, Sandwiches and Malted Milk Tablets.

Special Cable to the New York Times.

PORT MARNOCK, Ireland, Tuesday, June 24 - Major Charles Kingsford-Smith and his three companions took off from the beach here at 4:30 A.M. today (11:30 P.M., Monday, New York Daylight Saving Time), on what they hope will be a non-stop flight to New York. With 1,298 gallons of gasoline aboard, their plane, the Southern Cross, got into the air after a run down a three and a half mile stretch of packed sand on the beach here.

Day had broken a half hour before when the planks were finally released from the wheels and with a roar from the three powerful motors of the Fokker monoplane the four fliers began their great adventure across the Atlantic. Major Kingsford-Smith waved to a Free State officer who gave the signal to start and the beach runway was cleared. The eyes of thousands were on the machine as it taxied slowly to the red flag marking the runway.

Gradually gaining momentum, the Southern Cross rose easily and gracefully into the air shortly after the flag was passed. The crowd breathed a sigh of relief, for in the minds of all there had been some doubt whether the machine would lift its seven-ton load.

Once in the air, the plane flew over the beach, skirting Howth and Ireland's Eye Island, rising higher and higher. Circling back over the throngs on the beach, the plane roared over Dublin and on westward. Within a few minutes after the take-off the Southern Cross was lost to the sight of those on the beach.

Engines Function Perfectly.

It was at 3.33 that the engines were started, Major Kingsford-Smith listening to them attentively to assure himself they were running perfectly. It was daylight at 4 but some time was required to remove the planks beneath the plane's wheels and to make all final preparations.

Governor General James MacNeill of the Free State, Colonel Russell, other officials and members of the Irish Aero Club gathered to tell the aviators farewell.

Major Kingsford-Smith was the first to board the plane, climbing into the cockpit, followed immediately by Relief Pilot, M. E. Van Dyk. Then the navigator, Captain J. P. Saul and J. W. Stannage, the wireless operator, entered their cabin, after they had waved to their two other companions, whom they will not see again until the journey's end. Mr. Van Dyk started out wearing plus-fours, but the other three were in conventional flying garb.

So great was the demonstration of enthusiasm of the crowds thronging the beach that one girl fainted. Every moment of the final preparations was followed with the most intense interest by the throng.

Shortly before 3.30 A.M. Major Kingsford Smith and his crew, after a few hours' sleep, arrived on the beach, ready for the take-off as soon as they could get sufficient light. A growing tenseness in the atmosphere was noticeable as they made final preparations.

Early last evening Captain J. P. Saul, the navigator, motored from Dublin to bring his fiancee, Miss Zena Marchant, an Irish girl, to the beach to see the take-off.

"Yes," Mr. Saul said, "I brought her out here, but she will have to drive home alone."

Bids Daughter Good-Bye.

Mr. Saul, who is a widower, had bid his little daughter Pat good-bye before she went to bed last night. The devotion of his retriever, Kip, to his master was one of the most touching aspects of the take-off. The dog, which had accompanied Mr. Saul on many flights, seemed to sense that he was not going along on this one.

A rare photograph of Smithy in flight in the Lady Southern Cross, taken somewhere over Hawaii on 29 October 1934.

The Southern Cross flies past Mount Taranaki on arrival in New Zealand for the 1933 joyriding tour - one of the few air-to-air photographs of the famous trimotor that has survived

Wherever it landed in 1928, the Southern Cross was quickly engulfed in a sea of humanity - as here in Christchurch, New Zealand, after its historic Tasman crossing.

Chapter 4

Paddy Saul and the Southern Cross transatlantic flight

The circumnavigation of the globe and the men who crewed the Southern Cross

In 1930, Paddy Saul was navigator of the Southern Cross, which he flew with Major Charles Kingsford-Smith, on the second east to west Transatlantic flight, taking off from Portmarnock Strand, Dublin on the June 24th, 1930. The aircraft which they flew was a Fokker V11 Air Corps personnel provided ground handling facilities for the Southern Cross.

Paddy Saul became civil air traffic controller with the Department of Industry and Commerce as chief ATC officer and also officer in charge at Foynes in September 1943. His previous experience with the RAF as a navigation instructor proved invaluable to him.

There were nine men who made up the crews of the Southern Cross for the various legs of its major pioneering flights. On May 31st 1928, the aircraft took off from Oakland, California and flew west over the Pacific to Australia. The flight included landings in Hawaii and Suva. This was the first aerial crossing of the Pacific and was a decade ahead of its time. It was a superb illustration of organisational, piloting, radio and navigational skills as until that time, no aircraft had flown further from the American mainland than Hawaii. The crew for the Pacific Flight was Kingsford Smith, Charles Ulm, Jim Warner (radio) and Harry Lyon (navigator). Both Warner and Lyon were skilled U.S. Navy veterans. It was a top-flight team. Time spent in the air totalled 83hrs 38mins.

Once in Australia, a successful flight to New Zealand across the Tasman Sea followed. For this and the subsequent flight to England in 1929, the crew was Kingsford Smith, Charles Ulm, Harold Litchfield (navigator) and Tom McWilliams, a New Zealander (radio). For the final leg of the journey from Rome to England, the Wright Company engineer who prepared the engines, Cecil Maidment, joined the crew as a passenger. The Southern Cross then continued to Holland. In Holland, it was refurbished completely by the Fokker Company at its own cost. During this interlude, Kingsford Smith returned to Australia by sea.

It was then back to England for Kingsford Smith. In late May 1930, Kingsford Smith took the refurbished Southern Cross from Holland to Croydon with Evert van Dijk, Paddy Saul and Cecil Maidment. The crew was joined there by John Stannage, who completed the team. From Croydon, they flew to Baldonnel Aerodrome in Ireland. The Atlantic take off took place at 4.25am (BST) on June 24th. During the flight, the Atlantic fog and generally adverse weather created continuously dangerous conditions. Eventually, a successful landing was made at Harbour Grace in Newfoundland at 10.58am (BST) on June 25th after some 30.5 hours in the air.

Eventually, on July 4th, 1930, the Southern Cross landed at Oakland Airport, California, the starting point on May 31st, 1928 of the first Pacific Flight. It had circumnavigated the globe.

The crews of the Southern Cross were: Commander Charles Kingsford Smith; Co-Commander Charles Ulm; co-pilot Evert van Dijk; radio operators (3) - Jim Warner, Tom McWilliams and John Stannage; navigators (3) - Harry Lyon, Hal Litchfield and Paddy Saul.

The crew received the freedom of the city from the Mayor of New York, James Walker

The ground engineer who prepared the engines of the Southern Cross for all the major legs of its round the world flight was Cecil Maidment of the Wright Company. Born in the United Kingdom, Maidment had served in the Royal Flying Corps in World War One before joining the Wright Company in the U.S.A. He had serviced Charles Lindbergh's engine and the airman had shown his appreciation by presenting him with a gold watch.

Jonathan Patrick Saul was born in 1895 in Dublin. He joined the Mercantile Marine at the age of 14 and visited many parts of the world. One of his first long trips was made in an old sailing ship, the Belford, from Ireland to New York in 1913. He saw active service throughout World War One as a commissioned officer in a variety of units and obtained his Master's certificate.

Paddy Saul was no stranger to Australia. In November 1920, his marriage to Bertie May Hobden of Waratah, New South Wales, was celebrated at Donnybrook. About 1922, the family, which now included a newly born daughter, Pat, suffered shipwreck. His wife lost her life but he managed to save his daughter when she swept past him in a big wave. The Atlantic flight was the big adventure of his life and he later received the aircraft's chronometer as a personal memento. In World War Two, he gave invaluable service as a navigating instructor. On the establishment of Shannon Airport, he became the first control officer. Paddy Saul remained active in community affairs thereafter. In 1965, one of his last acts was to ensure the preservation of his Southern Cross chronometer by placing it in the hands of authorities at Brisbane Airport where the aircraft itself is exhibited. J.P. Saul died on June 22nd, 1968 at the age of 74. Portmarnock Public School in Dublin features the Southern Cross aircraft in its school badge. The badge commemorates the use by the Southern Cross of the beach at Portmarnock on June 24th, 1930 as the take-off point for the flight across the Atlantic. The landing took place at Harbour Grace, Newfoundland, on June 25th after the Southern Cross had been in the air 30 and a half hours. The 70th anniversary of this historic flight was marked by a ceremony at Portmarnock on June 24th, 2000. Smithy flew the Southern Cross to New York on June 26th. The crew was: Charles Edward Kingsford Smith, commander; Evert van Dijk, co-pilot; Jonathan Patrick Saul, navigator; John Stanley Warburton Stannage, radio operator. Smithy was an Australian; van Dijk, a Dutchman; Paddy Saul, an Irishman; and John Stannage a New Zealander. The crew received the freedom of the city from the Mayor of New York, James Walker. Each member was presented with an inscribed gold pin as a memento. An illuminated 'Scroll of Honour' signed by the Mayor set out the historical nature of the team's achievement.

Southern Cross at Baldonnel with the Irish Aero Club EI-AAA and an Aer Corp Vespa

The Southern Cross

Air Commodore Sir Charles Kingsford Smith, M.C., A.F.C. Photograph taken at Croydon Aerodrome. Topical Press

The flight team whose 1930 atlantic journey was the first wholly successfully to cross the ocean from east to west. from left: navigator Paddy Saul, Smithy, Co-pilot Evert van Dijk, radio operator John Stannage.

The Southern Cross seen here at Portmarnock Strand prior to take off for the USA. The aircraft is preserved in the Australian Museum in Canberra

The "Southern Cross" is prepared for fuelling at Portmarnock

Triumphal march accorded to the crew of the Southern Cross

The 'Southern Cross' Crew at Baldonnel. left to right Paddy Saul, Co-Pilot Evert van Dijk, Smithy, Radio-operator John Stannage

Stannage and Saul in the middle of members of the Irish Army Aer Corps

Portmarnock Strand. Photo courtesy of Local Studies Dept, Fingal County Libraries

Portmarnock Strand 1933. Collapse of Faith in Australia, an Avro 10.

Charles Lindbergh

Other famous aviators/aviatrix of the day

Charles Augustus Lindbergh

Charles Lindbergh flew the first solo non-stop, trans-Atlantic flight. He flew from the United States to Paris in May 1927. His plane was named the "Spirit of St. Louis". At one point on his journey he circled a fishing vessel and shouted down "which way Ireland?" but there was no reply. However his flight did bring him over the southern tip of Ireland, and he said that when he saw the green hills of Ireland that he knew that he had "hit Europe on the nose". Lindbergh described Ireland as ìone of the four corners of the worldî because of its importance in aviation terms at the time. Raymond B. Orteig had first offered a prize of $25,000 in 1919. Lindberg had left Roosevelt Airfield, Long Island, New York at 7.52 am on May 20th. And landed at Le Bourget at 10.00 pm (Paris time) on the 21st. of May 1927. The Spirit of St. Louis was a Ryan Model "NYP" and was specially designed for Lindbergh for this flight. It had a Wright Whirlwind J5-C engine of 220 horsepower. The wingspan was 46 feet and the top speed was 120 miles per hour.

The Spirit of St. Louis

Ruth Elder, actress and pilot: her attempt to fly the Atlantic in 1927 finished in the sea, but gained her considerable publicity

Amy Johnson, Amelia Earhardt and Jim Mollinson on a visit to Ireland, 1932

Amelia Earhardt signing autographs after landing at Culmore near Derry in May 1932

Lady Bailey - In 1929 she was the first woman to be awarded the Britannia Trophy for the year's most outstanding air performance. She made the first solo flight from London to Capetown and back. It was was hailed in the press as the greatest solo effort.

Amy Johnson - the first woman to fly solo from England to Australia 1930

Ruth Nicholls - established speed records in the United States

Amelia Earhardt - the first woman to fly the Atlantic

Maryse Bastié - a regular participant in solo flight record competitions in Europe

Amelia Earhardt - the most famous woman pilot of her day

Chapter Five

Irish Army Air Corps

Air Sons

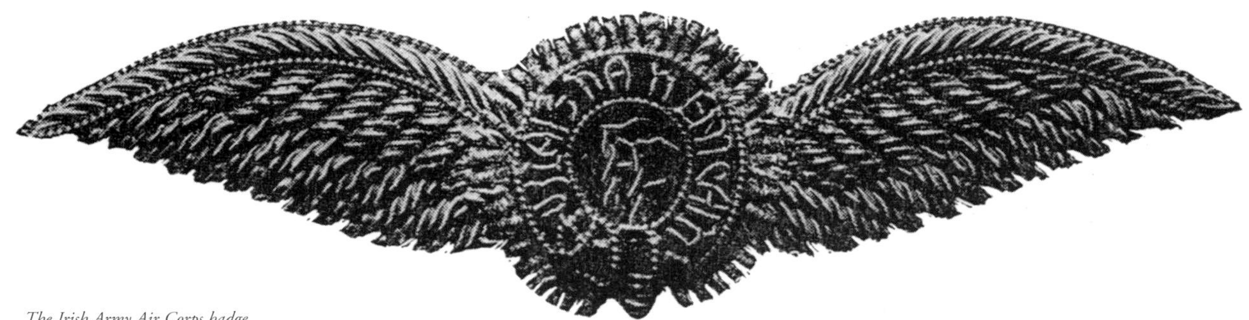

The Irish Army Air Corps badge

# of Ireland

Three of the four Gloster "Gladiators" operated

Avro 626s 1934

The director of Military Aviation, Commdt. G. J. Carroll; the C.O., Major J. J. Liston; and adjutant, Capt. D. J. Murphy, with the officers of the Army Air Corps. Aviation, 1935

Chapter 5

Irish Army Air Corps

Lieutenant James P. Twohig

Col. Charles Russell, ex-commanding officer of the Irish Army Air Corps. Served in the Royal Flying Corps. Founder member of the Irish Aero Club. Chief advocate during the 1930s of the concept of a national airline. Founded Irish Airways Limited

Lieutenant James P. Twohig, at the age of 26, was tragically killed near Baldonnel. He was one of the Irish Free State Army Air Corps' ablest and most daring pilots. The accident occurred when involved in formation flying. A wing of his machine, an Avro Cadet, tipped the wing of the plane next in line. The tragedy happened on August 5th, 1937 when he and some fellow pilots were preparing for an air display which was to take place in the Phoenix Park.

Colonel Charles Francis Russell

Colonel Charles Francis Russell was born in Dublin in 1896 and educated at the Salesian College, Farnborough. He served in the Royal Flying Corps from 1916 to the end of the war and then carried out aerial survey work in Northern Canada from 1919-1920. He was head of the Irish Free State Air Corps from 1922-1926 and retired in 1927. He organised the Irish Aero Club and founded Irish Airways Ltd., a company set up with the objective of operating a daily air service between Dublin and London.

Colonel Charles Russell, was chief of the Irish Free State Airforce as well as vice-chairman and honorary instructor of the Irish Aero Club, and from the 1920s and the 1930s was the main protagonist of the idea of a National Air Service in the Irish Free State. By a series of lectures, exhortations and, above all, demonstration flights, he speeded up the day when a national air service was possible. He promoted his concept unrelentlessly until officialdom began to believe in the idea. It is important that history recognises the cardinal role that Colonel Charles Russell played in the history of civil as well as military aviation in the Irish Free State. One of the notable experimental flights which Col. Russell flew was the first air mail flight from Galway to London, which took place on August 26th, 1929. Irish Airways Ltd. was the company which was responsible for the flight. Col. Russell left Oranmore, Galway at 8.30am in a Vickers Valiant Rolls-Royce aeroplane fitted with a 500 horse power Rolls-Royce Condor Vixen engine, carrying American mail from the German liner, Lloyd Karlsruhe, which had called to Galway.

Alfie Byrne 'The Lord Mayor of Dublin' in a characteristic attitude with Col. C. F. Russell

He got a huge send off from the large crowd, which included Mr. Patrick Hogan, Minister for Agriculture and other members of the Dail. The aircraft for this historic flight was placed at the disposal of Col. Russell by Sir Robert McLean, chairman of Vickers Aviation Ltd. His flight officer was Mr. Somers of Vickers Aviation Ltd. The aircraft, with its mail of 5,000 letters, landed safely at Croydon at 11.35 am and there to greet the crew were Major Atkinson, chief inspector of Vickers Aviation Ltd., as well as Mr. T. A. Smiddy, High Commissioner for the Irish Free State. Irish Airways Ltd. tried to secure a subsidy from the Irish Free State government in order to run a service from Dublin to London. The subsidisation of civil aviation was a key issue for Col. Charles Russell. The Government refused to accede to the frequent requests for such subsidies.

On October 22nd, 1932, Col. Russell was one of the organisers and a crew member of the air mail test flight which linked up with an air mail feeder flight from Oranmore in Galway and flew from Baldonnel to Templehof Aerodrome, Berlin. The feeder plane was an Iona National Airways 'Fox Moth', flown by Captain O. E. Armstrong of Kildonan Aerodrome. The plane, a triple engined Fokker F12 Royal Dutch Airliner, was flown to Berlin by Mr. J. B. Scholte and Col. Russell, with J. J. Denouter, wireless operator and Mr. P. Dunk, engineer.

The Martinsyde bearing the name "The Big Fella" at Baldonnel February 1923

Irish Army Air Corps aircrews being briefed at Fermoy, Co.Cork, during the early part of 1923. The aircraft shown are a Martinsyde Scout F.4. Buzzard, a Bristol F2B, and a pair of De Havilland D.H. 9s

To watch him flying on a summer's evening in Baldonnel in an Army Air Corps aircraft was an education in itself

Col. Russell, a man of great vision and a perfect spokesman for the advocacy of civil aviation, requested from the Government a sum of £10,000 in order to set up a company to operate as a national commercial aviation body. His repeated requests right through the late 1920s and most of the 1930s fell entirely on deaf ears.

Sir Alan Cobham first came to Ireland on the invitation of Col. Charles Russell, president of the Irish Aero Club and former commanding officer of the Irish Army Air Corps. Cobham came to Ireland with his flying circus in 1933. He had been a First World War pilot.

Captain Oscar Heron

Captain Oscar Heron was one of the best trained pilots of the Irish Army Air Corps. He was highly decorated, (D.F.C., Qua de Guerre, Belgium) and became an 'ace' as he shot down nine German aircraft, all of them Fokker D.7s. He was an excellent pilot, arguably the highest qualified pilot in the air corps. He was killed at a flying display in the Phoenix Park in 1933. His passenger, Private Tobin, was also killed.

Captain Fred Crosley

During World War 1, the Sopwith Camel was practically unmatched for manoeuverability and shot down more 'enemy' aircraft than any other type. In a Sopwith Camel F-1 the Canadian 'Air-Ace' Captain Roy Brown shot down and killed the Red Baron Manfred Von Richtofen

Fred Crosley flew in the First World War as a Camel pilot. He was, in the opinion of many, the best pilot of the day. He had what is described in flying as 'the hands of a surgeon'. (To watch him flying on a summer's evening in Baldonnel in an Army Air Corps aircraft was an education in itself.) Lieutenant James P. Twohig, Arthur Russell and Fred Crosley were instructors at the Irish Army Air Corps. The most active instructor was Russell. Captain Fred Crosley left the Irish Army Air Corps in 1931 or 1932 and joined Lady Dorothy Paget. He raced with her for a couple of seasons before going on to represent Shell-BP. Before that, he worked for a short time with one of the smaller aircraft companies. He retired around 1961 and went to live in Malta.

Lieutenant Arthur Russell

A Fairey 3F (the biggest machine in use in the Air Corps at the time - a day bomber and a reconnaissance aircraft and not suited to stunting), piloted by Lieutenant Arthur Russell, had just looped the loop, righted itself and then - to the horror of spectators - went into a violent spin. It nose-dived down through the trees into the garden of Miss Rose Gibson, close to Russell's own house in Rathgar. The aircraft immediately burst into flames and the fireball prevented helpless and distraught bystanders from rescuing the men. Only Sergeant Patrick L. Canavan, one of the three Irish Free State Army Air Corps pilots, escaped from the devouring flames, suffering severe burns. The third soldier, Private Daniel J. Twomey, as well as Arthur Russell, were burned to death, trapped in the inferno. Lieutenant Arthur Russell, aged 27 at the time, was a younger brother of Colonel Charles Russell. Arthur Russell had previous narrow escapes and many had marvelled at his hairsbreadth escapes from disaster.

The Fairey 3F was rather unusual in that it had a three seater cockpit and it could be fitted with floats. It was occasionally in Dun Laoghaire or at Skerries. There was as much construction in the floats as the machine - they were like canoes. Arthur's death was in 1934, while Oscar Heron died at the Phoenix Park air pageant in 1933.

Two Dead In Blazing 'Plane

NOSE-DIVE INTO GARDEN

ONE A BROTHER OF FAMOUS AIRMAN

ARMY MACHINE

"Daily Express" Special Correspondent.

DUBLIN, Monday.

TWO airmen were burned to death in a Free State Army airplane which nose-dived into a garden in Terenure-road, here, today.

One of them, Lieutenant Arthur Russell, brother of Colonel Russell who is to fly the Irish Free State's airplane in the Melbourne race, had hitherto borne a charmed life.

Burned to death with him was Private Daniel J. Twomey, aged twenty.

A third soldier, Sergeant Patrick L. Canavan, leaped from the cockpit after the airplane had crashed. He was severely burned.

The airplane, a Fairey Moth, was piloted by Lieutenant Russell, who, although only twenty-seven, had been in about a dozen previous crashes. His hairbreadth escapes in the past have been a by-word.

This time his luck deserted him.

He and Twomey were trapped in the blazing airplane, and were burned beyond recognition before their bodies could be recovered.

Before the crash the airplane looped the loop and then righted itself.

Immediately afterwards it went into a spin and nose-dived between a number of tall trees in the garden.

It was encircled by the garden wall

Hundreds of persons saw the airplane drop, including many children on their way home from school.

Pedestrians, tram drivers, and motorists ran into the garden and made frantic efforts to release the men.

Flames jumped twenty feet into the air.

Sergeant Canavan, who was lying clear of the wreckage, was hastily carried out of range of the flames.

Ambulances and fire brigades were called, and he was taken to hospital. Tonight he was reported to be making progress.

When the flames were under control the two charred bodies were taken from the wreckage and carried to military ambulances for transference to the military hospital at Arbour Hill.

News of the crash spread rapidly and all available police in the district were called out to deal with the crowd that assembled.

Mechanics arrived within an hour from Baldonnel, the headquarters of the Air Force, and took the twisted framework of the machine to pieces ready for removal.

Miss Rose Gibson, into whose garden the 'plane crashed, said tonight: "The machine passed over the house, and I heard two explosions followed by a crash. I rushed to the front, and saw that the airplane had crashed through the trees. Immediately it burst into flames. The blaze was so furious that I feared the house would take fire.

"Rescuers rushed up, but they could not do anything, as the fire was too fierce."

John Martin, another witness of the crash, covered his eyes while telling me of the rescue efforts made by himself and others.

"I shall never forget it to my dying day," he said.

Directly opposite the garden in which the crash occurred is Clarendon Court, the home of Colonel Charles Russell, Lieutenant Russell's brother. Col. Russell was formerly Officer Commanding of the Irish Air Force.

Next to the house of the crash is the home of Mr. Justice Meredith, who was recently appointed vice-president of the Saar Commission.

The machine narrowly missed the judge's house, a wing striking the wall separating the two houses.

The scene of Lieutenant Arthur Russell's death. His aircraft was engulfed in flames immediately on crashing into a garden in Rathgar

Johnny Maher, pictured with the Cumberbatch Trophy in 1950

Johnny Maher

Johnny Maher joined the Royal Naval Air Service in 1915. He was posted to Devonport and later to Portsmouth. He became an aide to Lieutenant R.B. Colmore - director of airships. After experience of fitting, mooring, flying in and parachuting from airships, he became an expert airman. In 1918, he became a petty officer, air mechanic first class. He also gained valuable experience flying and maintaining new aircraft. He returned to Ireland to join the newly formed Irish Free State Air Corps as a sergeant observer/maintenance engineer and was soon promoted to senior NCO. He was posted to Fermoy, Co. Cork but returned to Baldonnel in 1923.

Johnny Maher was appointed chief ground engineer with Aer Lingus in 1936. The new airline was operating from Baldonnel at the time. In addition to his 'A' licence to work on wood and metal aircraft, he also held a 'B' licence for their overhaul, a 'C' engine licence and an 'X' licence for parachutes, instruments and gliders. He had also responsibility for the maintenance of the terminal building and restaurant and fire-fighting ambulance and first aid service when Aer Lingus commenced their operations at Collinstown.

Maher left Aer Lingus in 1965. He then accepted a job with 20th Century Fox film producers, maintaining their fleet of World War One war fighterplanes at Weston Aerodrome, where he felt very much at home with the 'Blue Max' and the 'Red Barron'.

Joe Gilmore

Joe Gilmore completed the first successful parachute jump in Ireland at Baldonnel. He was also one of the first Irishmen to build his own aircraft. He had many miraculous escapes in his flying and non-flying ventures. These included escapes from motor cycle crashes, car crashes and air crashes. On one occasion at a parachute jump in Cork, his rip cord fouled and, in his own words, he "plunged like a stone, the earth rushing at me. I worked methodically at the harness and did not claw frantically at the gear. The chute checked me with a terrific jerk".

On one occasion at a parachute jump in Cork, his rip cord fouled and, in his own words, he "plunged like a stone, the earth rushing at me. I worked methodically at the harness and did not claw frantically at the gear. The chute checked me with a terrific jerk"

Baldonnel thrill - A photograph taken from the air by Irish Times staff photographer of Mr. Gilmore's parachute descent at Baldonnel on April 17th, 1933. This was the first parachute descent in Ireland and the first time that Mr. Gilmore, a member of the Irish Aero Club, had attempted the feat

Open Day at Baldonnel 1931

27 Miles Magisters operated by the Air Corps

Cavalry Captain Manfred von Richthofen

Aces - Knights of the Sky

Like the knights of old, World War 1 pilots fought first in single combat, man pitted against man, plane against plane. Aces were pilots who had shot down five or more enemy aircraft. The Red Baron, Manfred von Richthofen of Germany was the most famous with 80 victories. The other most noted were René Fonck of France, 75 victories, Edward Mannock of England, 73 and William Bishop of Canada, 72. In a strange contradiction, and like knights of old, the pilots of the First World War respected the enemy and honoured him for his bravery. For example, it is recorded that when a German aerial patrol, raided an air base in France and shot down an American pilot, on the day of his funeral the same patrol returned with white streamers attached to the wings of their planes and dropped flowers on the cemetery. But none was honored more than Baron Manfred von Richthofen. He was shot down behind Allied lines, killed by a single bullet, which pierced his heart. Twenty-year-old English Captain Roy Brown of 209 Squadron piloting a Sopwith "Camel" fired the bullet. It was the last year of the war. The date was the 21st of April 1918. The British with full military honours buried the Red Baron. The next day a British pilot flew over von Richthofen's squadron air base. He dropped an announcement of the great ace's death and a photograph of Allied pilots firing a last salute over his grave.

The all-red Fokker triplane of the German ace, Baron Manfred von Richthofen

German medal commemorating von Richthofen's victories

The Blue Max Fokker DI triplane

Chapter Six

The Irish Aero Club

Chapter 6

The Irish Aero Club

After an earlier abortive attempt to set up an aero club in Dublin in March 1927, with a committee led by Col. Charles Russell of the Irish Army Air Corps, further efforts were made in 1928. It was the immense euphoria which followed the successful 'Flight of the Bremen' which flew from Baldonnel Aerodrome to the United States in April 1928 (the first east/west crossing of the Atlantic) which provided the spark to generate sufficient interest to make up the numbers to have a successful aero club. Col. J. C. Fitzmaurice, who was a member of the Bremen crew, chaired a meeting on August 9th, 1928 at the Hibernian Hotel, Dublin, at which a provisional committee was appointed. Its task was to set up an agenda for consideration by an inaugural meeting, due to take place a short time later.

The new aero club, the Irish Aero Club, was formally inaugurated at a meeting at the Engineer's Hall, 35 Dawson Street, Dublin, on the evening of August 15th, 1928. Col. Fitzmaurice presided at the meeting.

The initial membership of the Irish Aero Club also included Captain Crossley, Messrs. McDunphy, Reddy, G. Finlay-Mulligan, Sheehan, W.A. Armstrong. Messrs. Fitzpatrick, Ready, Dunckley, Huet, Dr. G. Pepper and J. C. Malone. The committee included Senator Oliver St. John Gogarty and Osmond Grattan Esmonde. By September 19th, 1928, the club had 212 members on its books. Col. Fitzmaurice was president and Col. C. F. Russell was chairman.

Irish Aero Club. Ltd., Baldonnel Aerodrome, July 25th, 1933. DH.60G. 'Moth', EI-AAJ, (ex.G-ABOZ), believed to be the aircraft flown by the eminent Dublin surgeon and statesman, Senator Oliver St. John Gogarty, on the occasion when he collided with a sheep at the moment of touchdown at Baldonnel. Note damaged undercarrige and propeller. J.N.D. Photo courtesy of Mr. Pearse Cahill

Chapter Six *The Irish Aero Club*

Seán O hUadhaigh

The Irish Aero Club was not the first of its kind to exist in this part of Ireland. The Aero Club of Ireland was set up with its first aviation meetings held at Leopardstown Racecourse on August 29th and 30th, 1910. At this meeting successful flights were made by Captain Bertram Dickson, Mr. Cecil Grace and Mr. Armstrong Dexel. Later, the Irish Aero Club changed its meeting place to 22 Suffolk Street, Dublin and the then secretary, A.P. Reynolds, gave great service to the club.

The membership of the Irish Aero Club committee changed over the years. At the club's A.G.M. dated July 3rd, 1931, the following committee was elected: Captain J. P. Saul, vice-president; A. P. Reynolds, honorary secretary; Mr. D. Grattan Esmonde, T.D; Dr. G.E. Pepper, chairman and flying committee; Mr. C. Gleeson; Mr J. C. Malone; Mr. Storey; and Miss K. McCormack. Other prominent and active members over the years included Senator Dr. Oliver St. John Gogarty, M.D; The Lord Mayor of Dublin, Senator Alfred Byrne; Major S. Dunckley; Dr. S. V. Furlong; Mr. P. Gore-Grimes; Captain H. J. Hosie; Mr. E. J. Dease; and Mr. R. H. Hill.

Mr. Seán o hUadhaigh, president of the Irish Aero Club; Col. C. F. Russell, chairman, Irish Aviation Day Committee; Mr. S. T. Lemass, Minister for Industry and Commerce; and Sir Alan Cobham in the Fifteen Acres, Phoneix Park, Dublin. Courtesy Evening Mail

IRISH AVIATION DAY

12th May, 1935

AVIATION. MAY. 1935.

The Patron of IRISH AVIATION DAY

Mr. Sean F. Lemass, The Minister for Industry and Commerce.

SOME OF THE MEMBERS OF THE EXECUTIVE COMMITTEE FOR IRISH AVIATION DAY.
Left to right—front row—Mr. C. E. McConnell, Mr. Seán O hUadhaigh, Colonel C. F. Russell, Miss Hamilton, Major General Hugh MacNeill.
Left to right—back row—Mr. J. McAuley, Mr. Cecil Crowe, Mr. E. J. Dease, Captain H. St. G. Harpur, Mr. G. J. Bonass, Mr. J. J. O'Leary.

Irish Aviation Day, May 12th, 1935

Irish Aviation Day, May 12th, 1935

The programme of air displays for Irish Aviation Day took place in the Phoenix Park, Dublin on May 12th, 1935. The highlight of the occasion was the display of Flight Lieutenant Tyson, the crack aerobatic pilot of Sir Alan Cobham's Air Circus. He won the hearts of the huge crowd due to his skill and bravery. In his specially equipped Avro 'Tutor', he completed loops, slow rolls, half roll from the top of a loop, flying inverted from the top of a loop, the very difficult 'bunt' and outside loop and terminal velocity dive followed by a vertical upward spin. In 1934, Tyson flew from England to France upside down to commemorate the 25th anniversary of Bleriot's historic Channel flight.

He won the hearts of the huge crowd due to his skill and bravery

EI-AAA - The first aircraft acquired in 1928 by the Irish Aero club was an Avro Avian 504K trainer. This together with a privately owned Avian EI-AAB were the first civil aircraft registered in the State. The third was De Havilland Moth EI-AAC

Miss Joan Meakin, the famous woman glider, discussing the day's work with Mr. Ivor Price, the well-known parachutist

Iona Fleet at Dublin Airport in the 1990s

Chapter Seven

Chapter

Pearse Cahill

Chapter 7

Pearse Cahill

In 1957, Pearse Cahill approached Aer Lingus and the Department of Industry and Commerce for permission to build a hangar at Dublin Airport. Permission was granted and before the doors of the hangar were up, the first Piper Super Cub had been assembled. This Piper assembly work continued until 1961. Business began to grow steadily and Iona became for a time the only establishment in Ireland where light aircraft could have major repairs and overhauls carried out.

In 1965, Iona became the Cessna aircraft agent for Ireland and developed from being essentially an aircraft maintenance base to a flight training and air charter/taxi operator. In 1969, the air taxi business took a step forward when the first Cessna 310 six-seat twin-engined aircraft went into service.

Throughout the 1970s, Iona's air taxi business flourished and this resulted in the purchase of a Cessna 414A Chancellor III, pressurised eight-seat twin-engined aircraft for executive class travel. In 1974, Iona delivered eight Cessna aircraft to the Army Air Corps and also undertook specialised mechanical maintenance on these aircraft. All in all, the part played by Pearse Cahill and Iona in the history of Irish general aviation was a leading one.

All in all, the part played by Pearse Cahill and Iona in the history of Irish general aviation was a leading one

M. P. Cahill (Iona Special) after winning the Leinster Trophy, 1950. Photo Irish Independent

1950 LEINSTER TROPHY RACE

(WICKLOW—12 LAPS)

No.	DRIVER	CAR	HANDICAP Credit Laps	Mins.	No.	1	2	3	4	5	6	7
1	A. POWYS-LYBBE	2904 Alfa-Romeo s/c ...	Scratch		1							
2	T. L. H. COLE	5424 Allard	0	1	2							
3	S. H. ALLARD ...	3917 Allard	0	2½	3							
4	O. MOORE	1971 O.B.M.	0	4½	4							
5	R. BAIRD	1087 M.G. s/c.	0	6	5							
6	R. E. DORNDORF	1971 B.M.W.	1	3½	6	x						
7	W. LEEPER	1250 M.G.	1	3½	7	x						
8	A. R. SCOTT	1099 Ford	1	4	8	x						
9	C. W. E. MAUNSELL	2276 Talbot	1	4	9	x						
10	M. P. CAHILL	1287 Iona Special	1	4½	10	x						
11	T. N. LARGE	1250 M.G.	1	4½	11	x						
12	C. VARD	1250 M.G.	1	4½	12	x						
13	R. G. SHATTOCK ...	1496 Atalanta Special ...	1	5	13	x						
14	J. KEARNEY	1810 Vauxhall	1	5½	14	x						
15	A. L. YOUNG	1250 M.G.	1	5½	15	x						
16	G. A. MANGAN ...	1250 M.G.	1	5½	16	x						
17	N. E. GLEESON ...	1250 M.G.	1	6½	17	x						
18	MISS E. INGRAM ...	1250 M.G.	1	6½	18	x						
19	R. G. LOVELL-BUTT	1287 M.G.	1	7	19	x						
20	L. COLLEN	1250 M.G.	1	7	20	x						
21	K. MURPHY	1287 M.G.	1	7	21	x						
22	K. C. CAHILL	1089 Riley	2	0	22	x	x					
23	C. MARTIN	1089 Riley	2	0	23	x	x					
24	E. DOYLE	1098 T.M.C. Special ...	2	½	24	x	x					
25	L. G. EARL	995 Fiat	2	½	25	x	x					
26	J. G. STEVENSON ...	1267 S.A.R.	2	½	26	x	x					
27	E. CONNELL	1089 Riley	2	1½	27	x	x					
28	M. P. HEASLETT ...	1250 M.G.	2	2½	28	x	x					
29	L. CARVILL	1496 Riley	2	2½	29	x	x					
30	F. E. A. BIGGER ...	1122 Morgan	2	3	30	x	x					
31	R. EDWARDS	2120 Lancia	2	4	31	x	x					
32	J. J. FLYNN	939 M.G.	2	4	32	x	x					

The race card for the 1950 Leinster Trophy Car Race which Pearse Cahill won. Note the handicaps, the record of some of the other placings and the cars driven by the various drivers

PREVIOUS LEINSTER TROPHY WINNERS

WICKLOW CIRCUIT

1950

1—M. P. CAHILL, 1287 c.c. Iona Special 68.87 m.p.h.
2—T. N. LARGE, 1250 c.c. M.G. ... 68.86
3—C. VARD, 1250 c.c. M.G. 68.42
Fastest Lap—W. Baird, 1087 c.c. Meteorite 80.28

1951

1—J. M. HAWTHORN, 1496 c.c. Riley 78.19 m.p.h.
2—W. R. BAIRD, 1496 c.c. Maserati ... 81.28
3—B. McCALDIN, 1250 c.c. M.G. ... 68.90
Fastest Lay—Baird 84.58

1952

1—J. D. TITTERINGTON, Allard ... 78.36 m.p.h.
2—J. J. FLYNN, M.G. s/c 72.84
3—B. McCALDIN, M.G. 69.32
Fastest Lap—W. R. Baird, Baird-Griffin 85.06

1953

1—F. D. SMYTH, 1172 c.c. Ford ... 67.31
2—W. T. TODD, 1200 c.c. Todd Special 61.18
3—D. B. BEAUMAN, 1496 c.c. Riley ... 69.78
Fastest Lap—W. R. Baird, 4.1 litre Ferrari 77.17

1954

1—W. D. LACY, 1250 c.c. M.G. ... 67.30 m.p.h.
2—J. KELLY, 3442 c.c. Jaguar ... 81.37
3—J. TITTERINGTON, 1991 c.c. Triumph 75.10
Fastest Lap—Kelly 83.86

1955

1—D. R. PIPER, 746 Empire Lotus ... 75.98 m.p.h.
2—R. B. BLEAKLEY, 1172 c.c. Ford Special 66.32
3—F. D. SMYTH, 1172 c.c. Ford Special 71.90
Fastest Lap D. Beaumann, 2448 Connaught 82.94

1956

1—J. B. NAYLOR, 1484 c.c. Lotus/Maserati ... ... 82.14 m.p.h.
2—L. EARL, 2663 c.c. Jirano 75.59
3—A. C. O'HARA, 3442 c.c. Jaguar ... 75.30
Fastest Lap—P. Whitehead, 2991 c.c. Maserati 87.04

1957

1—B. EMERSON, 948 c.c. Buckler ... 68.93 m.p.h.
2—J. S. MACKENZIE, 1250 c.c. M.G. T.C. 63.31
3—D. J. CALVERT, 1290 c.c. Alfa-Romeo 74.55
Fastest Lap P. N. Whitehead, Aston Martin 88.31

Motor racing - Leinster Trophy winners, Wicklow Circuit 1950 - 1957

Pearse Cahill recieves the Colonel Fitmaurice award from Terry Rowan, Vice President, F.A.I. (the international controlling body for aviation) in 1981

Mr. Pearse Cahill in the cockpit of the D.H. Chipmunk Mark III

Cessna T303 Crusader

Cessna Titan Ambassador

Cessna Chancellor

Passengers boarding at Pearse Cahill's Iona National Airways, Dublin Airport

Embraer Bandeirante EMB-110 P1

Chapter Eight

Chapter

Iona National Airways Ltd.

Chapter 8

Iona National Airways Ltd.

Kildonan House, as it is and as it was when the aerodrome existed on its lands. A family by the name of Fitzpatrick occupied the house then. Mr. Ignatius Byrne became the occupant and the Byrne family continues in its occupancy today

Iona National Airways Limited's stay at Baldonnel was only intended to be a short one because it was a military aerodrome

Iona National Airways Ltd. commenced operations at Baldonnel Aerodrome in September 1930 with the Gypsy Moth G-ABBV (later to be registered as EI-AAK) and the Desoutter Mark II EI-AAD which was delivered on September 5th. The former was purchased for flying training, while the latter was earmarked for air taxi work, although not exclusively.

Iona National Airways Limited's stay at Baldonnel was only intended to be a short one because it was a military aerodrome and when the new hangar was built at the newly acquired aerodrome at Kildonan by contractors P & W MacLellan, structural engineers of Glasgow, Hugh Cahill moved his enterprise across to what was Ireland's first ever commercial aerodrome. The contractors also built a fine new clubhouse. The new enterprise settled in very well in its new home at Finglas. Hugh Cahill was no stranger to Finglas and his motor garage was only a few miles down the road at Cross Guns Bridge, Whitworth Road/Botanic Road junction, Glasnevin. By the time of the official opening of Iona National Airways Ltd.'s new aerodrome at Kildonan, Finglas on June 8th, 1931, the company had a fleet of three aircraft, namely Gypsy Moth G-ABBV (EI-AAK); Gypsy Moth EI-AAF, registered to Iona on June 3rd, 1931; and Gypsy Moth EI-AAG, registered to the company on June 2nd, 1931.

By the time of the official opening of Iona National Airways Ltd.'s new aerodrome at Kildonan on June 8th, 1931, the company had a fleet of three aircraft

Seamus Dolan T.D., parliamentary secretary to the Minister for Industry and Commerce, performed the official opening.

The chief pilot at Kildonan at the time of the official opening was M. F. Coogan, a former Air Corps officer. The administration of the new aerodrome was carried out at the Iona National Airways Ltd. and Flying School headquarters at Hugh Cahill's garage and showrooms, Cross Guns Bridge, Glasnevin. When Mr. Coogan retired as chief pilot at Kildonan, O. E. Armstrong took over the position. Kildonan Aerodrome had the use of 75 acres, giving a run of 600 yards in all directions.

Finglas Village, 1932 - as it was at the time when Kildonan Aerodrome was established.

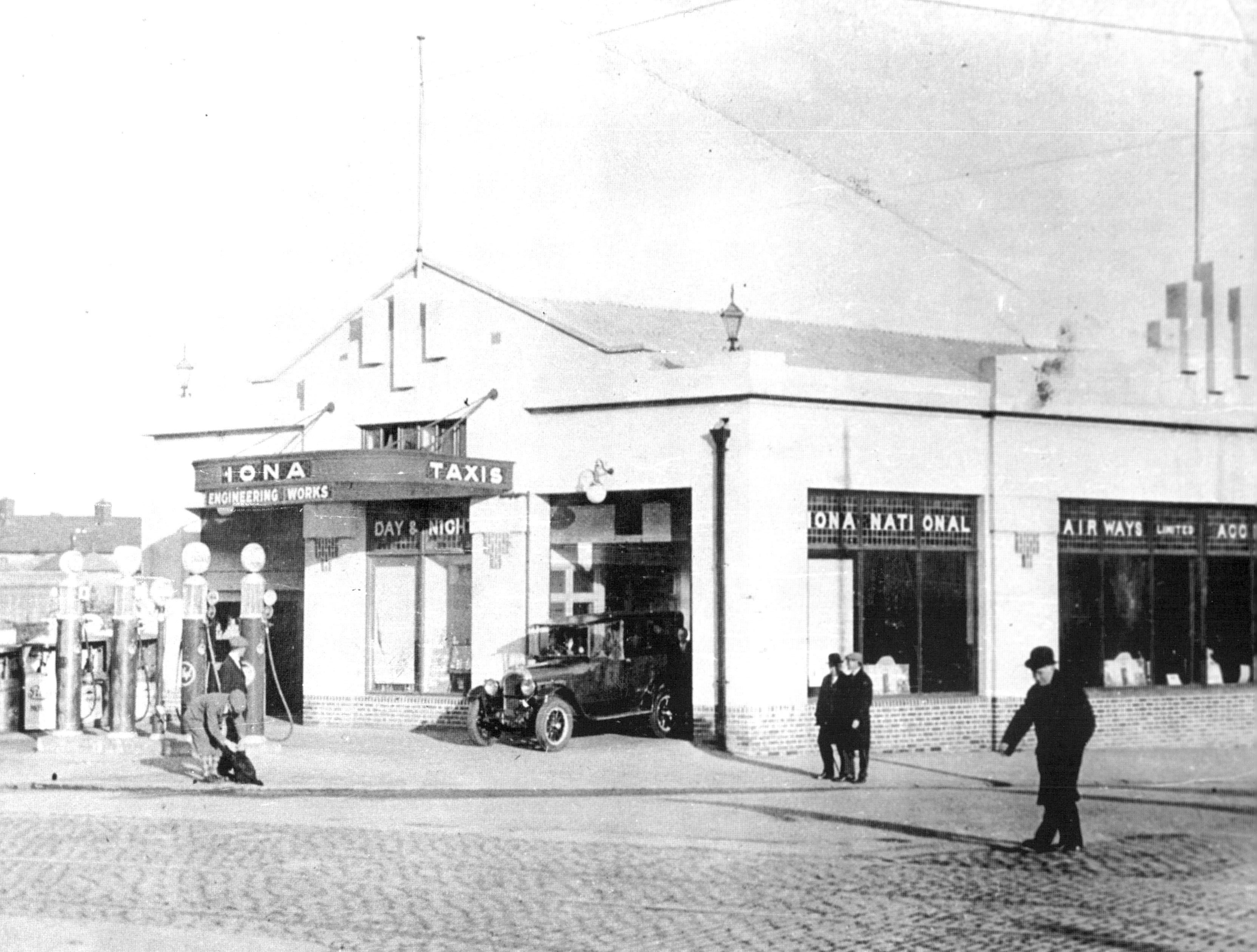

Iona National Airways Ltd. and Iona Engineering Works, Cross Guns Bridge, 1931

Details of this crash were kept secret because it is believed it was flown by an army pilot who shouldn't have been flying it! Pilot uninjured. Crashed at Ballisadare, Co. Sligo, early 1931. Arrived in Baldonnel on same day. Became EI-AAK

In June 1932, the Department of Industry and Commerce licensed Kildonan as a public aerodrome and customs facilities were established. The licence was granted in time to provide landing facilities for two very interesting aircraft which flew over from Heston. These were 9 Junkers F13 G-ABDC of Personal Flying Services, flown by Captain W. Ledlie, and a Hendy 302 G-AAVT. The Junkers remained at Kildonan for some time, providing joy-riding and sight-seeing flights during the Eucharistic Congress, which coincided with its visit.

Captain O. E. Armstrong resigned as chief pilot of Iona National Airways Ltd. in October 1932 and was succeeded by Captain Eric Stewart, a New Zealander, who took up the position in November. In August 1933, Lady Heath brought her Gypsy Moth G-ACBU to Kildonan, where it was based from then on. The following November, a Stinson Junior G-ABTZ purchased by Lady Cathleen Nelson was delivered to her at Kildonan, where it was also based.

In November 1933, Iona National Airways Ltd. decided to cease trading because Hugh Cahill was leaving the aviation business. Kildonan Aerodrome, the Iona aircraft and the staff were taken over by a new company set up by Lady Nelson, known as Everson Flying Services Ltd. The new company began its operations on December 1st, 1933.

Kildonan was officially opened on June 8th, 1931. It was the first civil and commercial aerodrome in Ireland

The Air Corps always flew at Baldonnel until 4.30 in the afternoons. You could have a prospective customer for a charter flight ringing up Hugh Cahill at Baldonnel, saying that they wanted a trip in half an hour's time to go to Cork. At Baldonnel, where the Air Corps was busy taking off and landing, it was often impossible for charter flights to get off the ground on time, and valuable custom was lost to Iona. Charter flights, planes milling around overhead and aerobatics could not be mixed. However, in spite of the obvious operational difficulties which were experienced, the DeSoutter made a remarkable number of charter and other flights before the operation was moved to Kildonan. Indeed, it is a tribute to both Hugh and the Air Corps that a high degree of co-operation was achieved between 1930 and 1931. The DeSoutter itself was sold before Hugh moved to Kildonan. Although quite busy in the number of trips it made, the DeSoutter was not busy enough to justify its retention as part of the Iona fleet. Consequently, it was sold. The aircraft which took its place was EI-AAP D.H. 83 Fox Moth, which was registered by Iona National Airways Ltd. on July 20th, 1932. Another aircraft which was eminently suited for the charter business was the EI-AAQ General Aircraft ST 4 Monospar ex. G-ABVS, registered in the name of O. E. Armstrong on February 20th, 1933.

O.E. Armstrong became the chief pilot at Kildonan, carrying out many of the aerodrome's most notable flights. Having gained immense experience at Kildonan, he went on to become the first and chief pilot of Aer Lingus when it was established. This vital link between Kildonan and Aer Lingus cannot be emphasised enough. In fact, the Aer Lingus edifice was built on the bedrock, as it were, of Kildonan pilots of the highest calibre, particularly O. E. Armstrong and Ivan Hammond.

Kildonan had been officially opened on June 8th, 1931. It was the first civil and commercial aerodrome in Ireland. The company, Iona National Airways Ltd., had three aircraft in operation at the time. They were: EI-AAF, EI-AAG and EI-AAK. Details of these aircraft are as follows:

This photograph was taken at the official opening of Kildonan Aerodrome. The company, Iona National Airways Ltd., had three aircraft in operation at the time. These were: EI-AAF, EI-AAG and EI-AAK

Business card of Hugh Cahill, managing director of Iona National Airways Ltd.

Perhaps this poster more than anything else captures the spirit of the aerodrome at Kildonan. The notion that flying is fun and the novelty of it comes across quite easily. There is no mystery, no barriers, complete openness: tea rooms, joy-rides and the thrill of it all. It must have been difficult to resist the invitation as there is a certain simplicity in the appeal. The aircraft in the poster is EI-AAK

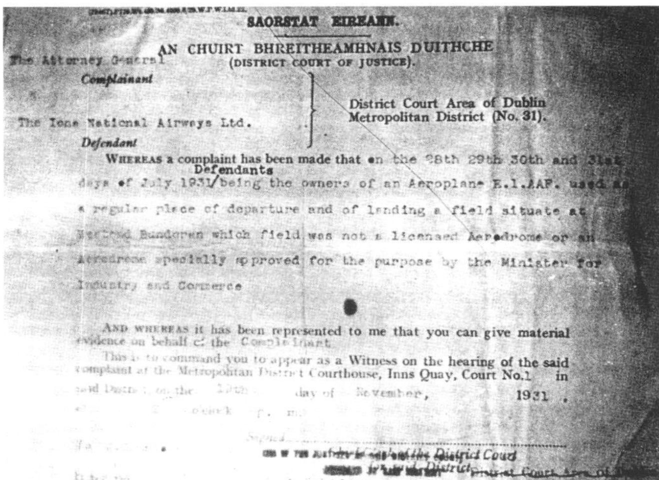

SAORSTAT EIREANN.

AN CHUIRT BHREITHEAMHNAIS DUITHCHE
(DISTRICT COURT OF JUSTICE).

The Attorney General
Complainant

The Iona National Airways Ltd.
Defendant

District Court Area of Dublin Metropolitan District (No. 31).

WHEREAS a complaint has been made that on the 28th 29th 30th and 31st days of July 1931 Defendants being the owners of an Aeroplane E.I.AAF. used as a regular place of departure and of landing a field situate at [illegible] Bundoran which field was not a licensed Aerodrome or an Aerodrome specially approved for the purpose by the Minister for Industry and Commerce

AND WHEREAS it has been represented to me that you can give material evidence on behalf of the Complainant

This is to command you to appear as a Witness on the hearing of the said complaint at the Metropolitan District Courthouse, Inns Quay, Court No.1 in said District, on the 10th day of November, 1931.

Signed ....
Justice of the District Court

This is a summons which Iona National Airways recieved for an unauthorised landing

THE IRISH TIMES, TUESDAY, JUNE 9, 1931.

AIR TAXI SERVICE INAUGURATED.

FLIGHTS ANYWHERE IN IRELAND.

A VIEW OF DUBLIN FROM THE SKIES.

THE first civil aerodrome in the Irish Free State was opened by Mr. Seumas Dolan, T.D., Parliamentary Secretary to the Ministry of Industry and Commerce, at Finglas, County Dublin, yesterday evening. The aerodrome is the new headquarters of the Iona National Airways and Flying School, Limited, of which Mr. Hugh Cahill is the managing director.

Mr. Cahill must be congratulated on his efforts to establish civil aviation in this country. For many years the Irish Free State has lagged behind other countries of the world in this respect. Until Mr. Cahill established the Iona National Airways there was no air taxi service here, although the Irish Aero Club were always prepared to use their machines as air taxis.

Mr. Cahill has selected a fine field which, with some alterations that he proposes to make, will make an excellent aerodrome in which big machines will be able to land and take off. He has constructed a hangar that can hold twenty aeroplanes, in addition to a large club-house, where ground instruction will be given to the members of the flying school.

The aerodrome is fully staffed and is in charge of a competent pilot, Mr. M. F. Coogan, who was, up to a short time ago, an officer in the Free State Army Air Corps. Mr. Coogan has been flying for several years, and has a first-class record.

ANYWHERE IN IRELAND.

At present Iona National Airways has three light aeroplanes, all D.H. Moths. They will be used for air taxi work in Ireland, and also for the purpose of instructing the pupils of the flying school

At a moment's notice it will be possible now to charter an aeroplane for a fast journey anywhere in this country. No cross-Channel work, however, will be undertaken until the new tri-engined passenger aeroplane, for which Mr. Cahill is negotiating, arrives.

Mr. Coogan took an *Irish Times* representative up for a short flight last evening for the purpose of demonstrating the suitability of the aerodrome.

Once in the air a magnificent view was obtained, with the City of Dublin almost underneath, and the coast line from Bray Head up to Lambay Island was clearly visible. A fine display of aerobatics was given during the evening by the Airways machines.

There was a large attendance at the opening of the aerodrome, which included some of the members of the Irish Aero Club, Dr. Pepper and Dr. S. Furlong. Mr. M. A. Doyle, the Aeronautical Engineer to the Free State Army Air Corps at Baldonnel, was an interested spectator.

'PHONES { DRUMCONDRA 298 / HEAD OFFICE 22586 } TELEGRAMS "WINGS" DUBLIN

Iona National Aerial Taxi Service and Flying School

CITY OFFICE: 26 Westmoreland Street Dublin

IONA ENGINEERING WORKS: Cross Guns Bridge, Glasnevin

To All Interested in Flying

Dear Sir, or Madam,

We should like to bring to your notice the fact that we have opened the above school which is equipped with the very latest type of machines.

One or two points we wish to emphazise—it is most important if you wish to take your "A" licence quickly, conveniently, and with the minimum of expense that you should be able to receive instruction according to your own convenience without a considerable loss of time. Our school is organized with this end in view, our Aerodrome situated as it is within 4 miles of the city can be reached in 15 minutes—a ring on the phone and the machine is ready awaiting your arrival at any hour of the day, or we can arrange to call for you with one of our motor taxis if you so desire.

It is our wish that all pupils pass out of the school with more than average ability to fulfil "A" licence tests.

There is no waiting list, no schedule of time to which you must adhere, the instructural experience available is unique and will enable the highest standard to be reached by all pupils.

Your consideration of the above remarks we trust will be received favourably.

Yours faithfully,

Iona National Aerial & Taxis Flying School Service

Application Form

I request my name to be included in the list of pupils for solo and Instructional Flying and I enclose remittance of £..............................
being subscription for year ending..............................193........
I am over / under 21 years of age.
I further agree to be governed by the Memorandum and Articles of Association and the Rules for the time being in force, and any which may hereafter be issued.

Signature..............................

Name in full..............................

Address..............................

....

Date..............................

Proposed by..............................

For Instructional and Solo Flying
£2 2s. 0d.

HIRING OF AEROPLANES

The hiring of all aeroplanes is on the understanding that H. Cahill accepts no responsibility for any damage or injury whatsoever that may occur to any member of the school while flying in the aeroplanes the property of the School.

Signed..............................

Date..............................

If under 21, the applicant must, in addition, obtain the signature of his / her parent or guardian below, as consenting to this application.

....
Parent / Guardian

Date..............................

PRINTED BY
THE ANGLESEA PRESS, 20 ANGLESEA STREET, DUBLIN.

Iona National Aerial Taxi Service and Flying School application form

No. 5003
TAXI TICKET.

7/-
FLIGHT.

Name..............................
If under age (21), Signature of Parent or Guardian.
....

Pilot..............................

Keep this Ticket to get back to Cross Guns Bridge.

DOLLARD, PRINTINGHOUSE, DUBLIN, LTD.

No. 5003
IONA
National Airways, Ltd.,
CROSS GUNS BRIDGE, GLASNEVIN.
CITY OFFICE:
26 WESTMORELAND STREET, DUBLIN.

VALID FOR ONE FLIGHT.

7/-

FLIGHTS will be given, as far as possible, in order of precedence of the above number. This Ticket must be given up before the Flight takes place.

IMPORTANT NOTICE.
(Subject to Conditions overleaf.)
The Company does not guarantee the performance of any journey, and shall not be held responsible for any loss or damage which may be occasioned by any delay or failure to complete any journey under notice.

Joy-riding at Iona: a ticket to ride

EI-AAF D.H.60G Moth, Reg'd. 3/6/31, Iona National Airways, c/ no. 1262, ex G-ABBG

EI-AAG D.H.60G Moth, Reg'd 2/6/31, Iona National Airways c/ no. 648, ex G-EBYV

Built as a D.H.60x Moth, but converted to 60G standard some time before sale to Ireland. Re-sold to the U.K. as G-EBYV in September 1932 and flown as such until withdrawn from use at Craulington, Newcastle, in October 1936.

EI-AAK D.H.60G Moth, Reg'd. 22/8/31, Iona National Airways c/ no. 1276, ex G-ABBV, C. Nelson, 22/3/35, Dublin Air Ferries

Operated in turn by Iona National Airways, Everson Flying Services and Dublin Air Ferries, until delivered to the U.K. on 7/4/36. Cancelled on 17/4/36 on sale to G-ABBV and flown as such until destroyed at Churchtown, Gloucestershire, on 15/7/39.

EI-AAK D H 60G Moth

The first aircraft acquired by Hugh Cahill was the Gypsy Moth G-ABBV and although registered in Hugh Cahill's name in July 1930, it continued on the English register during its first year of operation in the Irish Free State.

G.A.B.B.V. Gypsy Moth

On August 1st, 1931, this aircraft, piloted by Mr. Coogan and with a passenger from Belfast, crashed at Annaghmore, near Collooney, Co. Sligo. It was a minor accident and only slight injuries were sustained.

The head office of Iona National Airways Ltd. was at Cross Guns Bridge and the city office was 26 Westmoreland Street. The full title was Iona National Flying School and Motor Engineering Works. This was the original title of the company.

Some of the early names at Kildonan

Instructors at Kildonan included J.C. Coogan, J.M. Kearney (St. John Kearney) and Captain Eric Stewart, who was later killed at Newtownards when flying from Stranraer. J.R. Currie was both the ground engineer, instructor and aircraft designer.

In addition to the names mentioned above, a lot of the Air Corps officers flew at Kildonan. One of the familiar names in this regard was Paddy Hassett, who did much of his flying there.

EI-AAK, D.H.60G Moth, Reg'd. 22/8/31, Iona National Airways c/no. 1276, ex G-ABBV, 2/12/33, C. Nelson

22/3/35, Dublin Air Ferries

On June 5th, 1931, Iona Airways organised one of the first charter flights to the Isle of Man. The flight took place in a Gypsy Moth under the auspices of the Royal Irish Automobile Club. The purpose of the flight was to bring Mr. Crabtree, a well known racing driver, from a competition in the Phoenix Park to a similar competition in the Isle of Man. Joe Adams, who was manager of the Iona Garage at Cross Guns Bridge, signed the authorisation in this case. The price was one shilling a mile and the pilot's expenses were one pound. Mr. Crabtree was collected at the Phoenix Park by taxi and brought to Kildonan Aerodrome.

Imagine you have just purchased your ticket for your first ever joy-ride with Iona National Airways Ltd., Kildonan. It offers you the thrill of a lifetime and afterwards free transport back to the Iona Garage at Cross Guns Bridge. The only problem is that it is valid only until 1933, so you have probably missed the bus, and the flight

Another notable flight was an ambulance flight completed in the Fox Moth, D.H.83 EI-AAP, which in one day flew from Kildonan to Liverpool, then on to Croydon, Bristol, Cardiff, Cork and back to Kildonan. O.E. Armstrong was the pilot. Imagine you have just purchased your ticket for your first ever joy-ride with Iona National Airways Ltd., Kildonan. It offers you the thrill of a lifetime and afterwards free transport back to the Iona Garage at Cross Guns Bridge. The only problem is that it is valid only until 1933, so you have probably missed the bus, and the flight. The crowds flocked to Kildonan and the euphoria which was generated reached its high point in 1933, a year of pageants and joy-riding never surpassed. Pageants were organised by Iona National Airways Ltd., the Irish Aero Club and the impresario himself, Sr. Alan Cobham. People were caught in the grip of an irresistible urge to fly.

EI-AAP D.H.83 Fox Moth

In answer to the established need to provide for charter flights in the Irish Free State, Iona purchased D.H. Fox Moth EI-AAP. It was flown to Kildonan Aerodrome by William Gardner a pilot of Brian Lewis and Co, agents for de Havilland. This aircraft, the latest in the D.H. range, had seating accommodation for three passengers in an enclosed cabin. A fourth passenger could be accommodated on short trips such as joy-rides.

The importance of this aircraft in the development of civil aviation in the Irish Free State should not be underestimated. For the next six years, EI-AAP was the principal aircraft used for charter flights.

The Fox Moth was used extensively for scenic tours which included trips to the south-west and along the Shannon. Its life was not without incident and in August 1932, on one of these trips down the country, Captain O.E. Armstrong, chief pilot of Iona, hit a rock outcrop on landing in a field damaging the under carriage and breaking the propeller. Damage was slight and the Fox Moth was soon back in service.

EI-AAP, D.H.83 Fox Moth, Reg'd. 20/7/32, Iona National Airways c/no. 4003. New aircraft, 2/12/33, C. Nelson

22/3/35, Dublin Air Ferries

This aircraft was used for charter operations in turn by Iona National Airways, Everson Flying Services and Dublin Air Ferries, until shipped to England on 31/8/38. It was cancelled on 18/9/38 and later registered in the U.K. as G-AFKI. It was impressed by the RAF on 31/8/41 but no RAF serial number was allocated. Its final fate was unconfirmed but it was presumed scrapped.

EI-AAP Fox Moth

Kildonan Aerodrome during the Eucharistic Congress. This picture shows the Parnell Elf and also a British registered Junkers aircraft which was chartered by Iona National Airways Ltd. for about a month at the time of the Congress. June 1932

One of the notable charters completed by Captain O.E. Armstrong in EI-AAP DH 83 Fox Moth, took place on July 1st, 1933. The aircraft departed Kildonan Aerodrome at 6.30 a.m., flew to Liverpool and from there to Croydon, with a passenger.

There were many notable flights at Kildonan during the days of Iona National Airways Ltd. One of the achievements of Iona was to deliver photographs of important events quickly to England, including photographs of the Irish Sweeps draw for the Grand National. On Easter Sunday,1932, Mr. O.E. Armstrong, one of the few pilots permitted by the insurance companies to fly single engine aircraft on the direct route from Dublin to Holyhead, flew to Manchester with photos of the Republican parade and demonstration at Glasnevin.

Aircraft EI-AAF

In August 1931, a pilot and passenger in a light aircraft were injured when it crashed into a house while trying to land at West End, Bundoran. The accident happened at about 9pm on a Friday when the Moth aeroplane, belonging to Iona National Airways Ltd. which had been taking passengers for short flights in the course of the week, caught a wall with its tail and struck the home of Miss McAughey, a native of Sligo who resided alone.

The passenger in the plane, a Mr. John O'Doherty from Belfast, was injured. The pilot, Mr. Coogan, escaped with minor injuries. Both were removed to the Rock Hospital, Ballyshannon. There was a large crowd on the landing strip as the aircraft had been making its approach. They were waiting for trips in the aircraft at the time and it was suggested that their encroachment onto the landing strip had forced the pilot to go too close to the house in order to avoid them.

The particulars of EI-AAF are as follows:

EI-AAF, D.H.60G Moth, Reg'd. 3/6/31, Iona National Airways c/no. 1262, ex G-ABBG

Re-fuelling at Kildonan, D.H. Gypsy Moth, EI-AAK Dublin Air Ferries, Kildonan, 8/3/1935

Iona National Airways Ltd, Kildonan Aerodrome, summer 1931. Iona ground engineers, Mr. Mick Brady and Mr. Sheridan, with D.H.60. G. Moth, EI-AAG. Note: Gypsy 11 engine and high pressure tyres. Compare this photo with photo below where the same A/c. is fitted with an ADC. Cirrus 11 engine and 'doughnut' wheels. Weston photo, Dublin

Iona National Airways Ltd. Kildonan Aerodrome, c. early 1932.
From left: Mrs. John Horgan, Mr. Hugh Cahill, and Captain O.E. Armstrong, pilot. Name of passenger not known. A/c. D.H.60 'Moth', EI-AAG, here shown fitted with ADC. 'Cirrus' 2 engine and 'doughnut' wheels. Compare with photo, above of the same aircraft, taken in 1931. Photo from the private collection of Mr. Pearse Cahill

A/c. D.H.60 'Moth'. EI-AAG D.H.60G Moth Reg'd. 2/6/31, Iona National Airways c/no. 648 ex G-EBYV. Built as a D.H.60X Moth but converted to 60G standard some time before sale to Ireland. Re-sold to the U.K. as G-EBYV in September 1932 and flown as such until withdrawn from use at Craulington, Newcastle, in October 1936

The Iona fleet at Kildonan Aerodrome (from left): EI - AAP D.H.83 Fox Moth; EI-AAQ General Aircraft S.T. 4 Monospar; and two D.H. 60G Moths. Inset includes J.R. Currie, Tony Millea, Lilly Dillon, Kevin Sheridan and Mick Brady

Pearse Cahill, standing beside the giant Bristish Junkers cahter aircraft at Kildonan Aerodrome, on the occasion of the Eucharistic Congress. Pearse Cahill went solo on April 30th, 1933

The Eucharistic Congress took place in 1932. Dublin had never seen such a big crowd as that which congregated in the Phoenix Park that month. It was the most historic religious event of the 1930s that the country had witnessed. Kildonan Aerodrome was to the forefront in providing aircraft facilities for photographic assignments, joy-rides and sight seeing flights during the congress. Cappagh Hospital, Finglas has a unique link with this historic event as the specially built altar which was used to celebrate benediction at O'Connell Bridge in the evening was transported to the hospital for safe keeping. And today, it is preserved in pristine condition in the grounds of the hospital. Cappagh Hospital had a special place in the hearts of the pilots who flew at Kildonan. It was customary when flying over the hospital for the pilots to dip a wing and wave to the patients, who in the summer were wheeled out in their beds. For the patients, this was big medicine and they waved back enthusiastically. A special bond built up over the years between patients and pilots.

Kildonan Aerodrome during the Eucharistic Congress. This photograph includes a Parnell Elf, G-AAVT. June 1932

A British owned Junkers charter aircraft at Kildonan Aerodrome for the occasion of the Eucharistic Congress, which was held in Dublin in June 1932. Photo from the private collection of Mr. Pearse Cahill

A close-up shot of Junkers charter aircraft at Kildonan Aerodrome on the occasion of the Eucharistic Congress which was held in the Phoenix Park, Dublin in June 1932. Junkers was the first to introduce corrugated covering on the wings as well as the body and was a very safe machine to fly. The corrugation was for strength

A visiting craft (Junkers) at Kildonan for the Eucharistic Congress, 1932

The roads in the Phoenix Park, Dublin were thronged with people on the occasion of the Eucharistic Congress which was held in June 1932. Photograph taken from an aircraft of Iona National Airways Ltd.

The altar which was used to house the tabernacle at the benediction ceremony held on O'Connell Bridge after the ceremonies of the Eucharistic Congress in the Phoenix Park. It was transferred to the grounds of Cappagh Hospital, Finglas where it is perfectly preserved to this day

The Eucharistic Congress High Mass held in the Phoenix Park in 1932. Photograph taken from an aircraft of Iona National Airways Ltd.

Eucharistic Congress Evening Benediction Ceremony at O'Connell St. Bridge

Irish Independent report, Tues June 6th, 1933

Pageant took place Monday June 5th, 1933

Flying kit, 1930s advertisement

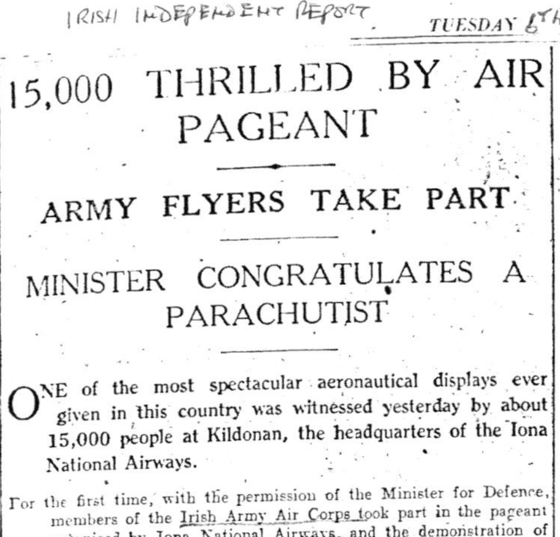

IRISH INDEPENDENT REPORT TUESDAY 6TH JUNE

15,000 THRILLED BY AIR PAGEANT

ARMY FLYERS TAKE PART

MINISTER CONGRATULATES A PARACHUTIST

ONE of the most spectacular aeronautical displays ever given in this country was witnessed yesterday by about 15,000 people at Kildonan, the headquarters of the Iona National Airways.

For the first time, with the permission of the Minister for Defence, members of the Irish Army Air Corps took part in the pageant organised by Iona National Airways, and the demonstration of aerobatic flying roused the spectators to great enthusiasm.

Another feature was the parachute descent by Mr. Joseph Gilmore, engineer of the Army Air Corps, who made a most spectacular landing after side slipping a grove of trees.

Crazy Flying

Mr. Elliot, of the Irish Aero Club, giving a display at the Air Pageant at Kildonan.
—*Irish Independent* Photo (C.)

On landing Mr. Gilmore had a most enthusiastic reception,

tion, they received wonderful appreciation from the public on landing.

The item of the evening in which the thousands of spectators seemed interested was the parachute descent by Mr. Gilmore, from a height of 2,500 feet.

BREATHLESS SPECTATORS.

He alighted from the 'plane west of the aerodrome, and the thousands of spectators stood breathless until the parachute opened out, and Mr. Gilmore made a perfect landing about 200 feet from a wooded portion of land on the eastern side of the 'drome.

Mr. Gilmore told an *Irish Independent* representative that to avoid the trees, at about 700 feet from the ground, he had to "split the wind" in the shoot, so as to avoid landing in the trees.

Mr. Gilmore also stated that the parachute was his own, and that he was ready to give demonstrations anywhere over the country.

THE OPEN RACE.

In the open race, for which Lady Nelson presented the Irish Cup, to be competed for annually, a replica being given in the interim to the winner, the following competed: Lady Heath, Mr. P. O'Brien, Mr. A. Woods, Mr. W. R. Elliott, and Mr. C. F. French.

The result was:

1—Mr. French.
2—Mr. Elliott.
3—Mr. O'Brien.
4—Mr. Woods.
5—Lady Heath.

So great was the rush for joy rides that after the contest it was found necessary to postpone the spot-landing contest, so as to give patrons an opportunity of taking part in the joy rides.

At one point in the competitions a 'plane passed over dropping showers of leaflets issued by Independent Newspapers, Ltd.

LANDING CONTEST.

Sunday night's landing contest, for which a cup was presented by Iona Airways, was won by Capt. O. E. Armstrong in a Puss Moth.

THE FLIGHT PAST.

The first event—the flight past—in which eight 'planes took part, proved most fascinating. Those participating were:—

Mr. W. R. Elliott, in a Gipsy I. Moth, Chief Instructor of Irish Aero Club;
Mr. C. J. French, Asst. Instructor I.A.C. (Gipsy I. Moth);
Lieut. A. Russell,
Lieut. Keane, and
Lieut. Twohig, officers of the Army Air Corps, in Avro Cadets;
Lady Heath (Gipsy Moth);
Mr. P. O'Brien (Fox Moth), and
Mr. Andrew Woods (Gipsy Moth).

During the flight-past Mr. Aiken, who was accompanied by Mr. Little, arrived and was received by Mr. Hugh Cahill, managing director, Iona National Airways, Ltd., and Capt. T. Young, manager.

MAP-READING RACE.

Several thousand people witnessed the start of the map-reading race contest, in which the competitors were:—Mr. W. R. Elliott (Gipsy I. Moth), Mr. C. F. French (do.), Mr. Andrew Woods (do.), and Mr. P. O'Brien (Fox Moth). For the race Marconi and Co. presented a wireless set.

Before the start of the race the competitors were handed a map of the course, and observers were stationed at pylons to report to the judges the progress and accuracy of the course followed by the competitors.

After a most exciting race,

Mr. O'Brien was declared the winner, with the others, in order: Mr. Elliott, Mr. French, and Mr. A. Woods.

FORMATION FLYING

TRIBUTE TO PILOTS' TRAINING

The demonstration of formation flying, given for the first time before the public by the Army Air Corps, was delightful, and showed the excellent training received by the pilots, who were Lieutenants Russell, Keane, and Twohig.

During the demonstration one gentleman interested in aviation told an *Irish Independent* representative that the perfect formation gave the impression of barrack square drill.

At high and low altitudes the pilots gave an excellent demonstration of 'plane manipulation in perfect formation.

OBSTACLE RACE

The obstacle race proved highly interesting. The participants were Lady Heath, Mr. P. O'Brien, Mr. C. F. French, Mr. W. R. Elliott, and Mr. R. J. Currie.

The pilots had to stand 25 yards away from their machines, put on flying garb, from that spot carry a glass of water each to the machine, and then start the engines to take part in the race.

The prize was a canteen of cutlery presented by Mr. Hugh Cahill, Chairman and Managing Director, Iona Airways, Ltd.

After an exciting race, Mr. Elliott was declared the winner, with Mr. French second.

Mr. W. R. Elliott then gave a wonderful demonstration of crazy flying, and on landing received plaudits from the thousands present.

THRILLING AEROBATICS.

One of the most spectacular events of the evening was the demonstration given by Lieutenants Russell, Keane, and Twohig,

who amazed the crowded throng by aerobatics, which included looping the loop, inverted flying, gliding, nose diving, falling leaf, and formation flying—in fact, every trick know to aviators.

This being the first occasion on which Army Air pilots gave such a demonstra-

The judges in all the events were:—Gen. Hugh MacNeill, Assistant Chief of Staff, Mr. M. A. Doyle, B.Sc., Eng., Aeronautical Engineer, Army Air Corps; Comndt.

A 2,500 Feet Jump

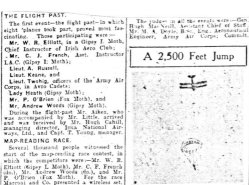

A parachute descent (a picture taken just after the parachute had opened) by Mr. Joseph Gilmore at the Air Pageant at Kildonan.
—*Irish Independent* Photo (C.)

O'Carroll, Director, Military Aviation, and Major J. J. Liston, O/C. Army Air Corps, Baldonnel.

The catering was carried out by Mrs. Lawlor and Sons, Naas.

Aeronautical display, Kildonan, Monday June 5th, 1933

Advertisement of the 1930s

Iona 'Fox-Moth' EI-AAP and Mr. Joseph Gilmore, prior to making a parachute descent at a Kildonan air display. Weston Photo, Dublin

Mr. Gilmore making his parachute descent

National Aero Club (Irish Free State)

A meeting was held at Kildonan Aerodrome on May 21st, 1933, where it was decided to set up an aero club for pupils of the Iona Flying School. The new club was named the National Aero Club (Irish Free State). Lady Cathleen Nelson was elected chairperson and president. Vice-presidents were: Mrs. Wilkinson; Mr. Hugh Cahill; Lady Heath; Sir James Nelson BT; Mr. R. Everett; Mr. Conway and Captain Young. The committee elected was: Lady Heath, Messrs. Peterson, Donoghue, Gleeson, Hayes, Hill, Kearney and Young.

The first parachute jump from an aeroplane in Ireland was made by Mr. Gilmore on April 17th, 1933 at Baldonnel Aerodrome. Mr. Gilmore was a ground engineer in the Army Air Corps and was a native of Ardglass, Co. Down. The pilot of the aircraft on this occasion was Mr. Raymond Quilter and the aircraft was Gregory Quilter's own plane, he being the inventor of the parachute which was new. Gregory Quilter had been trying to interest the Army Air Corps who were still using the old American. Irving 'chutes, which were massive and cumbersome, though made of pure silk.

George Weston, aviation photographer supreme, with a smile on his face, ready to take to the air. His camera was his friend. He is pictured here in front of an Iona National Airways Gypsy Moth

Photograph of George Weston, without whose images the history of Kildonan would be very incomplete. George lived at number 10 Idrone Terrace, Blackrock, Co. Dublin. Chris Bruton photo

Baldonnel thrill - A photograph taken from the air by Irish Times staff photographer of Mr. Gilmore's parachute descent at Baldonnel on April 17th, 1933. This was the first parachute descent in Ireland and the first time that Mr. Gilmore, a member of the Irish Aero Club, had attempted the feat

Air display, Kildonan, June 5th, 1933. Photo shows a section of the spectators around the hangar area. Aircraft on the ground (far left) is one of three Avro 'Cadets' of the Air Corps' aerobatic team, as flown by Lieuts. A. Russell, J. Twohig and W. Keane

Air pageant, Iona National Airways Ltd, Kildonan, June 5th, 1933

Flying Contests at Kildonan Aerodrome
Finglas, Dublin

(Under the Auspices of the Iona National Flying Services, Ltd.)

FOR WHIT MONDAY, JUNE 5TH, 1933

APPLICATION FORM

ARRIVAL CONTEST (To Arrive at 7 p.m. 4th June)

Machine Gypsy Moth Owner Hugh Cahill esq Lettering EI-AAK

Engine ~~DH63~~ G. Moth Engine No DH63 Insured yes Pilot's Licence No 19..

Load Carried — Pilot G. R. Currie & G. Weston Fee 5/-

Pilot's Signature G. R. Currie

OPEN RACE

Machine .... Owner .... Lettering ....

Engine .... Engine No .... Load Carried .... Fee 5/-

Pilot .... Pilot's Licence No ....

Pilot's Signature ....

MAP RACE

Machine .... Owner .... Lettering ....

Engine .... Engine No .... Load Carried .... Fee 5/-

Pilot .... Pilot's Licence No. ....

Pilot's Signature ....

OBSTACLE RACE

Machine .... Owner .... Lettering ....

Engine .... Engine No. .... Load Carried .... Fee 5/-

Pilot ________ Pilot's Licence No. ________

Pilot's Signature ________

SPOT LANDING CONTEST

Machine Gypsy Moth Owner Mr H. Cahill

Pilot G. Weston Fee 1/-

Pilot's Signature G Weston

BALLOON BURSTING CONTEST

Machine Gypsy Moth Owner Mr H Cahill

Pilot G Weston Fee 1/-

Pilot's Signature G Weston

Flying Contests at Kildonan Aerodrome application form, June 5th, 1933

The Monospar twin-engined monoplane (Pobjoy) taking off at Kildonan

A side view of the Monospar twin-engined monoplane (Pobjoy) taken at Kildonan Aerodrome, Finglas

A view of the Monospar twin-engined (Pobjoy) taken from the rear

A Monospar in flight

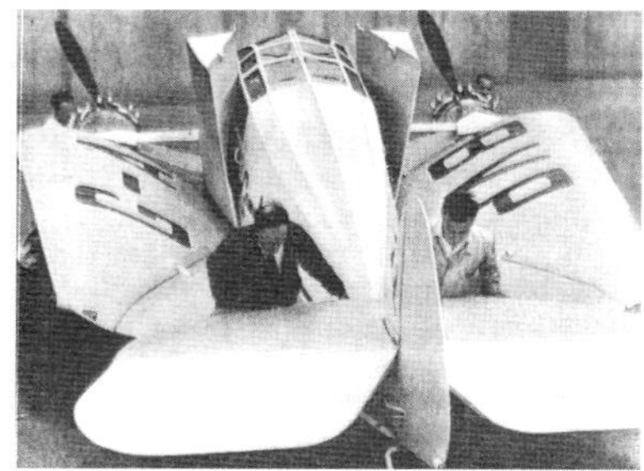

A Monospar with wings folded

EI-AAQ, General Aircraft S.T.4 Monospar, Reg'd. 20/2/33, O. E. Armstrong, c/no. S.T. 4/6, ex G-ABVS

Cancelled 2/11/33 upon re-sale to G-ABVS. Flown as such until scrapped at Ford in 1939.

A Monospar

EI-AAQ. G. A. Monospar ST.4.

F. & F/S. Silver-doped overall, but of a shade darker than that usually to be found on F/S Markings: (M.) deep cream.

The Currie Wot Aircraft Aireymouse G-APNT

While working in Ireland for Iona National Airways, J.R. Currie designed the single seater Currie Wot in the mid 1930s and built two aircraft, both of which were destroyed in an air raid in 1940. The design was resurrected in 1958 by Viv Bellamy and a further eight aircraft were built over the next 14 years. This is the Aireymouse at Weston which was made famous by Harold Penrose in a book of the same name. G-APNT is responsive, light on the stick and forgiving. The Wot's capacity of 11.5 gallons at a burn rate of four gallons per hour gave it a distance span of about two and three quarter hours at 70mph

Food for isolated Meath. The roads being impassable as a result of the recent snow-storm, airways service had to send food supplies to isolated areas in Co. Meath. Photo shows the plane being loaded at Kildonan Aerodrome, Finglas. Irish Independent, 1/3/33.

Food for isolated Meath

As a result of blizzard conditions, the whole country was blanketed in snow. Nine people had already died and several others were reported missing. Because of severed cables, there was no direct telephone or telegraphic communications between Dublin and the west and north of Ireland. County Meath was the worst hit and communications with this area were virtually non-existent.

Iona National Airways Ltd., in response to an appeal by the Lord Mayor of Dublin, Alderman Alfie Byrne T.D., provided an aircraft free of charge, as well as the services of two pilots, Captain Stewart and Captain T.L. Young. Food, provided free by Messrs. Alex Findlater and Co. Ltd., a well known Dublin firm, included 200 loaves of bread and 20lbs. of tea. They were flown by Iona to isolated villages including Dunshaughlin, Nobber, Summerhill and Balivor.

While Hugh Cahill answered the call of the Lord Mayor of Dublin and the prayers of the snowbound inhabitants of the plain of Moynalta, Jack Craigie, founder of Merville Dairy, sent out his men to fell trees for fuel so that no family in Finglas would perish from the sub-zero temperatures that the heavy blanket of snow had brought. Particular attention was paid to the old and the needy, usually the first victims of hypothermia.

J.R. Currie was the co-inventor of the Currie-Wot aircraft. Currie-Wots were later converted for the picture, The Blue Max, where they were made to look like an SE 5 A of the First World War.

The Master of Sempill, a very famous aviator of the day, made a number of flying visits to the Irish Free State. When he visited Kildonan as guest of Iona National Airways Ltd., he was director of National Flying Services in England. He had been invited over by the Institute of Motor Traders of the Irish Free State. His schedule included a reception by the Lord Mayor, Alderman Alfie Byrne at Kildonan Aerodrome and an aerial reception by planes of the Free State Army Air Corps and Iona National Airways Ltd. Also included was a banquet in his honour by the motor trade in the Dolphin Hotel. A highlight of his visit was a lecture delivered in the Physics Theatre of University College Dublin on 'Co-operation between Aviation and the Motor Trade'. During the lecture, he showed films in connection with Graf Zeppelin's flight to South America.

Going solo at Kildonan

Going solo at Kildonan was a very big occasion. The successful aviator was met by the members as he or she taxied in and was cheered to the clubhouse, congratulated by all. (Afterwards, a visit to one of the local public houses was essential to do justice to the occasion.) The 'Upper Floods' was the most popular and most convenient to the aerodrome, being located at the top of the main street in Finglas Village. Not to be confused, of course, with the 'Lower Floods', which was situated at the bottom of the hill at the lower part of the main street in the village. Mick Brady, one of the engineers at Kildonan, went solo in 1935 and appropriately Flood's facilities, the upper house, were availed of. A silver tankard was presented to the successful soloist and drinks were shared from it. Mick had started off as a motor mechanic at Hugh Cahill's Iona Garage in Glasnevin.

Photograph of Mick Brady, ground engineer with A/c EI-AAK at Kildonan, Finglas

Mick Brady, ground engineer at Kildonan, carries out a major engine overhaul. Photo: Chris F. Bruton

Ground engineers Mick Brady and J.R. Currie hard at work in the hangar at Kildonan. Photo: Chris F. Bruton

Pearse Cahill went solo on April 30th, 1933. During the period March 19th to April 19th, 1935, when Dublin Air Ferries operated at Kildonan, the following pilots went solo:

Mr. Culleton of Galway after 7 hrs. 45mns.

Ms. Denise Beattie after 7 hrs. 20 mns.

Mick Brady, assistant ground engineer, after 6 hrs. 30 mns.

Miss Katherine Bayley Butler.

Mr. Little, Mr. L.U. Smith, Mr. E.J. Gleeson.

Hugh Cahill knew quite well that it would be very difficult, if not impossible, to sustain his project until the aviation market firmed up. Unless, of course, there was the possibility of some kind of State subsidy. In England, the flying clubs were subsidised and at home the Irish Aero Club, of which Hugh was a member, was pushing very strongly for a subvention. Hugh was fully aware of this and a subsidy for the new club at Kildonan would have probably made his venture viable in the long term. But the door was closed on both Hugh and the politically active Irish Aero Club. The main fear in the minds of the Government was apparently the fact that a proliferation of flying clubs and aerodromes might in some way constitute a security risk and that the role which they would fulfil in training future pilots for the defence force could not make up for the risk which they regarded as very real. They felt flying was primarily for the defence force and that they should not encourage the proliferation of the flying clubs. What key members of the Air Corps wanted was a State company and it would take another five years to achieve this. Col Charles Russell was the outspoken and constant advocate of this concept. It was the only option which gained favour because it provided for state control which was regarded as essential.

The following poster, which was published in the early 1930s, shows the attitude of the establishment and the reaction of the flying enthusiasts. The Irish Aero Club had held out some hope for a while but eventually despaired of any prospects of a change in the Government's attitude. When this, the premier flying club with the most clout and close to the ear of the Government failed in its efforts, what hope then had Hugh Cahill got. He was, comparatively speaking, a freelance in the arena of the flying world.

A poster indicating the State's refusal to fund the flying clubs

The credit must go to Hugh Cahill for visualising the day when you could hire air taxis. To Hugh Cahill fell all the difficulty and hassle of finding a suitable airfield, within reasonable distance of the city, in this case five miles from the city centre. The ground had to be inspected and passed as being suitable as an aerodrome. Then he went to the expense of providing a very good, purpose-built hangar. He sank a fuel tank with an appropriate dispensing pump and hose, suitable for aircraft. Although these appear very run of the mill in the modern context, we are talking about the 1930s and Hugh started with no equipment, stock, aircraft or buildings. The project was solely of his conception and his investment. He started with green fields, his ideas and his savings and took all the risks. Only down the road was the ex-R.A.F. Collinstown Aerodrome, with hangars, landing strips and all the back-up facilities. It was disused at the time. Hugh established a very nice set-up for a commercial operation and flying club. Unlike Britain, where the flying clubs were subsidised from 1925 onwards, the Free State Government provided no State aid whatsoever, until the coming of Aer Lingus. The State did not give a penny to Hugh Cahill, to Lady Nelson, or to Lady Heath, directly or indirectly. They had to stand on their own two feet.

Iona National Airways had already ceased its operations by August 1933 when Lady Nelson, a new operator,who had already been a regular user of the aerodrome, took over. She formed a new company called Everson Flying Services Ltd.

The air pageant fatality at Phoenix Park: ambulance men attending to Private Tobin. Captain Oscar Heron and Private Richard Tobin were killed. Irish Independent photo

EI-AAG

Chapter Nine

Hugh Cahill's role in aviation history

Aerial photograph of Kildonan Aerodrome, taken during the days of Everson Flying Services, 1934. Photo shows Lady C. Nelson Miles 'Hawk', EI-AAX (EX-G-ACNX) and D.H. 80A, the 'Puss Moth', G-ABDL, as used by Captain O. E. Armstrong. Photo from Pearse Cahill collection

Chapter 9

Hugh Cahill's role in Irish aviation history

In years to come, as the locational limitations of Dublin Airport become more apparent in the light of new advances in the field of aviation and new demands for air travel, it may become apparent that subsequent aviation planners should have built on Hugh's dream location before it was surrounded on its southern flank by new developments, and by an electricity station to the north.

Careful planning was one of the most important attributes of Hugh Cahill. When he decided to set up Kildonan Aerodrome, he had travelled every inch of Dublin and its hinterland. He had searched high and low. He had flown over the land, drove around it and walked large tracts, until he knew that Kildonan fitted the bill more so than any other. When the Ice Age had retreated many centuries ago before the first settlers came to this area, it left a vast plain - the plain of Moynalta - which stretched out for miles like a huge tapestry of multiple shades of green and gold. It was as if the High Kings of Tara, the eventual rulers of the Island of Ireland, had rolled out a giant carpet, which enveloped the whole lands, uninterrupted by hill or vale. Hugh looked out and he saw that it was good for what he wanted, good for his creation - Kildonan Aerodrome.

In years to come, as the locational limitations of Dublin Airport become more apparent in the light of new advances in the field of aviation and new demands for air travel, it may become apparent that subsequent aviation planners should have built on Hugh's dream location before it was surrounded on its southern flank by new developments, and by an electricity station to the north.

Hugh Cahill was the father of Irish commercial aviation. When he set up Iona National Airways Ltd., his place in the aviation hall of fame had been assured. Hugh chose an excellent location for his aerodrome - it was located in open country as far as the eye could see.

Mr Cahill was an entrepreneur in the classical sense of the word. He did not have the benefit of market research as we know it today - it was not possible to be sure if the timing was right. Hugh reverted to his former occupation as a motor mechanic at his garage at Cross Guns Bridge, also called 'Iona'. But not before he had achieved many notable aviation feats and sown the seeds of deep interest in the heart and mind of his son Pearse, which in good time would take root and blossom into a thriving business - Iona National Airways situated at Cloghran, adjacent to Collinstown Airport. Hugh was first and foremost a businessman and when the time was right he sold his aviation business interest.

Yet in a very short time the successes of Iona National Airways Ltd. were formidable. The company lasted from 1930 to 1933 and in that time commercial aviation had been firmly established. Charter flights took place on a regular basis. A flying club, the Dublin Aero Club, had been established. Hugh Cahill hosted Sir Alan Cobham's first Irish air display at Kildonan on July 2nd, 1933. Iona pioneered commercial aerial photography, banner towing for advertising and novelty features such as the dropping of a football from an aircraft to start Gaelic football matches at Croke Park and Mullingar.

By means of the many pageants held by Iona at Kildonan and other locations, Hugh played a key role in bringing aviation to the masses. Flying was not solely the preserve of the elite.

During the Eucharistic Congress which took place in the Phoenix Park, in 1932, Kildonan was used as a landing place for large and small aircraft. Photographs were taken of this historic occasion from Iona aircraft.

Perhaps Hugh Cahill's most remarkable and ambitious enterprise was the inauguration of a passenger and mail air service linking up with the cities of Cork and Galway and the Atlantic liners and thence via Dublin, London and Rotterdam on to Berlin. Iona Fox Moth EI-AAP, piloted by Captain O.E. Armstrong, flew from Galway to Baldonnel. And a giant three engined KLM FOKKER monoplane, piloted by Captain Scholte with 13 passengers on board, waited there ready to complete the final leg of the 825 mile journey.

Anthony Fokker

This flight was intended by Hugh Cahill to be the beginning of a new European flying network. However, due to the lack of financial support from governmental sources, which would have been necessary to sustain this type of advanced service, the opportunity for a link-up between the west and the east of Ireland and the rest of Europe and the Atlantic lines was lost.

In a matter of three years, Hugh Cahill had secured his place in Irish aviation history. In true entrepreneurial style he had set up Ireland's first commercial aerodrome and initiated many and varied enterprises. Hugh was instrumental in popularising flying and preparing the ground so that others could in time reap the benefits. Aer Lingus was to be the main beneficiary as several of Iona's former pilots went on to play key roles in the development of the new national airline.

Captain O.E. Armstrong, pilot of the Iona aircraft Gypsy Moth EI-AAP, which flew mail and passengers from Galway to Baldonnel to link up with the giant Fokker monoplane owned by the Dutch Airline KLM and captained by Captain Scholte. This aircraft flew on via London and Rotterdam to Berlin, on what was its inaugural flight

EI-AAP, which took part in the above inaugural flight

Col. Charles C. Russell of the Irish Army Air Corps (second from right) with the crew of the KLM Fokker monoplane which flew air-mail from Baldonnel to Berlin. The full crew was: J.B. Scholte, pilot; J.J. Denouter, wireless operator; Col. C.F. Russell, ex. O.C. Irish Army Air Corps; and P. Dunk, engineer

Galway-Dublin-Berlin Flight—Photograph taken at Oranmore, **Galway, this morning.** Mr. C. **Lynch, Postmaster of Galway,** handing the bag of mails to Capt. O. E. Armstrong, **who piloted the "Feeder" plane to Baldonnel.** The two passengers are Mrs. P. Kenny and Miss Kitty Curran.

(Photo by Air from Galway).

The first leg of the Galway-Dublin-Berlin flight. Photograph taken at Oranmore, Galway, on the morning of the flight. Mr. C. Lynch, postmaster of Galway, handing the bag of mail to Capt. O.E. Armstrong, who piloted the 'feeder' plane to Baldonnel. The two passengers are Mrs. P. Kenny and Miss Kitty Curran. Photo by air from Galway

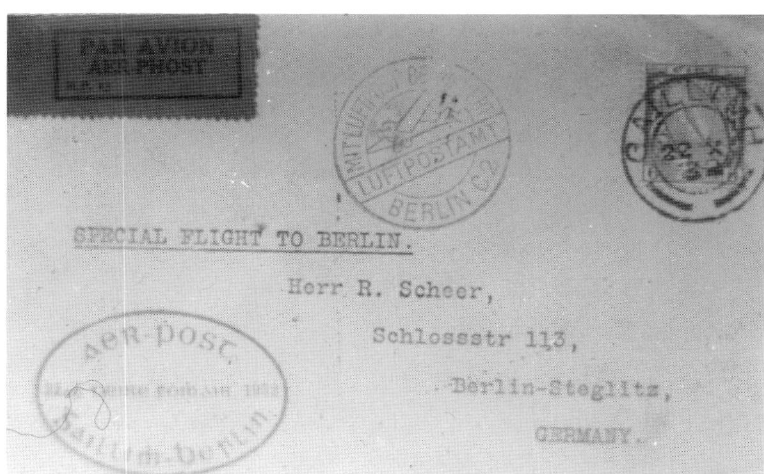

A photograph of a postcard sent by one of the passengers on the Berlin flight. The postcard shows the special Irish air-mail stamp for the occasion. The date of this historic flight was October 22nd, 1932

The special air mail stamp to commemerate the special demonstration flight, from Galway, via Baldonnel, to Berlin. Hugh Cahill, Col. Charles Russell and O. E. Armstrong, chief pilot at Iona National Airways, Kildonan, played the key roles in this fine venture

Envelope of letter sent with Galway/Berlin Air Mail Stamp. Galway - Berlin historic flight, October 22nd, 1932

First air mail, flight Galway-London, April 26th, 1929

The first airmail service between Ireland and the UK was flown between Oranmore Aerodrome outside Galway to London's Croydon Aerodrome on 26 August 1929. The moving spirit behind this trial was Colonel Charlie Russell who, with 'Mutt' Summers, the chief test pilot of Vicker's Aviation, collected American mail which had arrived in Galway on the German liner Karlsruhe. Seen here: the Postmaster is handing up one of the bags of US mail to Russell at 7.30am. The Vixen touched down at Baldonnel at 8am and was en route to Croydon, via chester, at 8.30. where it arrived at 11.37.

Hugh Cahill had little time for diplomatic niceties. He was impatient to realise his dream of air taxis and flying machines

EI-AAP, D.H.83 Fox Moth, Reg'd. 20/7/32, Iona National Airways, c/no. 4003. New Aircraft 2/12/33, C. Nelson 22/3/35, Dublin Air Ferries

Used for charter operations in turn by Iona National Airways, Everson Flying Services and Dublin Air Ferries, until ferried to England on 31/8/38. Cancelled on 18/9/38 and late registered in the U.K. as G-AFKI. Impressed for the RAF on 31/8/41. No RAF serial number allocated. Final fate unconfirmed, but presumed scrapped.

EI-AAP, D.H.83.Fox Moth

F. dark red and light green, F/S silver doped. The light green of the upper surface of fuselage extended from Prop. boss, through the full width of the centre section, tapering rearward to the rubber-post. This A/c never flew at Kildonan in any colour-scheme other than that detailed above. (Aero-Ireland, Vol. 2, No. 6, page 22 by Liam Byrne.)

The first leg of this historical flight began in Oranmore, Co. Galway. Iona National Airways pilot, O.E. Armstrong, took off in darkness on a bitterly cold damp morning with his cargo or air mail and his two passengers, Mrs. Peggy Kenny and Miss Kitty Curran. In the Iona Fox Moth feeder cabin plane, he flew through blinding rain to link up with the triple engined Fokker F. 12 PH-AID Royal Dutch Airliner which flew on to Templehof Aerodrome, Berlin.

Hugh Cahill had major involvement in the organisation of this historical flight. Col. Charles C. Russell of the Irish Army Air Corps was heavily involved on the operational side and was part of the crew which flew from Baldonnel to Berlin. The aircraft was a KLM-three engined Fokker monoplane PH-AID. The full crew was: J.B. Scholte, pilot; J.J. Denouter, wireless operator; Col. C.F. Russell, ex. O.C. Air Corps; and P. Dunk, engineer.

Hugh Cahill was not a seasoned member of the Irish Aero Club, made up of socialites and politicians. It was an exclusive club slow to accept those who had not been bred, as it were, into the system. Hugh Cahill had little time for diplomatic niceties. He was impatient to realise his dream of air taxis and flying machines. He saw his venture as strictly business. But what was needed for the ultimate success of such a project in the Irish context, equally as much as risk capital and entrepreneurial skills, was the diplomacy to woo the senior political and social membership of the Irish Aero Club. It was impossible to succeed in this mammoth task without influencing this leadership to put its weight and the weight of its colleagues in high places behind the project at Kildonan.

Hugh Cahill, can also be judged on a record of safety, second to none. The ground staff, the management, the pilots, the instructors and the trainees of the three companies which operated at Kildonan-Iona National Airways Ltd., Everson Flying Services and Dublin Air Ferries - collectively were responsible for a safety record never before or after surpassed. There were no fatalities resulting from Kildonan's operations, either at home or abroad.

In 1930, Hugh Cahill and his friend J.C. Malone visited the Desoutter aircraft factory at Croyden, London. Here Hugh purchased a DeSoutter Mark II monoplane, the first Irish commercial aircraft, registered EI-AAD.

Portrait of Hugh Cahill

Chapter Ten

Ireland's first commercial aircraft

Chapter 10

DeSoutter II VH-BQE ex EI-AAD & VH-UEE

Ireland's first commercial aircraft

DeSoutter Mark I : crashed at Bootle, Liverpool, 1930 on delivery flight to Baldonnel to Iona Aerial Taxis and Flying School. Hugh Cahill left and press reporter

The DeSoutter Mark II EI-AAD was a replacement for the DeSoutter Mark I G-AATX (c/n D18) which never made it to Dublin. After leaving Croydon, it was damaged in a forced landing at Barfield Farm near Bootle in Liverpool. From there it was taken back by rail to the DeSoutter plant at Croydon, where it was repaired and sold to another customer. Instead, the Desoutter Mark II EI-AAD (c/n D30) was sent to replace it and arrived at Baldonnel on September 5th, 1930. It was registered in Hugh Cahill's name on October 20th, 1930 and had the name 'Iona National Air Taxis and Flying School' on its side. The aircraft was registered on October 20th, 1930 and was the property of the newly formed Iona National Air Taxis and Flying School, a company which Hugh had set up while operating at Baldonnel Military Airfield. In the same year, Hugh bought a De Havilland Gypsy Moth which he used for charter and air taxi service.

De Soutter Mark II at Curragh 1930

The Desoutter Mark II, Ireland's first commercial aircraft, never flew from Kildonan, which was soon to be the home of Iona National Airways Ltd., but made many commercial flights from Baldonnel, where Iona was based between 1930 and 1931. Baldonnel was the Irish Army Air Corps' Aerodrome and Iona could not operate a commercial venture from there on a permanent basis. This would have been made clear to Hugh Cahill by the authorities from the outset of his commercial undertaking. After seven months, the DeSoutter was sold. It was probably too large for the volume of business which was generated at the time, although it had made a surprising number of flights, including a flight to Paris. Iona National Airways Ltd. was registered as a limited company while still at Baldonnel in 1930. This was necessary in order to make any commercial flights.

DeSoutter II, EI-AAD with a member of the Irish Army Air Corps at Baldonnel,1930, EI-AAD DeSoutter mk. II Reg'd. 20/10/30, H. Cahill c/no. D. 30. New aircraft, cancelled in May 1931, sold in England, becoming G-ABOM in September. Sold in Australia as VH-UEE in December 1932, later being re-registered VH-BQE. Currently registered as such in the early 1960s and now preserved at Launceston, Tasmania as VH-UEE

DeSoutter II EI-AAD: Hugh Cahill bids farewell to passengers ready to board for a charter flight to England. Photograph taken at Baldonnel 1930

The first aircraft of Iona National Airways Ltd., the DeSoutter II EI-AAD, a high-winged monoplane and a D.H. Gypsy Moth, pictured at Baldonnel, 1930. Included in the photograph are Pearse Cahill (extreme left) and Mr. Tyndall, Iona's first pilot (third from right)

The following is the background and brief history to Ireland's first commercial aircraft and some of the relevant dates associated with the aircraft while it was in its Iona phase:

Test flight - 30/08/30 - at Sealand.

Sealand to Baldonnel, 05/09/30.

Baldonnel to Skerries, 08/09/30, 45 mns. This was the day when Pearse Cahill had his first flight.

Baldonnel to Manchester via Holyhead, 1 hr. 45mns.

Tyndall was the pilot of these early flights, an ex RAF pilot.

Joy-riding at the Curragh, 5/10/30 and 08/10/30.

Joy-riding at Drogheda, 26/10/30.

Baldonnel to Manchester, 21/04/31.

Stag Lane to Paris, 28/04/31.

The aircraft was locked up at Stag Lane on the 04/05/31.

After the flight to Manchester, above, on April 21st, subsequent flights were from Stag Lane, which was the de Havilland Aerodrome.

It was out of commission until December 26th, 1931 when it was sold.

In England in 1929, Marcel DeSoutter formed the DeSoutter Aircraft Co. to manufacture the Dutch designed Koolhoven F.K. 41 high-wing light aircraft under licence. The design was modified by Desoutter's chief engineer, C.H. Handasyde, and in this form was produced as the DeSoutter monoplane. Mr. Handasyde had been designer in the firm of Messrs Martin and Handasyde which produced Martinsyde aircraft during World War One.

In 1930, Handasyde made improvements - a D.H. Gypsy 111 engine in place of the earlier versions Cirrus Hermes, redesigned ailerons and tail surfaces and provision for wheel brakes. The prototype of the modified design first flew in June 1930 and was known as the DeSoutter II.

This DeSoutter II when it came off the production line bore the constructors number D.30. (It went to the Irish Free State and was the first commercial aircraft in that country). With registration marks EI-AAD, it was operated on charter by the owners, Iona National Air Taxis and Flying School. After seven months in Ireland, it was registered in England as G-ABOM (owner not known). In December 1931, it was sold and shipped to Australia soon afterwards.

On March 11th, 1932, the DeSoutter II was added to the Australian register of civil aircraft with the marking VH-UEE. The owner was Mr. L. McKenzie Johnson, who gained the mail contract between Launceston and Flinder Island. On June 7th, 1932 he flew the first of the bi-weekly services to Whitemark on the island. The aircraft was named 'Miss Flinders'. In September 1932, the Holyman brothers began a service to the island with the De Havilland D.H. 83 VH-UJM 'Miss Currie'. In October, Johnson and the Holyman Brothers combined to form Tasmanian Aerial Services Pty. Ltd. and extended their services. When Johnson left the company to be a flying instructor with the Tasmanian Aero Club, the firm was renamed Holyman Airways Pty Ltd. With gradual expansion of services and acquisition of other airlines, the company developed to become Australian National Airways (ANA).

After a period with aero clubs, Mr. Johnson became flight superintendent for ANA, and then Victorian manager. When Ansett - ANA was formed in the later part of 1957 - he became Victorian manager for the Matson Line in 1958. At the annual conference of the Royal Aero Club Federation of Australia in Launceston from April 16 - 20th, 1958, L. McKenzie Johnson was re-elected president of the federation for the eighth successive year. However, he died suddenly at his home in Melbourne on April 25th, 1958. When Holyman Airways was expanding, the DeSoutter 11 had been sold to the de Havilland Aircraft Pty. Ltd in Sydney in mid 1935. There was a succession of owners and charter operations in the years leading up to and following the second world war.

In 1951, the Department of Civil Aviation allotted a new registration VH-BQE to the aircraft. VH-UEE conflicted with ICAO recommendation that registration markings should not include two or more E letters in succession (probably because it might be confused with the international radio signal in which a succession of E letters means erase previous signal). In 1957, it was sold to Rain Air Taxis, Sydney, NSW, but from mid-1961 at least, it lay idle in a hangar gathering dust at Bourke, NSW.

In March 1966, it was transported to Melbourne and on March 26th, 1966, the dismantled aircraft was flown to Launceston Airport within Ansett ANA's ATL Carvair VH-IMJ. It was restored and placed on display in a hall within the new airport terminal of Lauceston as a memorial to the pioneer air services in Tasmania.

For list of Australian registered owners see below:

References

Register of Civil Aircraft, Department of Civil Aviation, British Civil Aircraft Vol. 1; A.J. Jackson, History of Australian Aviation, S. Brogden, Air Pictorial, May 1950.

Journal of Aviation Historical Society of Australia Vol. 11, P68, June 1961.

Details from Civil Aircraft Register of Ireland:

Registered marks	EI-AAD
Type of aircraft	DeSoutter 11
Previous identity	New Aircraft
Constructor's No.	D. 30
Cert of registration No.	4
C of A No.	2647
Category and Sub Division	Normal (d) (e)
Owner's full name & address	A. H. Cahill, Prospect Villas Glasnevin, Dublin 11.
Nationality	Irish
Usual station of aircraft	Baldonnel
Date of reg	30/10/1930
Remarks	Sold as G-ABOM, cancelled 5/1931

Added to British Civil Aircraft Register as G-ABOM, 1/9/1931. Struck off 12/1931
Extracts from Australian Civil Aircraft Register:

11/3/1932 VH-UEE	L. Mck. Johnson, Western Junction, Tasmania. 'Miss Flinders'
18/10/1932 VH-UEE	Tasmanian Aerial Services Ltd., Launceston, Tasmania. Holyman Airways Ltd., Launceston, Tasmania.
18/7/1935 VH-UEE	Struck off register; sold to de Havilland Aircraft Ltd., Sydney, NSW
23/7/1935 VH-UEE	J.J. Larkin, Sydney, NSW
18/8/1936 VH-UEE	G.P. Hoskins, c/o Airlines of Australia, Townsville, Qld.
15/11/1938 VH-UEE	J. Pater, Warragul, Vic
24/4/1939 VH-UEE	C.D. Pratt, Melbourne, Vic
28/9/1946 VH-UEE	Wollonggong & South Coast Aviation Services, Wollonggong, NSW
6/8/1951 VH-UEE	Struck off Register; withdrawn from service
30/8/1951 VH-BQE	New registration marks allotted
25/1/1952 VH-BQE	South Coast Airways Ltd., ,Wollonggong, NSW
5/1/1953 VH-BQE	W.E. James, Wollonggong, NSW
14/7/1953 VH-BQE	Airmech, Bankstown Airport, NSW
14/5/1954 VH-BQE	R.C. Burt, Baradine, NSW
25/5/1956 VH-BQE	Australian Aircraft Sales, Sydney, NSW
17/1/1957 VH-BQE	Rain Air Taxis Ltd., Sydney, NSW
5/9/1961 VH-BQE	Struck off register; withdrawn from use

The aircraft was originally fitted with a D.H. Gypsy 111 engine. When it was a new registration in August 1951, the engine was shown in the register as a D.H. Gypsy Major 1. At some stage late in its career (probably when owned by Rain Air Taxis Ltd.), the DeSoutter II was named 'Jeerbin'. It bore this when an AHSA member saw the aircraft in hangar at Bourke, NSW in June 1961. After its long industrious and illustrious service in Australia, and due to the onset of old age and a scarcity of spare parts, the little pioneer aircraft of Irish and Australian aviation was retired. Fittingly, it was restored and made a prime exhibit at the official opening of the new terminal building at Launceston Airport, Tasmania on October 29th, 1966 where it is still exhibited today. The little Iona emigrant pioneer had earned its prominent position as a show-piece. Kildonan, Finglas and Lauceston, Tasmania have a lot to talk about. Many possibilities suggest themselves - cultural exchange and twinning possibilities. Perhaps the little aircraft might spend a little time in Ireland at some stage with appropriate celebrations of its achievements in pioneering civil aviation in Ireland and Australia - and of course the families of the pilots who flew the DeSoutter Mark II would be part of a great celebration.

EI-AAD, DeSoutter mk. II, Reg'd. 20/10/30, H. Cahill c/no. D.30, new aircraft

Cancelled in May 1931, sold in England, becoming G-ABOM in September. Sold in Australia as VH-UEE in December 1932, later being re-registered VH-BQE. Currently registered as such in the early 1960s and now preserved at Launceston, Tasmania as VH-UEE.

DeSoutter II VH-BQE ex EI-AAD & VH-UEE on exhibition at the terminal building at Launceston Airport, Tasmania, Australia

DeSoutter II VH-BQE ex EI-AAD & VH-UEE on exhibition at Lauceston Airport, Tasmania

Chapter Eleven

Chapter

Sir Alan Cobham's first Irish air display

Chapter 11

Sir Alan Cobham's First Irish Air Display

Sir Alan Cobham

Sir Alan Cobham

Mr. Hugh Cahill (right), proprietor of Iona National Airways Ltd., with Sir Alan Cobham, left, on the occasion of Cobham's first Irish Air Display which took place on July 2nd, 1933

Mr. Hugh Cahill pictured with Alderman Alfie Byrne T.D., Lord Mayor of Dublin, who performed the official opening of the Cobham Circus at Kildonan. This picture, however, was not taken at Kildonan, but at the Irish Army Air Corps headquarters at Baldonnel

Sir Alan Cobham chose Kildonan as the location for his first Irish air display, which was held on July 1st and 2nd, 1933. The public responded to the pre-display advertising which included a flight over the city of Dublin the day before. The citizens looked up in amazement and disbelief at this truly wonderful and unprecedented spectacle. Most of the aircraft had not been seen in Ireland previously. An estimated 14,000 spectators turned out to see the aerobatics at Kildonan on that Sunday. Alderman Alfie Byrne T.D., Lord Mayor of Dublin, performed the official opening. Cobham provided the commentary himself, describing each act in detail. He was the organiser of this highly successful National Aviation Display or circus as it was popularly called, which did so much to popularise flying. Cobham was a pioneer aviator in the classical mode. Following his historical flight to Australia, he was knighted in 1926 and went on to accomplish further noteworthy feats in aviation. He was, furthermore, a major achiever in the technological sphere of aviation and invented a new technique for in-flight re-fuelling.

The use of the giant aircraft of the day dispels the myth that Kildonan Aerodrome was a tiny airfield. On the contrary, it was able to accommodate the largest aircraft available. These ex Imperial Airways machines had been used to fly such routes as Cairo to Bombay. Cobham's air pageant contained the best aircraft available, piloted by the best pilots. It was colourful in every sense of the word, as demonstrated in the breathtaking aerobatics of the pilots and the brightly painted aircraft. His display demonstrated a dozen different aircraft types, from the tiny Cierva Autogiro piloted by A.C. Rowson to the huge Handley Page HP 33 Clive 1 GABYX with a seating capacity of 22. It was powered by two 550 h.p. Bristol Jupiter 1X engines. The Cierva was the world's first autogiro, a two seater, designed by the Spaniard Don Juan de La Cierva, in 1923. Also included in the display was the prototype Airspeed Ferry G-ABSI, appropriately named 'Youth of Ireland', a three-engined 10 passenger biplane coloured silver and green. Prominently featured also was the Handley Page W10 G-EBMR with two Napier Lion 450 h.p. engines and passenger capacity of 16 persons. Built in 1925, it had been formerly flown with Imperial Airways. On the smaller scale were the three AVRO 504 ks: a DH 83 Fox Moth G-Acey; a DH 82 Tiger Moth; and a DH 60 Gypsy Moth G-ABUB, used by Jim Molinson to set up a new long distance record from Australia to England in 1931. The de Havilland prototypes G-ABRC and G-ABUL were also included in the Cobham fleet.

Pearse Cahill and John N. Duggan (captain), recall another aircraft which Cobham had in Dublin, where they saw it in flight. It was a very unusual aircraft and a very good one. It was the Blackburn Lincock, a single seater fighter which had been turned down by the R.A.F. This aircraft, they both recall, was over at the first show. It was painted red and "went like hell". It was, they say, the first aircraft to do an upward spin. Built as a result of a private venture, produced in the hope that the R.A.F. would buy it as a light fighter for which it was absolutely ideal. The R.A.F., however, turned it down. There were only about eight of them built, painted red with wings silver doped. It flew over Dublin and along the Gresham and "several women in O'Connell Street fainted at the sight ", not being accustomed to that kind of flying. When it disappeared down behind the buildings, they waited in trepidation for the bang which of course never came and when they revived, they stood in awe and could not believe their eyes or their ears. That was a "terrific machine". It was part of the Cobham Circus, according to the recollections of both Pearse and John. They remembered it well.

The fleet of Sir Alan Cobham's Flying Circus on the ground at Kildonan Aerodrome, prior to the Cobham Air Pageant, July 2nd, 1933

Mr. Hugh Cahill and his daughter standing in front of one of Cobham's Hanley-Page Clive 22 seater air liners at Kildonan Aerodrome, Finglas, July 2nd, 1933

Detail of Imperial airways aircraft of the day

F. Handley-Page O.B.E. :
head of the famous Crinklewood firm

Rolls Royce cars business card

The advert of the Handley Page HP 42 signalled the beginning of luxurious air travel. Imperial Airways, to whose order the HP 42s were built, introduced the type on both its European and Far Eastern Routes, commencing in June 1931

The scale of some of the aircraft type that Cobham flew

DETACHED A 6488

National Aviation Day Display

Organised by

Sir ALAN COBHAM, K.B.E., A.F.C.

VALID FOR ONE FLIGHT

Complimentary Ticket

PER PASSENGER.

SUBJECT TO CONDITIONS OVERLEAF

Issued by National Aviation Day, Ltd., **Grand** Buildings, Trafalgar Square, London. W.C.2.

To be Retained by Passenger.

Conditions Governing All Flights and Subject to which only Passengers are accepted.

1.—By accepting a ticket on taking part in a flight passengers shall be deemed to have accepted the following Conditions which constitute the terms of the contract of carriage subject to which only National Aviation Day Ltd., (hereinafter called "the Company") accept passengers.

2.—The expression "the Company" shall throughout these conditions be taken to include National Aviation Day Limited, its servants and agents, and any other publishing or other company, firm or individual, their respective servants and agents, by or through whom any flight is arranged or who are otherwise in any way concerned or connected with flights the subject of these Conditions.

3.—No liability whatsoever is accepted by the Company in connection with the carriage of passengers or luggage or in connection with services ancillary to such carriage. It is a condition precedent to the acceptance by the Company of passengers or luggage for a flight that the passenger renounces for himself and his representatives and dependents all claims for compensation for damage (including death, injury, loss and delay) caused or alleged to have been caused during or in connection with the carriage, either directly or indirectly, to passengers or their belongings, or to persons who, except for this condition, might have been entitled to make a claim, and whether or not any such damage is alleged to have been due to the negligence of the Company.

4.—Any passenger under the age of 21 years must notify the Company to this effect and obtain the signature of his/her guardian, or other person duly authorised, on the form at the foot of these conditions prior to the flight. In default of evidence to the contrary the Company shall be entitled to assume that passengers are over 21 years of age. The Company shall be under no obligation to verify the credentials of the party completing the form annexed to these Conditions on behalf of passengers under 21.

5.—The Company reserves the right to refuse to carry any passenger or luggage on any flight and to cancel any flight, and shall be under no obligation in respect of such refusal or cancellation beyond returning to the passenger the price paid for the ticket.

6.—Passengers must comply with all the Company's regulations and the instructions of the Company's officials, and will be held liable for the consequences of any breach or non-observance of such regulations and instructions.

Certificate for completion by parent, guardian or other duly authorised person when passenger is under 21 years of age.

I agree to.................................taking a flight subject in all respects to the foregoing Conditions.

Signature of parent, guardian or other person duly authorised (see Condition 4 above)..................

Date.................................

Cobham Air Display ticket

The Cobham Circus fly-over

The Cobham Circus fleet in formation at the air pageant display flyover held under the auspices of Iona National Airways at Kildonan Aerodrome on July 2nd, 1933

At the Cobham display, Kildonan, a stuntman standing on the upper wing of an Avro 504K

A wing-squatter performing at an Iona air pageant

Some looked away, unable to take anymore, some felt weak and fainted

The first aircraft to arrive at Kildonan was Tiger Moth G-ABUL, flown by Sir Alan Cobham himself, followed by the Handley Page HP 33 Clive G-ABYX; Handley Page W10 G-EBMR; Airspeed Ferries G-ABSI and 'BSJ'; Fox Moths G-ACEX, G-ACEY and G-ABWF; Avro 504 G-ABVH; Moth G-ABUB; and Cierva autogiro G-ABGB. There was also a mongoose-engined Avro 504 as well as the Blackburn Lincock, remembered by Pearse Cahill and John Duggan.

About 15,000 people attended the Cobham Air Circus at Kildonan. The display started proper with a fly past of the aircraft spearheaded by the giant HP33 Clive 1.

Then followed a whole series of heart-stopping aerobatics. The brightly coloured yellow Tiger Moth, piloted by Flt. Lt. Turner Hughes, flew upside down over the crowd then rolled over, climbed steeply, rolled over and dived at the crowd in the inverted position, amid screams and applause. The sound of the engine could scarcely be heard over the noisy crowd. This was quickly followed by stunned silence and amazement as Martin Hearne climbed out of the cockpit of the in-flight Avro 504, got up onto the top wing and waved to the crowd. They were too scared to return the salute. To the further disbelief of the throng, the pilot immediately completed a loop with Hearne perched on the wing without harness. Hearne was glued to the aircraft, the crowd was glued to the ground as if transfixed. Some looked away, unable to take anymore, some felt weak and fainted. Cobham and his team seemed to thrive on the adulation shown by the crowd and even more daring feats followed.

Flight Lieutenant Geoffrey Tyson caused hearts to jump with inverted flying a few feet above the ground. Bunts, outside loops, terminal velocity-dives and impossible upwards spirals, were all executed by him with uncanny precision. Tyson was one of the stars of the Cobham flying circus. He could pick up a handkerchief from the ground with the help of a hook attached to the tip of the wing of the Tiger Moth which he flew.

A key element of the Cobham pageant was the participation of the crowd. Lt. H.C. Johnson, chief pilot of the mammoth-like red and white H.P. 33 Clive 1, ferried passengers about for seven shillings and sixpence. It cost one pound for an acrobatic thrill in the open cockpit of the Avro 504. Captain Joe King could hardly cope with the great demand for flights in the exceedingly popular silver and green Airspeed Ferry G-ABSI, 'Youth of Ireland'. The flights continued until the last man, woman and child were satisfied. Nobody was disappointed. The sky was already beginning to darken when the last flight landed and the pilots mingled with the crowd. No questions were too trivial to be answered and nobody was too shy to ask, such was the tremendous rapport which developed between Cobham's team and the people. All communication barriers were broken down.

Slowly, the crowd wended its weary way down towards Finglas Village full of adulation, where a shuttle of buses and taxis was ready to ferry them home. Sore limbs and tired eyes could now be rested and look forward to the next Kildonan air display. The pilots and their back-up team sat down to a well deserved rest and a feast fit for a king. This display was an outstanding success and a credit to Hugh Cahill and the Kildonan staff. The Irish Aero Club also participated in the event.

When Cobham was finished in Dublin, he moved down the country for what was a whole series of air pageants. But it was at his Limerick display that tragedy struck. Two of the stars of the show were Geoffrey Tyson, one of Cobham's leading men, who was piloting a Fox Moth, and Mr. William R. Elliott, the first full time instructor of the Irish Aero Club. It was said that there was deep-seated rivalry between the two going back to their days in the R.A.F.

Elliot was piloting one of the Aero Club machines for joy-rides, while Tyson was stunting. Elliott was apparently flying into the sun at the time and in the difficult visibility resulting, did not see Tyson dive. Tyson's machine tore the wing off Elliot's plane. There was general anger at Tyson's performance and towards the Cobham circus, on the part of the people of Limerick who felt that far from being an accident in the normal sense, it was one which was totally avoidable. Cobham's camp had to be protected by the police that night because it was felt that citizens of Limerick in their anger might take the law into their own hands. Although the official enquiry, held later, purported to clear Tyson completely of any negligence, this was not the opinion generally, for it was felt that Tyson was to blame.

Tributes made at the time show in what high esteem Mr. William Elliott had been held by those who knew him.

Sir Alan Cobham's first Irish air display, Iona National Airways Ltd., Kildonan Aerodrome, July 2nd. 1933. City of Melbourne, H.P. W10

The Blackburn Lincock aerobatic machine was part of the Cobham air display

One of the Handley-Page 'Clive' 22 seater air liners of Sir Alan Cobham's Air Circus, prior to the air display. Former Imperial Airways aircraft, they were named, 'Youth of Australia' and 'Youth of New Zealand', the latter pictured above. Photo: Pearse Cahill collection

Joy-riders over Dublin at the Cobham air pagaent. Photo courtesy of Pearse Cahill

A SINCERE FRIEND

TRIBUTE TO THE DEAD PILOT

In an interview with an *Irish Independent* representative last evening, Mr. T. O'B. Kelly, Sec., Irish Aero Club, said Capt. Elliott, was a most capable and careful pilot.

He was a very sincere friend, and always had the interests of the Irish Aero Club at heart.

The Club did not participate in any flying events yesterday.

Mr. Kelly, in company with Mr. French, will fly to Galway this morning in an Aero Club 'plane to take part in the Cobham display.

They will go from Galway to Bundoran, and intend to return to Dublin on Wednesday.

IN MEMORIAM

WILLIAM ELLIOTT

(Chief Instructor, Irish Aero Club).

(BY A PUPIL.)

(OLIVER St. John Gogarty, Senator.)

It's not the unreached or unseen;
It's not the "What he might have been";
It's neither this nor that, because
We loved him for the man he was:
A sail top-gallant of the air,
High Admiral of the atmosphere!
Honour his ensign: when he sailed
Or landed, still his flag was nailed.
He worked long-tried, and wearied not;
Perfection was the least he taught;
And he could make your spirit stir
By dint of simple character:
Cheerful, trustworthy, clean and bold;
He makes his grave a mine of gold;
And heedless schoolboys may forget
Great names, remembering Elliott.

FATHER'S PATHETIC WAIT.

"The last I saw of my son," said Mr. William Ower, Senr., "was when he got into the 'plane with Capt. Elliott, and it moved off.

"**I stood waiting, waiting, for I was to be the next passenger. . . . But the 'plane did not return. Instead, somebody told me my son was killed.**"

Mr. J. M. Bell, Baldonnel, ground engineer to the Irish Aero Club, said the 'plane piloted by Capt. Elliott was in perfect condition when it took the air. He examined it every morning.

Roger Heins, who said he saw the collision from a bus, stated that the machines were travelling in opposite directions. The under-carriage of one struck the other 'plane about a mile from the city.

Dr. Louis Humphreys said Capt. Elliott's body had a lacerated wound on the forehead and poll and a compound fracture of both legs. Ower's body had several injuries, also to the head and legs.

Sympathy was voted to the Aero Club and to the families of the dead men.

The chief mourners were:—Miss Swinger (sister-in-law), Mr. Geo. Withers.

THE ATTENDANCE.

The attendance included:—

Army Air Corps—Major Liston, O.C.; Capt. P. Quinn, Capt. Heron, Lieut. A. G. Russell, Lieut. W. J. Keane, Lieut. J. P. Twohig, Cadet D. K. Johnston.

Directors, Irish Aero Club—Capt. H. J. Hosie, Messrs. P. Grimes, J. McCaulay, Cecil Crowe, Brian Rogers, T. O B. Kelly, Sean O hUadhaigh.

Members, Irish Aero Club—Mr. R. Hill, Mr. S. Murphy, Senator Oliver St. John Gogarty.

Iona National Airways, Ltd.—Capt. Young, Mr. O. E. Armstrong, Mr. Sheridan, Mr. Woods.

68th Dublin Troop, Boy Scouts were represented by Mr. J. J. McLaughlin, Scoutmaster, and Mr. J. Hughes, Assistant-Scoutmaster.

General Public—Mr. J. Tighe (Shell and B.P. Co.), Mr. T. W. Kerrigan (Dunlop Rubber Co.), Dr. W. J. Chapman, Mrs. H. J. Hosie, Mrs. Heron, Mrs. J. McCaulay, Miss M. Finn, Mr. and Mrs. C. F. French, Rev. J. Furlong, C.C. , Mr. J. Kavanagh, Lady Heath, Mr. G. A. Williams, Mr. J. M. Bell, ground engineer to the Aero Club.

Tribute to William Elliot by Oliver St. John Gogarty

Sir Alan Cobham

Chapter Twelve

Chapter

Everson Flying Services

Chapter 12

Everson Flying Services

Everson Flying Services badge

Everson Flying Services Ltd. took over Kildonan Aerodrome, as well as the aircraft of Iona National Airways Ltd. It retained the staff who were employed at the aerodrome. The new company started operations on December 1st, 1933. The two aircraft, Moth EI-AAK and Fox Moth EI-AAP, were registered to Lady Nelson on December 2nd of that year. the new company also had the use of Lady Nelson's Stinson G-ABTZ and Lady Heath's Moth G-ACBU, which was later registered as EI-AAW. The company's chief pilot was J.R. Currie; Lady Nelson purchased a Miles Hawk G-ACNX which was delivered to Kildonan on February 24th 1934 and registered EI-AAX a month later. This aircraft which was used for instruction remained at Kildonan until December 1934 when it was sold.

EI-AAW, D.H.60G Moth, Reg'd. 29/5/34, Lady Heath, c/no. 1849, ex ZS-ADB, G-ACBU

This aircraft had been based at Baldonnel in British marks from at least August 1933 and was used for charter work by Everson Flying Services. Crashed and destroyed by fire at Stone, Staffordshire, on 26/11/35, en route Dublin - Speke - Croydon.

EI-AAX, Miles M.2 Hawk, Reg'd. 26/3/34, C. Nelson, c/no. 24, ex G-ACNX

Delivered as G-ACNX on 24/2/34. Returned to the U.K. on 18/12/34 and cancelled two days later, being restored as G-ACNX. Crashed at Malnesbury, Wiltshire, on 12/4/35, but later repaired. Impressed for the RAF as DG578, then to an instructional airframe as 2617M. Everson Flying Services, Ltd., obtained a Percival Gull G-ACJW on lease, for the months August and September 1934. The company had also the use of Moth EI-AAR owned by E.J. Dease. In November 1934, chief pilot J.R. Currie returned to England and Mr. A. Griffith took over his position as chief pilot at Kildonan.

EI-AAR, D.H.60G Moth, Reg'd. 1/5/33, E.J. Dease, c/no. 1030, ex G-AAEA

Shown in the official records as crashed on 21/12/34 and is believed to be the aircraft used by Everson Flying Services which crashed on 21/12/34 at Roffery, near Saintfield.

Lady Heath purchased a Gypsy Moth G-AASY which arrived at Kildonan on December 21st, 1934. It was later registered EI-ABE.

EI-ABE, D.H.60G Moth

F. two-tone, upper half emerald green, lower, light green, fin and rudder, same colours. Wings and tail-plane, silver-doped. M. same colours as F. but in reverse order to background colour,ie; half and half.

EI-ABE, D.H.60G Moth, Reg'd. 1/3/35, Lady Heath, c/no. 1048, ex G-AASY, 20/2/37, Dublin Air Ferries

Delivered to Ireland as G-AASY on 21/12/34. Cancelled on 7/2/38 upon re-sale as G-AASY. Impressed for the RAF as AW128 and later to an instructional airframe as 4490M.

On Saturday December 22nd, 1934, the Moth EI-AAR, which was owned by E.J. Dease and in use by Everson Flying Services Ltd., crashed and was written off on a flight to Belfast. The machine was piloted by James Bell, a pilot at Everson Flying Services, who was also carrying a passenger. Unable to locate Newtownards airfield in the fog, the pilot landed in a field at Roffery near Samplefield, Co. Down. The landing was without incident but the aircraft was wrecked on the attempted take-off from the field. Both pilot and passenger, however, escaped without serious injury. In January 1935, Everson Flying Services ceased trading.

Everson Flying Services Ltd. began business on December 1st, 1933, with Lady Nelson, wife of Sir James Nelson as the owner. Mr. J.R. Currie, A.R.A.C.S.I., was appointed manager in charge of flying services. Chief pilot and instructor, G.E.N. (George) Everett was a close associate of Lady Nelson in the Everson Flying Services venture. Both names can be identified in the title of the new company, i.e. Everett and Nelson. Among those present at the official opening were Senator Dr. St. John Gogarty and Mrs. Gogarty, Captain H. St. G. Harpur, Irish Shell and Lady Heath. Although the main emphasis in the new enterprise was on instructional work, charter flights were also very much part of the business. A Miles Hawk was acquired to cope with the demand for training and instruction. J.R. Currie was ably assisted by Mr. F.W. Griffiths. Mr. M.J. (Mick) Brady oversaw the engineering. Captain W. Hamilton, chief of the transport department of Independent Newspapers Ltd., a qualified pilot, took a special interest in the new company. The Miles Hawk trainer was collected from Mr. Miles, designer of the Miles Hawk, by J.R. Currie at Woodley Aerodrome, Reading at the end of February, 1934.

One of the Everson Flying Services Ltd. air displays was held on April 10th and 11th, 1934, at Kildonan. These displays were called 'At Home' displays. At this event, the first aircraft designed and built by an Irishman, the 'Spirit of Erin', created by Mr. Charles V.L. Foley of Sligo was exhibited. Besides Lady Nelson's, husband Sir James Nelson, Mr. R. Everett and those already mentioned, many others took an active part in promoting club activities at Kildonan Aerodrome, including Captain T. Young, Mrs Wilkinson, Mr. Conway, Messrs. Peterson, Hill and Kearney.

Tiger Noth in Royal air Force markings

Happy days at Everson Flying Services, Kildonan (from left): Bill Lonergan; third from left, Ivan Hammond beside Oonagh Scannell, later to marry Ivan; Denise Beatty, Katherine Bayley-Butler, soon to become Sr Katherine; George Bell, on the extreme right; and Mr. Peacock

Everson Flying Services
KILDONAN AERODROME
FINGLAS, DUBLIN
Telegrams: "Flying, Dublin."
Telephone: Finglas 5.

Proprietress: LADY NELSON
Chief Pilot: Fred. W. Griffith.

SOLE AGENTS IN IRISH FREE STATE FOR MILES HAWK

Everson Flying Services Ltd. 1933 to 1935 was the second of three companies which operated from Kildonan Aerodrome. One surviving piece of documentation, is a 17 page brochure published by the company promoting the services on offer. The brochure was printed in Ireland and published by J.E. Mulligan & Co., Abbey Buildings, Middle Abbey Street, Dublin.

This advertisement shows that Lady Nelson was the proprietress and that Fred. W. Griffith was the chief pilot of Everson Flying Services Ltd. The company was a sole agent in the Irish Free State for the 'Miles Hawk' aeroplanes.

J.R. Currie - designer of the Curie-Wot aircraft

Some of the Everson Flying Services fleet outside the hangar at Kildonan (from left): EI-AAP D.H.83 Fox Moth; EI-AAK D.H. 60G Moth, ex G-ABBV; and Miles N.2. Hawk, ex G-ACNX. (Weston photo)

John R. Currie.
A.R.Ae.S.I.

EVERSON FLYING SERVICES,
KILDONAN AERODROME,
DUBLIN.

Business card of J.R. Currie

Everson Flying Services Ltd. 1933 to 1935 was the second of three companies which operated from Kildonan Aerodrome

Mick Brady, ground engineer, at the propeller of EI-AAP in front of the hangar, Kildonan, Finglas

Felix Vaitkus, pilot of Lockheed Vega which crashed near Ballinrobe

J.R. Currie standing beside EI-AAP Fox Moth at Kildonan, Finglas

On September 22nd 1935, Dublin Air Ferries Moth EI-AAW flew down to Ballinrobe to assist Felix Vaitkus. Vaitkus had crashed near the Mayo town while attempting to fly from New York to Lithunania in a Lockheed Vega. The Moth was damaged while landing in a nearby field and had to be sent back by lorry for repairs to Dublin.

The Lockheed Vega, which on a flight from New York to Lithuania - piloted by Felix Vaitkus - crashed near Ballinrobe Co. Mayo - September 1935

Lady Nelson and Mr. George Everett ready to board Lady Nelson's 'Stinson' aeroplane, clearing customs at Kildonan. Everson Flying Services Ltd.

The following are extracts from Everson Flying Services promotional brochure:

The Home of Everson Flying Services

Have you ever experienced the joys of flying? Words cannot describe it and you can rest assured that it is very invigorating. The Everson Flying Services caters for the popular type of flying and joy flights can be had for as low as 2/6 each.

Have you ever experienced the joys of flying? Words cannot describe it and you can rest assured that it is very invigorating. The Everson Flying Services caters for the popular type of flying and joy flights can be had for as low as 2/6 each

Admittance to the aerodrome is free and you can spend a pleasant afternoon at the aerodrome by merely watching the flying. Saturday and Sunday are two days when exhibitions of stunting are given and the air on the drome is most refreshing. You can spend as much time as you like at Kildonan. After a while you will feel the spell working and will want to experience the joy and refreshing experience of a joy flight.

Short pleasure flights may be had at any time at 2/6, 5/- and 10/- each. A flight over Dublin is recommended and one can easily pick out the various places of interest.

There is no feeling of height and no dizziness as some people imagine, only a blissful sense of security and a certain strangeness that is most pleasant.

The pilots at Kildonan are fully licensed and have had years of experience. A little talk with one of them will make you feel at home, so when you feel like it "come up and see us sometime".

A flight of fancy is nothing compared to a flight in one of the Everson Flying Services aeroplanes and you are always welcome to the drome any time.

Air travel

A large number of people have recently been spending their holidays at the Kildonan Aerodrome learning to fly and have enjoyed the spirit that exists at the drome. Others have taken a flying holiday and have found that travelling by air is much more comfortable than any other method of travel. A trip round the lakes by air is most refreshing and another recommended trip is round the Wicklow Hills. These trips are becoming very popular and lately a number of people have taken advantage of these trips and have now made it a habit of taking a flight every week. Flying is better than a tonic and much more enjoyable.

A large number of people have recently been spending their holidays at the Kildonan Aerodrome learning to fly and have enjoyed the spirit that exists at the drome

The Fox Moth used by Everson Flying Services is a three-four seater and the cabin is separated from the pilot and quite private. It is also heated and the seats are most comfortable.

A telephone in the cabin connects with the pilot so that the passengers can at any time enquire where they are or hold a conversation during flight. This machine is becoming very popular with honeymoon couples and recently several honeymoon trips have been accomplished in this machine. It has a top speed of 100 miles per hour and the average time Dublin to London is about three hours. Compare this with other methods of travel and you will always find favour for air travel.

An Everson school machine

The Miles Hawk monoplane is the latest type of aircraft produced. It is constructed on entirely new lines and is exceptionally strong. One of these machines is used in the school for instructional work and is very popular with the pupils owing to the easy handling and graceful appearance.A similar machine fitted with a more powerful engine made second place in this year's King's Cup Race in England at a speed of over 140 miles per hour. This machine, with the exception of the engine, is identically the same as the machine used at Kildonan. Fitted with a Cirrus 111 engine, this machine costs only £450 ex works and is very economical, using only four and a half gallons of petrol per hour at 90 miles per hour.

The mechanical upkeep is very low as owing to the absence of wires and strutts there is very little to maintain: an occasional spot of oil on the wheels being all that is necessary. The wings of this machine fold back and it can be housed in a shed no bigger than an ordinary garage. It is an ideal machine for the private owner. Anyone who has flown a Miles Hawk is loud in praise of its flying capabilities and a number of these are owned by private individuals who find that it gives no trouble. A 12 months' guarantee is given with each machine and the Everson Flying Services are equipped to give any service in respect of repairs and overhauls.

EI-AAP, D.H.83 Fox Moth, Reg'd. 20/7/32, Iona National Airways c/no. 4003. New aircraft, 2/12/33, C. Nelson, 22/3/35, Dublin Air Ferries

Used for charter operations in turn by Iona National Airways, Everson Flying Services and Dublin Air Ferries, until ferried to England on 31/8/38. Cancelled on 18/9/38 and later registered in the U.K. as G-AFKI. Impressed for the RAF on 31/8/41. No RAF serial number allocated. Final fate unconfirmed, but presumed scrapped.

EI-AAP, D.H. 83. 'Fox Moth'

F. dark red & light green, F/S. silver-doped. The light green of the upper surface of fuselage extended from Prop. boss, through the full width of the centre section, tapering rearward to the Rudder-post. N.B. This A/c. NEVER flew at Kildonan in any colour scheme other than detailed above (vide: 'Aero-Ireland', Vol.2, No. 6, page 22. by Liam Byrne).

EI-AAX, Miles M.2 Hawk, Reg'd. 26/3/34 C. Nelson, c/no. 24, ex G-ACNX

Delivered as G-ACNX on 24/2/34. Returned to the U.K. on 18/12/34 and cancelled two days later, being restored as G-ACNX. Crashed at Malmesbury, Wiltshire, on 12/4/35, but later repaired. Impressed for the RAF as DG578, then to an instructional airframe as 2617M.

EI-AAX, Miles M.2. 'Hawk'. (ex. G-ACNX) & EI-ABQ (ex. G-ACMX)

F. standard Miles red (lighter than EI-AAP, 'Fox Moth') and high gloss finish. F/S. Silver-doped.

Miles Hawk M.2. EI-AAX, owned by Lady Nelson

Chris F. Bruton photo of EI-AAX

Extracts from Everson Flying Services promotional brochure:

The Flying School

Anyone who is over 17 years of age can become an aeroplane pilot so long as he has ordinary intelligence. It is easier to fly an aeroplane than to drive a motor car. There are no guards to worry you and no obstructions to hinder you. Flying is becoming more popular every day as shown by the increasing membership of the Everson Flying Services School. Several ladies are now on the list of pilots by the Everson Flying Services and are proving that flying is by no means confined to the males.

The instructors at the school are very thorough in their work and ensure that every pupil receives a thorough training. The cost of learning to fly is not so great as most people imagine and several pupils are spending only 10/- per week and some even less. So taken on this basis it places flying within the reach of almost everybody.

As a rough guide, a novice requires about 10 hours' instruction and at the end of this period he should be able to fly by himself. A further period of three hours is required by the authorities before he can apply for his pilot's licence. Once in possession of a pilot's licence you become a member of the exclusive circle of aviators and able to show that you actually can fly. There are quite a number of people who say they can fly, but the production of a licence dispels all doubt. Think how nice it is for you to be able to show to your friends your pilot's licence. If you have any doubt whether you will ever fly take a trial lesson for 10/-.

EI-AAX in flight

Some types operated by Everson Flying Services

The staff of the Everson Flying Services are all fully qualified in their respective occupations, the pilots holding current pilot's licenses and have had years of experience in flying. They have trained a considerable number of pilots and are exceptionally keen on their work. They are medically examined every six months by the official authorities and under no circumstances is a pilot allowed to carry passengers without his licence being up-to-date. They have carried out a good number of cross sea and country flights and are experienced instructors. The ground staff are carefully selected for their abilities and every job done on a machine is inspected several times before the certificate of airworthiness is signed. A long period of apprenticeship is spent by each ground engineer whose job it is to certify the machines are airworthy. The present staff have been with the firm since its inception and have carried out their duties unfailingly. The management is proud to state that no accident has occurred due to negligence of the staff. The chief pilot has had a wide experience of aviation. Visitors to the aerodrome will find that the staff are very obliging in every respect and no one need feel uneasy about asking questions on any subject pertaining to flying.

EI-AAX / G-ACMX

Business flights

A number of business flights have been carried out by the Everson Flying Services and in particular travellers who miss the boat have found the E.F.S. has been able to take them to their destination before the ordinary means of travel. A large number of flights are made each month across the Irish Sea and the time taken to reach Liverpool from Dublin is 11 and a half hours. This trip is often undertaken and the pilots at Kildonan are experienced in sea crossing flights.

When a machine leaves Kildonan a priority telegram is sent to Holyhead notifying them of the departure and when the machine crosses Holyhead a telegram is sent back to Kildonan notifying them of the safe crossing. Thus in the event of the machine meeting with any untoward accident the authorities at each end are informed at once and action taken to ensure the safety of the passengers. The machines are fully insured and every precaution taken to ensure the complete airworthiness of the aeroplane before it leaves the ground. Every day a thorough inspection is carried out on the entire machine and engine and a certificate signed by a fully qualified and licensed engineer. The pilot also signs this certificate and no defect is allowed to occur on any machine belonging to the Everson Flying Services.

Travel by the E.F.S. and be sure of getting there fast, sure and certain. The charge for the service is very low at 9d. a mile and all enquiries are welcomed.

G-ACBU, D.H.60G. Moth, 'The Silver Lining'. (later EI-AAW. on Irish Reg.)

Travel by the E.F.S. and be sure of getting there fast, sure and certain. The charge for the service is very low at 9d. a mile and all enquiries are welcomed

Personal A/c. of the late Lady Sophie Heath. Colour scheme as G-ACBU silver-doped overall, the F. colour being very slightly darker than the F/S. As EI-AAW, same as for EI-AAE, (The name, 'The Silver Lining', was deleted) F. blue, but of a slightly darker shade c., F/S. silver-doped.

EI-AAW, D.H.60G Moth, Reg'd. 29/5/34, Lady Heath c/no. 1849, ex ZS-ABD, G-ACBU

This aircraft had been at Baldonnel in British marks from at least August 1933 and was used for charter work by Everson Flying Services. Crashed and destroyed by fire at Stone, Staffordshire, on 26/11/35, en route Dublin - Speke - Croydon.

EI-AAT, Spartan I 3-seater, Reg'd. 15/6/33, J.M.J. Kearney c/no. 61, ex G-ABRA, 2/12/33, C.H. Gates

Cancelled on 5/2/35 as crashed.

Throughout the Everson Flying Services period at Kildonan, during which Lady Nelson was in charge from 1933 onwards, Lady Heath kept her aircraft at Kildonan.

Photograph showing G-ACBU D.H. 60G. Moth. 'The Silver Lining'. (Later EI-AAW on Irish Reg. Also included is EI-AAT Spartan 1 - three seater

Everson Flying Services 1934. Inside the Hangar at Kildonan Aerodrome. Included in the photograph are: Back row: Mick Brady, Tony Millea and A. White. Middle row: third from right, Lily Dillon; fifth from right, Bill Lonergan. Front row: second from left, Fr. Furlong with his dog Bruno; Captain Hamilton, fifth from left; J.R. Currie, seated beside Lady Nelson; Lord Nelson; and Fred Griffith

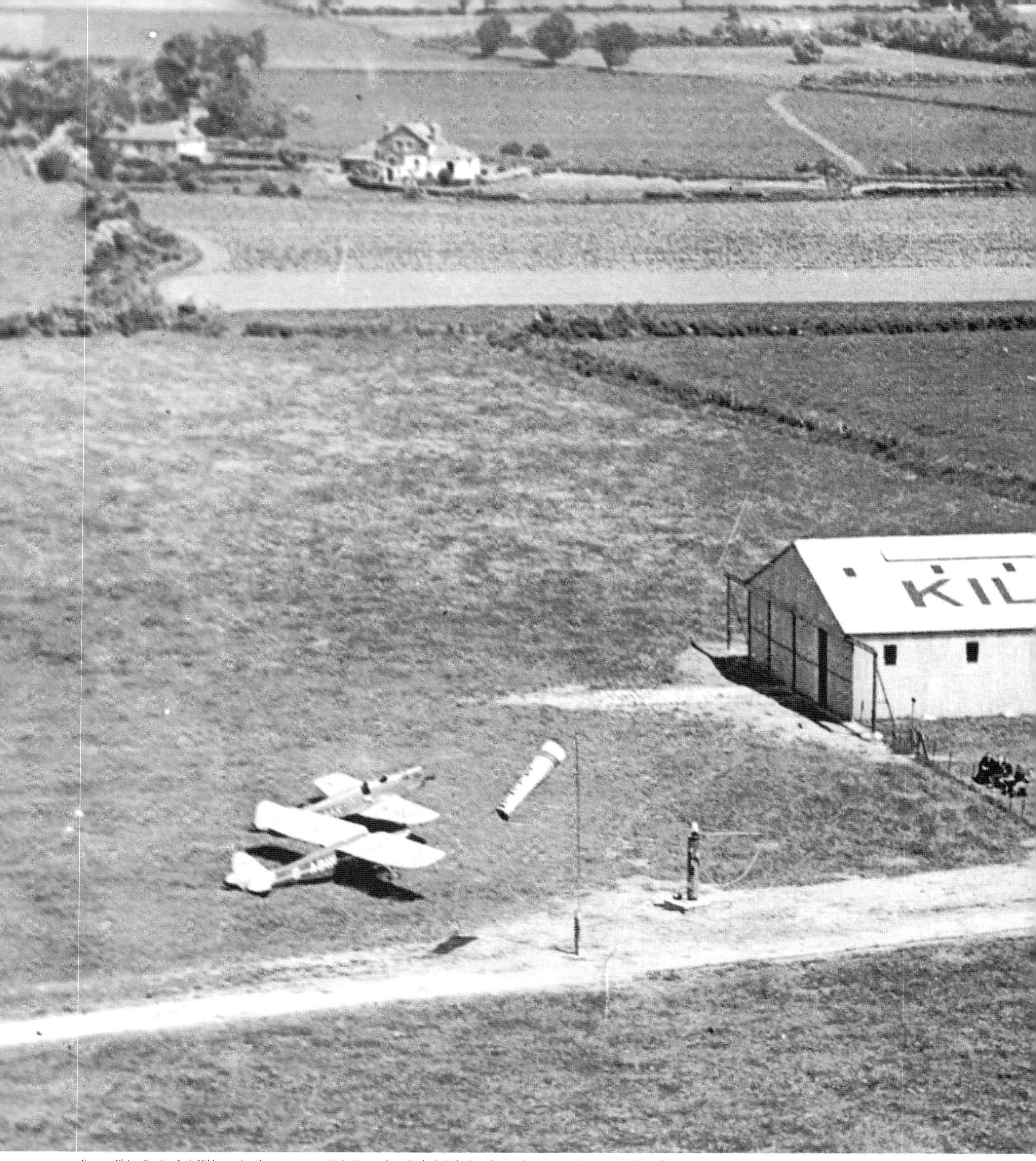

Everson Flying Services Ltd, Kildonan Aerodrome, summer 1934. A/c. in photo: Lady C. Nelson's Miles Hawk, E.I. - A A X (ex G-ACNX) and D.H. 80A. Puss Moth G-ABDL, as used by Captain O.E. Armstrong.
Weston Photo, Dublin *Photo from Pearse Cahill and Oonagh Scannell collection*

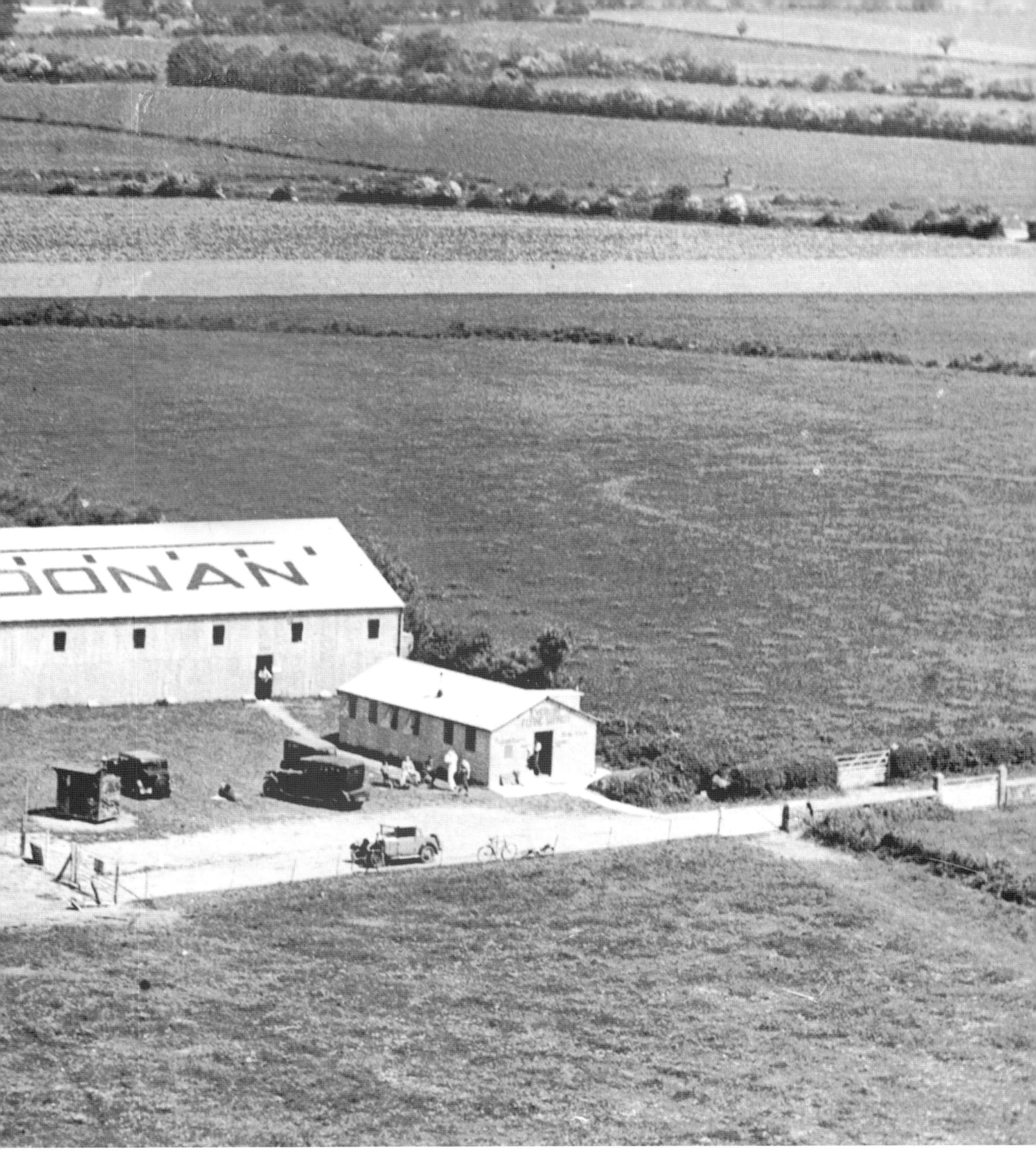

From left: Mick Brady, Oonagh Scannell (Hammond), Sr. Katherine Bayley, Denise Beattie and Jack Williams

The De Havilland " Puss Moth" (inverted Gypsy engine)

D.H. 80A Puss Moth G-ABDL, as used by Captain O.E. Armstrong. Photo taken in the hangar at Kildonan in 1934. Everson Flying Services Ltd.

Lady Mary Heath, Amy Johnson, and her sister Eleanor watch Amy's husband, Jim Mollison, take off. A reporter is intent on their reactions.

Jim Mollison checks his De Havilland Moth "The Hearts Content" at Portmarnock prior to his record breaking solo flight to Australia.

Some of the staff at Kildonan Aerodrome, Everson Flying Services, 1935 (from left): Mick Brady, Dermot Duffy, Fred Griffith, J.R. Currie, George Kennedy and Kevin Sheridan. A/c D.H. 80A. Puss Moth. Weston photo

Geraghty's, The Royal Oak, Finglas. Photo courtesy of Kinane Studio Photographers, 34 Berkeley Road, Phibsboro, Dublin 7. Tel: 830 45 98

Finglas in the 1930s advertising from Everson Flying Services promotional brochures

MONTGOMERY & SONS
VICTUALLER and
CONTRACTOR
Main Street, FINGLAS

All Meat killed for this Establishment
Passed by Veterinary Inspection

Buy Your Needs Here
P. J. Flood,

Select Wine and Spirit Bar
Grocery and Hardware

Bona-Fides Supplied until Last
Bus at Midnight.
LOWER HOUSE
FINGLAS

THE "FLYING" HOUSE
Geraghty's
The Royal Oak
Finglas

None But The Best Drinks
Served
Special Rooms, Special Drinks
Special Attention
Spacious Parking for Motorists

FOR GOOD VALUE
TRY
Patrick Flood,
FAMILY GROCER

: TEA, WINE AND :
SPIRIT MERCHANT

UPPER HOUSE
FINGLAS

New Co. Dublin Flying Service

Lady Nelson with (on left) Mr. John R. Currie, A.R.A. C.S.I., chief instructor and Mr. George Everett at the inauguration of Everson Flying Services Ltd., Kildonan Aerodrome, Finglas

Chapter Thirteen

Chapter

Dublin Air Ferries Limited

Dublin Air Ferries badge

Chapter 13

Dublin Air Ferries Limited

Official opening of Dublin Air Ferries, Kildonan, Finglas

The official opening of the operations of the new company Dublin Air Ferries took place on March 2nd, 1935. The Right Honourable, the Lord Mayor of Dublin, Alderman Alfred Byrne T.D., officiated at the ceremony.

Eleven machines were present on the aerodrome for the opening, including those of the firm. Among the visiting machines were Lady Nelson with her Stinson. Mr. Watson and Mr. Bradbrooke flew a two-engined Monospar, with Mr. Scott as passenger. Mr. Watson represented Lord Wakefield's Castrol Oil. Miss Hallina from Cork, with her Gypsy Moth; Major Dease and Miss Dillon, with their Klemm Swallow representing the Klemm Company. Major Dease was the principle pilot and instructor of the Cork Aero Club. Mr. Gates, a private owner of a Spartan, was present. Mr. French, chief instructor of the Irish Aero Club, was with Mr. Cormack, the Canadian trade commissioner. Mr. P. Hyland flew Mr. O.Grattan Esmonde's Gypsy Moth to the opening. Mr. Culleton, of Galway, whose machine, a Redwing, was undergoing its C. of A. here, was present. Before the opening, a formation of three machines, piloted by Mr. Scott, Mr. French and Mr. Hyland, flew over from Baldonnel. After the opening, a fly past of all machines took place. Thereafter, joy-riding and stunting were the order of the day.

Kildonan Aerodrome had in fact been taken over by Lady Heath and Jack Williams in February. Before it was officially launched as Dublin Air Ferries Ltd., it went under the title of Free State Air Ferries Ltd. Lady Heath was the chairperson and Mr. G.A.R. Williams, her husband, was a director of the company.

The chief ground engineer was Mr. James Bell. The new company had plans for special lectures on aviation for Thursdays, special courses for ground engineers and instruction in air navigation to be given by Captain J.P. Saul, who flew the Atlantic with Air-Commodore Sir Charles Kingsford Smith from Portmarnock in 1930. When Dublin Air Ferries took over at Kildonan there were some 100 pupils receiving instruction.

When Everson Flying Services ceased trading in January 1935, Lady Heath and her husband Jack Williams became Kildonan's new owners. The new enterprise, first called Free State Air Ferries, became Dublin Air Ferries. The fleet of the new company comprised two aircraft which had served the previous two Kildonan companies, namely Gypsy Moth EI-AAK and Fox Moth EI-AAP, together with Lady Heath's two Gypsy Moths, EI-AAW and EI-ABE. The latter two became part of the D.A.F. fleet and they flew under the title, 'Dublin Air Ferries, Kildonan, Finglas'. The Right Honourable Lord Mayor of Dublin, Councillor Alfie Byrne, performed the official opening which took place on the March 2nd, 1935. The ceremony included an air display which was performed by the Irish Aero Club. Besides the Fox Moth and three Gypsy Moths of DAF, other aircraft present included Lady Nelson's Stinson G-ABTZ, which finally bid farewell to Kildonan and Ireland in May of that year; Ruth Hallinan's Gypsy Moth EI-ABB, which had come up from Cork; Klemm Swallow EI-ABD of Major Dease; Spartan EI-AAT of Corkman C.H. Gates; Robinson Redwing EI-ABC; and Moth EI-AAC belonging to Grattan Esmonde, who had come from Galway. A twin-engined Monospar also attended the ceremony. It had come from Heston, England.

The following are some details of these aircraft:

EI-AAK D.H.60G Moth, Reg'd. 22/8/31, Iona National Airways

C/no 1276, ex G-ABBY, 2/12/33, C. Nelson, 22/3/35, Dublin Air Ferries

Operated in turn by Iona National Airways, Everson Flying Services and Dublin Air Ferries, until delivered to the U.K. on 7/4/36. Cancelled on 17/4/36 on sale to G-ABBV and flown as such until destroyed at Churchdown, Gloucestershire, on 15/7/39.

EI-AAP D.H. 83 Fox Moth, Reg'd 20/7/32, Iona National Airways

c/no. 4003. New aircraft, 2/12/33, C. Nelson, 22/3/35, Dublin Air Ferries

Used for charter operations in turn by Iona National Airways, Everson Flying Services and Dublin Air Ferries, until ferried to England on 31/8/38. Cancelled on 18/9/38 and late registered in the U.K., as G-AFK1. Impressed for the RAF on 31/8/41: no RAF serial number allocated. Final fate unconfirmed, but presumed scrapped.

EI-AAP. D.H. 83 Fox Moth.

F. dark red and light green F/S. Silver-doped. The light green of the upper surface of fuselage extended from Prop. Boss, through the full width of the centre section, tapering rearward to the rubber-post. N.B. This A/c never flew at Kildonan in any colour-scheme other than that detailed above.

EI-AAP DH 83 Fox Moth

The De Havilland 83 Fox Moth was of wooden construction with accommodation for four passengers in an enclosed cabin. The Fox Moth first flew in January 1932 and the first and only example of this type of aircraft to be registered in Ireland was EI-AAP, bought new from de Havilland by Hugh Cahill's Iona National Airways in July 1932. It was one of a total of 98 such aircraft built before the Second World War. EI-AAP was used by Iona National Airways Ltd. for its air taxi and charter services and was powered by a 130 h.p. Gypsy Major engine. When Iona's operations at Kildonan were taken over by Lady Cathleen Nelson and George Everett, under the company name, Everson Flying Services Ltd., the aircraft were also acquired by them. EI-AAP was registered in the name of Lady Nelson and Everson Flying Services was painted onto the Fox Moth. EI-AAP continued to play an important role with Dublin Air Ferries until the company ceased to exist in August 1938 when it was flown to England where it was registered G-AFKI. In 1941, it was impressed into the RAF.

D.H. Fox Moth

The D.H. Fox Moth was affectionately known at Kildonan as the 'Honeymoon Express' because of the number of couples who used it to go away on their honeymoon.

EI-AAW D.H. 60G Moth, Reg'd 29/5/34, Lady Heath C/no 1849, ex ZS-ADB, G-ACBU

This aircraft had been based at Baldonnel in British marks from at least August 1933 and was used for charter work by Everson Flying Services. It crashed and was destroyed by fire at Stone, Staffordshire, on 26/11/35, en route to Dublin - Speke - Croydon.

G.-ACBU. D.H. 60G Moth, The Silver Lining. Later EI-AAW on Irish Reg.

Personal A/c. of the late Lady Sophie Heath. Colour scheme as G-ACBU silver-doped overall, the F. colour being very slightly darker than the F/S. As EI-AAW, same as for EI-AAE, above. The name, 'The Silver Lining', was deleted.

EI-ABE D.H.60G Moth, Reg'd 1/3/35, Lady Heath, 20/2/37, Dublin Air Ferries

Delivered to Ireland as G-AASY on 21/12/34. Cancelled on 7/2/38 upon re-sale as G-AASY. Impressed for the RAF as AW128 and later to an instructional airframe as 4490M.

EI-ABE. D.H. 60G Moth

F. two-tone, upper half emerald green, lower, light green, fin and rudder, same colours. Wings and tail-plane, silver-doped. M. same colours as F., but in reverse order to background colour. i.e; half and half.

EI-ABB D.H. 60G Moth, Reg'd 1/3/35, Miss R. Hallinan C.A.C., C/no. 1142, ex G-AAKW

Delivered in Irish marks on 25/11/34 as a replacement for EI-ABA. Ferried to the U.K. on 7/4/37 and cancelled on 9/4/37. Restored as G-AAKM. Subsequently sold abroad as VT-AFU. Impressed for the RAF in India on 10/9/42 as MA953; struck off charge on 28/8/47.

EI-ABD Klemm L.25C-1A Swallow, Reg'd 22/3/35, E.J. Dease C/no. 28, exG-ACZK 29/1/36, Miss L. Dillon

On the outbreak of war in 1939, this aircraft was in the U.K. and was later impressed for RAF service, still wearing Irish marks. Cancelled from the Irish register on an unknown date 'after warnings to the owner'. Last heard of at RAF Henlow in January 1947.

Going solo at Kildonan

During the period between March 19th and April 19th, 1935, the following went solo:

Mr. Culleton of Galway 7 hrs 45mns

Miss Beattie 7 hrs 20mns

Mr. Mick Brady 6 hrs 30mns

(assistant ground engineer)

Miss Bayley Butler, Mr. B. Little, Mr. L. U. Smith, Mr. E.J. Gleeson

EI-ABC Robinson Redwing 11, Reg'd 17/4/35, W. H. Culleton C/no 4, ex. G-ABMJ

Cancelled on 12/5/35 as crashed. The remains were disposed of as scrap and subsequently re-appeared with various modifications under the auspices of a Mr. Foley, who presented it as a new design. In this guise it was called 'The Spirit of Erin'.

EI-AAC, D.H. 60 G Moth, Reg'd 11/4/29, O.G. Esmonde C/no. 1000. New aircraft 26/2/37, Dublin Air Ferries

Original colour scheme: fuselage (F.), light blue & silver; flying surfaces (F/S.), silver-doped. From 1937 onwards, F. dark blue, N.B. This a/c. was always a 60G Moth and was fully operational throughout 1937 and in 1938 - up until September.

Cancelled from the register on 5/4/37. Stored until ferried to England, 1/9/38, later registered as G-AFKA, impressed for the RAF as DG582 and became an instructional airframe as 2592M. Struck off RAF charge on 16/11/45.

Robinson Redwing

In May 1935, Dublin Air Ferries held an Irish aviation camp at Kildonan which lasted two weeks, with lectures, practical demonstrations in flying and social events in the evenings. Tents were used to accommodate visitors to the camp. A few weeks before the camp, Jack Williams had flown a special flight to be first with photographs of the fire in the Hospital Sweepstakes premises for the British evening papers in Manchester. The fire happened on April 24th.

Colour of aircraft

In the April 1936 issue of Aviation, under the heading 'Dublin Aero Club', the following observation was made: "Mr. Fred Hill's scarlet Miles Hawk is back with us once more from a rather long stay in England and makes a cheerful note of colour among our green machines."

EI-AAW

On Tuesday November 26th, 1935, while on a charter flight to Croydon with passenger Nora Wilson, Jack Williams, the pilot of the aircraft EI-AAW, had to make an emergency landing shortly after refuelling at Speke Aerodrome in Liverpool. While over Stone in Staffordshire, the aircraft's engine caught fire. The couple escaped to safety from the plane which had successfully landed when it burst into flames.

EI-AAK

On April 7th, 1936, EI-AAK was flown by Nora Wilson to Hansworth where it was overhauled and sold, assuming its original registration number, G-ABBV. Dublin Air Ferries was left with just two aircraft at this stage, namely Moth EI-ABE, which was originally registered in Lady Heath's name and Fox Moth, EI-AAP, which had faithfully served all three companies which had carried out operations at Kildonan Aerodrome.

EI-ABN (G-AEFU)

The fleet of Dublin Air Ferries Ltd. was supplemented in May 1936 with the arrival from Hansworth of an aircraft not yet seen in this country, a Japanese Aeronca, C. 3, G-AEFU, which was registered in the name of Rev. Fr. J. Furlong, Catholic curate in Finglas Village. It is understood that Fr. Furlong and Lady Heath were joint owners of this aircraft. Fr. Furlong used his plane for instructing members of the Tramway Aero Club, which Lady Heath and himself had recently set up at Kildonan.

Aeronca

The last picture taken of George Kennedy with Aeronca Japenese monoplane at Kildonan 1938. Weston photo

Aeronca J.A.P. advertisement

Flying Priest, Fr. Joseph Furlong, C.C., of Finglas, Co. Dublin, Ireland's only Flying Priest, was subsequently appointed parish priest of Kilcullen, Co. Kildare, by the Archbishop of Dublin. Fr. Furlong was one of the first amateurs in Ireland to receive his flying licence. His dog Bruno always accompanied him on his flying trips

An Aeronca, similar to that owned by Fr. Furlong, shot in flight

Dublin Air Ferries Ltd., Kildonan Aerodrome, c. summer 1936. Prominent pilot members of Dublin Air Ferries Ltd. and the Dublin Aero Club (from left): Lieut. 'Andy' Woods, Irish Army Air Corps; Capt. R. G. Williams (Lady Heath's husband); Mr. George Kennedy; and Mr. J. R. Currie, later to gain renown as the co-designer of the Currie-Wot light aeroplane. Weston photo, Dublin

DUBLIN AERO CLUB

FURTHER

FROM OUR AIR CORRESPONDENT.

A meeting of the recently-formed Dublin Aero Club was held at Kildonan on July 21st last, at which a committee was appointed, with the following flying members:—The Rev. J. Furlong, Finglas; Mr. Plant, Mr. Lowendes, Mr. Gleeson, Mr. B. Greene, Miss Scannell, Miss Beattie, Mr. Kelly, Mr. Barry, Mr. G. Kennedy, Captain Hamilton, Lieutenant Bell (hon. secretary, National Aero Club).

There are three machines at the disposal of the members of the Club.

Irish Times 24/7/35

The Dublin Aero Club

The Dublin Aero Club was formed in 1935 for pupils of the flying school formerly operated by Dublin Air Ferries Ltd., whose aircraft and instructors were availed of for training purposes. The number of members at the time was 140 persons.

A general meeting of the newly formed Dublin Aero Club was held at Kildonan Aerodrome on Sunday February 2nd at which the club was duly constituted and the following officers were elected:

President, Captain Hamilton; vice-president, Mr. W. Gleeson; Committee - two directors of the Dublin Air Ferries Ltd.; Mr. L.U. Smith, Miss N. Wilson, Father Furlong, Mr. Barry Egan, hon. secretary and treasurer, Miss K. Wilson.

Other members who served on the committee were: Mr. Maginnis, Mr. Lowndes, Mr. Plant, Miss Scannell, Miss Beattie, Mr. Kelly, Mr. Kennedy and Lieutenant James M. Bell. Lady Heath and Jack Williams, as owners of the company, were automatically members. Mr. Lowndes was a motor cycle racing champion and established a world speed record on a Norton in France. His wife was also a member of the Aero Club.

'A' Licence

At the beginning of 1936, two sisters, Miss K. and N. Wilson of Lanmore, Shankill, went together to Baldonnel to be tested for their 'A' licence and duly passed. The two qualified on the same day, which is probably the first time that this happened in the Irish Free State. Miss Bayley-Butler, who became Sr. Katherine, successfully passed the test shortly afterwards.

Tramway Aero Club

The Tramway Aero Club was formed in 1937 to cater for the needs and aspirations of employees of the Dublin United Tramways Company. The aircraft and instructors of Dublin Air Ferries Ltd. provided the training facilities. There were 80 members at this time.

Shortly after Aer Lingus commenced scheduled flights to England, in May 1936, Dublin Air Ferries shut down its operations on a temporary basis "for change of direction and re-organisation" (September 1936). The Dublin Aero Club also ceased to exist during the period of the close-down of operations of DAF. Before it re-opened, DAF bought Grattan Esmonde's EI-AAC aircraft following his death. The company recommenced its operations in March 1937, with three aircraft: Moth, EI-AAC; Gypsy Moth EI-ABE; and Fox Moth, EI-AAP. EI-AAC was soon sold in England in April 1937 and the other two aircraft were grounded for a time, having been damaged in separate incidents. Gypsy Moth EI-ABE was sold in England in February 1938 and when Fox Moth EI-AAP was flown to England for sale on August 31st, 1938, Dublin Air Ferries shut down its operations. A notice was issued by the Department of Industry and Commerce on December 20th, 1938 stating that Kildonan Aerodrome was closed.

Dublin Air Ferries Ltd, the third and final company at Kildonan, started in 1935 and finished up in 1938. Mary Lady Heath, A.R.C. SC. I., F.R.G.S., had been managing director of the company and her husband, G.A.R. Williams, had been director and flying manager. Lady Heath was known as Sophie to close friends and her husband Jack. Dublin Air Ferries had owned four aircraft, three Gypsy Moths and the ex-Iona Fox Moth Alpha Papa EI-AAP. They had employed three pilots. Operations included charter flights, training school, the Dublin Aero Club, the National Irish Junior Aviation Club and the Dublin Tramway Club.

He flopped but hung there for a moment and Christ almighty! The petrol from the centre section tank started to spill and you could see a plume of smoke where some of it had got onto the exhaust

Lady Heath, Ireland's greatest aviatrix, had chosen Kildonan as the place to communicate, to a multitude of willing pupils, her enthusiasm for flying and her great technical and professional expertise. Her work was not one in vain. For example one of her pupils, Ivan Hammond, later became chief pilot of Aer Lingus. Her organisational skills and enthusiasm were passed on to people like Chris Bruton, one of the most prominent members of the National Irish Junior Aviation Club, and who for many years played a key role in the clubs which cultivated the increasing interest in flying in what was at the time the Irish Free State.

Captain J.N. Duggan recalls that one day while Arthur White was flying one of the Kildonan aircraft, watched by Jack Williams and himself, he attempted a loop right over the aerodrome. " He went up but did not have sufficient speed to go over the top. He flopped but hung there for a moment and Christ almighty! The petrol from the centre section tank started to spill and you could see a plume of smoke where some of it had got onto the exhaust. Jack got terribly agitated. We stood dumbfounded because we thought actually that Arthur was going to disappear in a burst of flames. Anyway, he completed the loop, such as it was and landed. Jack was out there to meet him. Words and gesticulations were plenty. The end result was that Jack grounded him. Arthur's reaction was to go over and join the Irish Aero Club.

He bought EI-AAU, the particulars of which are as follows:

EI-AAU D.H. 60G-111 Moth, Reg'd. 19/9/33, Irish Aero Club

C/no.5032. New aircraft 30/3/38, A. White

Delivered in Irish marks on 18/9/33 as a replacement for the Gypsy Moths lost in accident earlier in the year. Sold to a private owner in 1938 and cancelled on 2/7/38, on which date it crashed at Kilcool, Co. Wicklow. The damaged remains were sold in the U.K., rebuilt. The aircraft reappeared as G-AFWX and was scrapped at Gatwick in 1946.

De Havilland Gypsy Moth in flight

EI-ABD Klemm L.250-1A Swallow, Reg'd 22/3/35, E.J. Dease

C/no. 28 ex G-ACZK, 29/1/36, Miss L. Dillon

On the outbreak of war in 1939, this aircraft was in the U.K. and was later impressed for RAF service, still wearing Irish marks. Cancelled from the Irish register on an unknown date "after warnings to the owner". Last heard of at RAF Henlow in January 1947.

Cruising speed, 98 m.p.h., top speed, 112 m.p.h. landing speed 30 m.p.h. Pobjoy 80-90 h.p. 'Cataract' engine.

B.A. 'Swallow', open two-seater monoplane, in flight

EI-ABD: a close-up of the cockpit

EI-ABD: a side view of the aircraft

EI-ABD: a frontal view of the aircraft

By March 31st, 1937, Dublin Air Ferries Ltd. had a new board of directors: J.N. Duff, T. Jackson and J.M. Clarke (managing director). The following letter of J.M. Clarke - to the 'Adjutant', 7 State Army Air Corps, Baldonnel - concerned modifications which were required to be carried out to Fr. Furlong's plane, the Aeronca G-AEFU. It is clear from the letter that the Aeronca had not yet been registered in the Free State at this time. The names Lady Heath and Jack Williams do not appear on the official notepaper as they had by then sold their interest in Kildonan Aerodrome.

MANAGING DIRECTOR
MARY LADY HEATH,
A.R.C.SC.I., F.R.G.S.
DIRECTOR:
G. A. R. WILLIAMS,
(FLYING MANAGER).

Dublin Air Ferries Ltd.
KILDONAN AERODROME
FINGLAS
Co. DUBLIN

TELEPHONE:
FINGLAS 5.
DAY & NIGHT.
TELEGRAPHIC ADDRESS:
"FLYING." DUBLIN.

Picture of letterhead. Note this was the official headed notepaper of Dublin Air Ferries Ltd.

DIRECTORS: J. N. DUFF. T. JACKSON. J. M. CLARKE, (MANAGING DIRECTOR).

DUBLIN AIR FERRIES, LTD.

AERODROME:
KILDONAN,
Finglas, Co. Dublin.
Telephone: FINGLAS 5.
Telegrams: "FLYING DUBLIN"

Head Office:
1, STH. FREDERICK STREET,
DUBLIN.
Telephone: DUBLIN 95864.

EI-ABN Aeronca C.3, Reg'd 16/6/37, Rev, J. Furlong

C/no. A.609, ex-GAKFU

Cancelled from the register on 22/11/55 and subsequently scrapped at Weston.

The Aeronca had a very high wing loading and was powered by a 38 hp engine. It was underpowered and consequently had no aerobatic licence. Few people were allowed to fly the Aeronca: 4444, George Kearney, Bill Lonergan and Captain J.N. Duggan were among the few.

The Dublin Aero Club

When Dublin Air Ferries ceased business operations, the members of the Dublin Aero Club moved over to Weston Aerodrome near Leixlip, Co. Dublin. This aerodrome was set up by Captain P.W. (Darby) Kennedy, who also was amongst the original pre-war staff pilots of Aer Lingus, with O.E. Armstrong, Ivan Hammond ('Hammy') B.T. O'Reilly and Noel McCaulay. Darby Kennedy became chief pilot with Aer Lingus. He left Aer Lingus for a time to concentrate on his aerodrome at Weston but later returned to Aer Lingus and until recently was still flying at Weston.

Marjory Bayley-Butler, posing for a photograph outside the hangar of Dublin Air Ferries Ltd. The photograph shows the Dublin Air Ferries Ltd. sign in the background .

George Kennedy taken with a Gypsy Moth at Kildonan Aerodrome, Finglas

DIRECTORS: J. N. DUFF. T. JACKSON. J. M. CLARKE, (MANAGING DIRECTOR).

DUBLIN AIR FERRIES, LTD.

AERODROME:
KILDONAN,
Finglas, Co. Dublin.

Telephone: FINGLAS 5.
Telegrams: "FLYING DUBLIN"

Head Office:—
1, STH. FREDERICK STREET,
DUBLIN.

Telephone: DUBLIN 95864.

JC/JA/324

The Adjuntant,
Free State Army Air Corps,
BALDONNEL.

31st March, 1937.

Dear Sir,

Some weeks ago you advised us that you were prepared to carry out modifications on the engine bearers of our Aeronca aircraft G-AEFU.

We shall be glad to know when we may send the machine over to your workshops at Baldonnel to have the necessary work done, and in view of the fact that the aircraft is due for C. of A. renewal on the 15th April, we shall be glad to know if you could do this work also.

It is our intention, after C. of A. has been completed, to register this aircraft in the Free State.

Thanking you in anticipation of your early reply,

Yours faithfully,
DUBLIN AIR FERRIES LTD.

J. M. Clarke

MANAGING DIRECTOR.

Modifications were necessary to make the aircraft 'safer'. The Aeronca was difficult to handle, was inherently unstable and had a tendency to stall on landing

C.A. 466.

SAORSTAT EIREANN.

DEPARTMENT OF INDUSTRY AND COMMERCE.

CIVIL AVIATION NOTICE.

No. 3 of 1935.

HIGH GASHOLDER AT DUBLIN

A. Obstruction to Air Navigation.
B. Direction signs for aircraft.

It is hereby notified:—

A. 1. A high gasholder has been erected at DUBLIN, and constitutes an obstruction to air navigation. The following are particulars :—

Position			Height	Description
Lat.	Long.	Local		
53° 20′ 44″ N	6° 14′ 22″ W	3¾ miles W. of the Poolbeg Lighthouse, on S. side of River Liffey.	260′	Circular, 136′ in diameter, dark grey in colour.

2. Pilots should exercise caution when flying in the neighbourhood of the gasholder in conditions of bad visibility.

B. 3. White direction arrows have been painted on the top surface of the gasholder, pointing respectively to KILDONAN and BALDONNEL Aerodromes, as indicated on the sketch overleaf. It should particularly be noted that the angles shown are from True North, not Magnetic North.

By direction of the Minister for Industry and Commerce.
JOHN O'BRIEN, *Director*.

TRANSPORT AND MARINE BRANCH,
14 St. Stephen's Green, N.,
DUBLIN, 11*th April*, 1935.

(6519T).M580.Wt.387/P107/35.3.250.5/35.W.P.W/Ltd.22.

Front of Civil Aviation notice

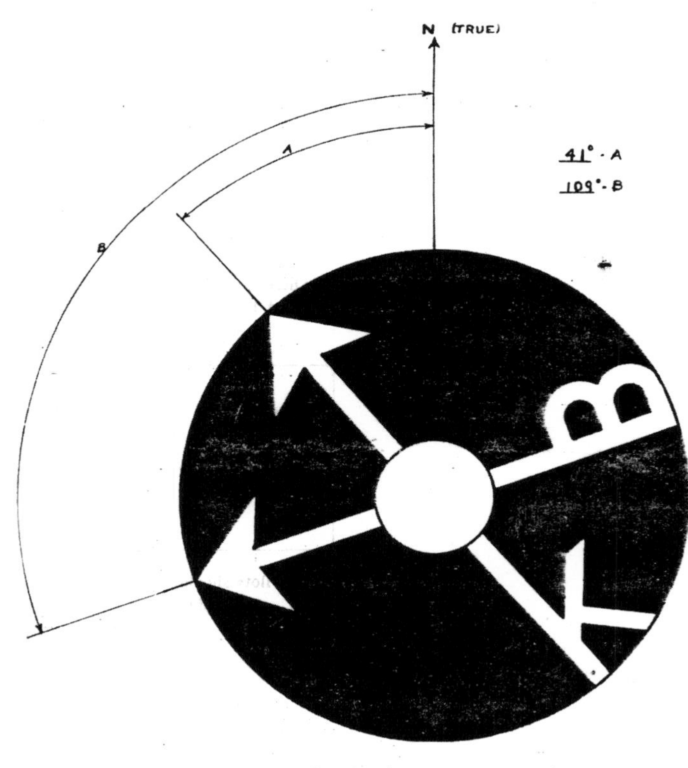

Back of Civil Aviation notice

WHERE DUBLIN WON ITS WINGS

John J. Dunne remembers the pioneer days of flying — in Finglas!

DUBLIN
DIASPORA
eblana·dyflinn·dubh linn
baile atha cliath·dublin·988-1988

It was a small, old-world village then, a cluster of quaint cottages, a little church crowned by a bell, and a holy well. It was a timeless place, snuggling back into its long history, and although Strongbow had once routed the Irish here and King Billy, after the Boyne, had mustered his troops close by, nowadays nothing much happened.

That was Finglas in the early 1930s, an isolated hamlet about five miles from the centre of Dublin. Then the enterprising Cahill family acquired a field just off the Ashbourne road (the old coaching road to Drogheda) about a mile north of the village and, in a way, nothing was ever quite the same again. That field became Kildonan Aerodrome, home of Iona National Airways, Ireland's pioneering airline. It was also to be the ~~first~~ base of ~~the Irish Aero Club and of its offshoot~~, the National Irish Junior Aviation Club.

The 'aerodrome' was simply a large grassy field, flat enough to be used for the take-off and landing of the tiny aircraft of the day, mostly primitive Puss Moths and Gypsy Moths, some with small cabins but usually with open cockpits. A large shed served as the solitary hangar. There was a petrol pump and a white canvas bolster attached to the top of a pole, the elementary wind-indicator known as a windsock. This was Hugh Cahill's dream: it was the grassy 'tarmac' from which Irish aviation took off.

As teenagers — before that term was coined — we were wildly enthusiastic about our National Irish Junior Aviation Club (the 'National' was later dropped from the title). Every Friday evening in summer we cycled out to Kildonan, or took the single-deck bus that then alone served Finglas village, and trudged the remaining mile along the Ashbourne road to the aerodrome.

There, the airmen and engineers working for Iona lectured us on various aspects of flying, using the firm's aircraft and equipment for demonstration purposes, while occasionally distinguished aviators would come. During the winter months the visits to Kildonan were replaced by lectures in the old Moira Hotel in Trinity Street. On one special occasion, when the Cobham Flying Circus visited Dublin, Sir Alan himself, hero of such record flights as London to Capetown and back in 1926 and other epic trips to Australia and India, fired our youthful imagination

Today, names survive through the clouds of time that are closely associated with those early Kildonan days: Hugh Cahill, J C Malone, John Horgan, the pioneering aerial photographer, Captain O E Armstrong, who was later to sign on as Aer Lingus's first pilot, Cahill's chief pilot M F Coogan and an enthusiast named Weston, (George, I think) who lived in a tall old house on Richmond Road in Fairview.

The dominant personality at Kildonan, however, as far as we teenagers were concerned, was the flamboyant Lady Mary Heath, who had started our unique club.

Born Sophie Mary Pierce in Newcastle West, Co Limerick, in 1897, she was the first woman to hold the British Air Ministry's 'B', or Commercial Licence which she got in 1926, the year she set up a world altitide record for light aircraft at 17,000 feet. In 1928 she made the first solo and light aeroplane flight from Capetown to Cairo and set up a further world altitude record for light planes at 23,000 feet. She had also been second pilot to the fledgling Dutch airline KLM and flew on all of its expanding European routes. While on a lecture tour in the United States in 1929 she entered for the National Air Race at Cleveland, Ohio, but crashed through a factory roof at more than 100mph.

Recovered from her extensive injuries, but still with steel plates in her skull, she came to Dublin as chief instructor to Iona National Airways. It was then that her enthusiasm for flying, and her desire that it should be accepted by young people, prompted her to form her unique aviation club for teenagers.

She was accompanied home to Ireland by her husband, G A R Williams, with whom she eventually took over Kildonan, renaming the company Dublin Air Ferries in 1935. Williams was Lady Heath's third husband.

Sophie Pierce was no stranger to tragedy. Her childhood had been blighted by a devastating family trauma and it seemed that a grim irony would pursue her to the end of her days. Her death came in May 1939, not in the air, where she had so often diced with danger, but in St Leonard's Hospital, Shoreditch, London, from injuries received in a fall from a London tramcar.

It was an era of 'air pageants' or 'air displays', those pioneering years of the 1930s, and many such events took place at Kildonan. A familiar figure at the aerodrome then was an early enthusiast, Father Furlong of Finglas, who became known as 'The Flying Priest' and with whom the present writer made his first-ever flight over Dublin city at night in a tiny Puss Moth, at a cost of half-a-crown!

Many gallant Irish men and women have added lustre to the pages of aviation history

Yet, once — and not so very long ago at that — it was all centred upon a tiny field near Finglas village. It is only fitting, therefore, in this Millennium Year that Dublin should be credited with providing the take-off to it all in the now almost forgotten name of Kildonan.

John J Dunne remembers the 'Golden Days' of flying at Finglas

Chapter Fourteen

Chapter

Kildonan -
The Aer Lingus connection
by
Oonagh Scannell (Hammond)

Chapter 14

Kildonan - The Aer Lingus connection

I started my flying at Kildonan as a member of the National Irish Junior Aviation Club, founded in May 1933 by Lady Heath, for the purpose of promoting aviation among young people. My sister Grainne was also a member at the same time.

Kildonan was a lovely little airfield where so many were happy. There were constant comings and goings and Air Corps pilots would also call in to see us. We had a cook, George Morris, who was marvellous at his job. Fitzpatrick's house was at the end of the landing strip. They bred horses.

The main period of my apprenticeship at Kildonan was during the time of Dublin Air Ferries Ltd. when Lady Heath and her husband Jack Williams managed the place. Every Sunday morning we flew in formation over the city. I remember Lady Heath very well and the tremendous commitment she had to promoting flying in Ireland. She gave every encouragement to me and showed many touches that were very considerate to the members at Kildonan as well as her acquaintances and friends. I remember Lady Heath sending a telegram to Lord Heath, to whom she had previously been married. It was the occasion of his third wedding. The telegram read: "From Mary the first to Mary the third." It was typical of her sense of humour.

It was difficult to get to Kildonan - bus to Finglas and then a mile walk. If we were lucky and a group of us were travelling together, we would hire one of Parkes' immaculately turned out taxis - shiny, sparkling, comfortable and smelling of new leather and polish inside. Parkes' was a garage on the main road at the top of the hilly village. If four of us shared, we travelled in state in our specially liveried chauffeur driven taxi, all for the princely sum of sixpence each.

I remember little incidents at Kildonan, like the day we decided to plant flowers around the outside of the clubhouse. The ground was rough. My husband Ivan saw our predicament and lent us a hand. When Ivan dug up the telephone cables, which obviously he was not meant to do, we laughed till we cried. They were quickly repaired because they were so vital to the operation of an aerodrome.

At weekends, there were lots of joy-rides for five shillings. We used to call them 'once around the graveyard', i.e. Glasnevin Cemetery. The Fox Moth took four passengers. We also had the Miles Hawk and the Gypsy Moth.

In those days in Kildonan we had a lot of waiting around for our turn, sometimes due to bad weather and sometimes due to pupils making bad landings, which necessitated minor repairs to the aircraft. But we did not mind this as it was all part of the learning process. In those days we were never bored. We did not know the meaning of the word.

Kildonan was small and beautiful. I felt like a big fish in a small pool, part of a select band of pioneers, as it were. Then there was that kind of family spirit, where everyone helped out - a kind of comraderie - which it is difficult to explain. You felt safe and secure in Kildonan like you do in your own home with your family around you. All the summers were sunny and all the people were happy. I had two special friends at Kildonan - Miss Marjory Bayley Butler and Miss Denise Beattie.

Pictured (from left): Mr. Michael (Mick) Brady; Miss Oonagh Scannell (later to become Mrs. Ivan Hammond); Miss Marjory Bayley-Butler (later Sr. Katherine); and Miss Denise Beattie. Dublin Air Ferries, August 8th, 1936. John. J. Horgan photo

The occasion for this photo, taken during the first week of August 1936, was the entry of Sr. Katherine to the convent of the Sisters of Charity, Milltown, Co. Dublin. Sir Katherine was received into the order on August 18th, 1936.

I went solo on the Easter Monday 1935 after three take-offs and landings. I was the first soloist in the Miles Hawk and I was the first to fly in that aircraft at Kildonan. When I taxied up to the club house, all the boys congratulated me, except for one, who interested me very much. He stayed in the hangar while I completed my solo run. He was the last to congratulate me. His name was Ivan Hammond, later to become my husband. Ivan was practising for his commercial licence at the time. Thereafter, I flew with Ivan continually while he clocked up the hours for his 'B'. Several times we were in trouble with Captain Currie. On one occasion, when he checked the fuel gauge, he knew that we had landed somewhere. In fact, we had landed at 'Clonswords' Ballyboughal, where Ivan's brother lived. Though we had fun at Kildonan, flying was a very serious business. We knew we had the best in terms of the back-up staff, all experts in their respective fields.

Ivan did a lot of joy-rides and trips to Liverpool and Manchester with business people. When we married I promised that I would not follow my flying career. Ivan never liked to see me fly.

I remember very many people at Kildonan, too numerous to mention. Captain Hamilton, transport manager of Independent Newspapers, was a pilot with Kildonan and sometimes flew the papers down the country. Lady Nelson took a great interest in Kildonan also.

EI-AAK, with J.R. Currie, in front, and Oonagh Hammond at the rear

The Dublin Aero Club was formed at Kildonan in July 1935 and at a special meeting called for that purpose, the following committee was formed: The Rev. J. Furlong, C.C. Finglas; Mr. Plant; Mr. Lowndes; Mr. Gleeson; Mr. R. Greene; Miss Scannell (myself); Miss Beattie; Mr. Kelly; Mr. Barry; Mr. G. Kennedy; Captain Hamilton; and Lieutenant Bell (hon. secretary, National Aero Club). This meeting took place on July 21st, 1935.

When Ivan was about to join Aer Lingus, he got a glowing commendation from Ireland's greatest aviator and something which we have treasured. Lady Heath took a personal interest in furthering people's aviation skills and interests.

Oonagh Hammond, standing on the wing of EI-AAK

So when Ivan joined Aer Lingus in 1937, it was small and discrete just like Kildonan. There were only about 12 people employed. Sean O'hUadhaigh and Mr. Jerry Dempsey were the head office staff. There were three engineers, including Johnny Maher and Nobby Rafter. The only pilots were Eric Armstrong and Ivan. For his first six months in Aer Lingus, Ivan was a part time pilot. He worked in the hangar as an engineer and when he was needed he flew as a co-pilot on a DH86. He also flew charter flights in the Rapide. When it came to chartering the Rapide, Ivan used to do most of the work himself. He would take a phone call, fix the price with the customer, collect the money, make the flight and pay the money to the company. Ivan had instructions from Sean O'hUadhaigh to fix the price himself at a rate which would ensure that the company did not lose money. This is just the way it was at the start. No sophisticated planning here - just enough to keep the company ticking over.

Iona National Airways
request the pleasure of the company of
Mrs. Una Hammond
to join with us in celebrating
53 years as Irelands Oldest Airline
in our
Newly Refurbished Clubhouse
at Cloghran Co. Dublin
on 2nd December 1983
Charles J. Haughey Esq.
will perform the opening ceremony

7·00pm *R.S.V.P. Tel. 378323 / 375228*

Oonagh Hammonds invite to the celebration of 53 Years as Ireland's oldest airline

This is a letter received by Ivan Hammond from Lady Heath on the occasion on the birth of his son. Note the warmth of her congratulations to Oonagh and her ever willingness to help members of the Dublin Aero Club.

Spelthorne St Mary's.
Thorpe. Nr Chertsey.
Surrey.

August 21st 1936.

Dear Mr Hammond,

I was very glad to get your letter, and to know that all is well with you. What do you call the new son ?

Please give Oonagh a big hug from me and tell her I am prouder than ever of her !

I wish I had known when you were in England, and would have loved to have seen you. Let me know next time you are over !

Let me know when you are coming over again.

On Monday next I am becoming Bridge hostess and Secretary to the Aviation Club. 41A Albemarle St W.1. The Dublin Aero Club will get a notice from me in the near future that they can become members when they come over. The tel; is Regent 4565. You can look me up there whenever you like.

Tons of the best wishes to you both.

Sincerely yours

S Mary Heath

Letter received by Ivan Hammond from Lady Heath on the occasion of the birth of his son

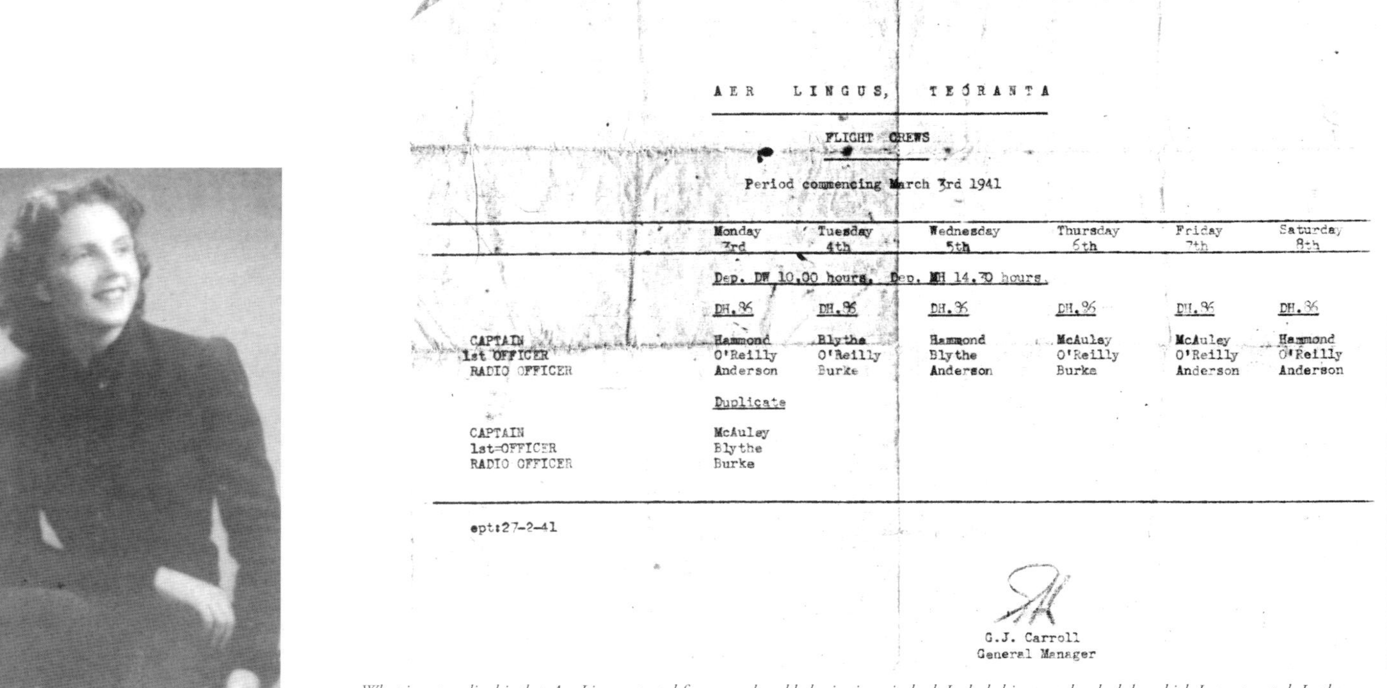

Captain Hammond

AER LINGUS, TEÓRANTA

FLIGHT CREWS

Period commencing March 3rd 1941

	Monday 3rd	Tuesday 4th	Wednesday 5th	Thursday 6th	Friday 7th	Saturday 8th
	Dep. DW 10.00 hours.	Dep. MH 14.30 hours.				
	DH.86	DH.86	DH.86	DH.86	DH.86	DH.86
CAPTAIN	Hammond	Blythe	Hammond	McAuley	McAuley	Hammond
1st OFFICER	O'Reilly	O'Reilly	Blythe	O'Reilly	O'Reilly	O'Reilly
RADIO OFFICER	Anderson	Burke	Anderson	Burke	Anderson	Anderson
	Duplicate					
CAPTAIN	McAuley					
1st=OFFICER	Blythe					
RADIO OFFICER	Burke					

ept:27-2-41

G.J. Carroll
General Manager

What is not realised is that Aer Lingus started from very humble beginnings, indeed. Included is an early schedule, which Ivan operated. In the formative years of Aer Lingus, things had the Kildonan feeling. The scale of the operation was small and everyone was very special

Sheila Broderick-The first Aer Lingus hostess

A group photo taken at Kildonan, Finglas, in front of Fr. Furlong's Aeronca aircraft (from left): Ivan Hammond; Captain J.N. Duggan; Johnny Maher (Aer Lingus' first engineer); Rev. Fr. Furlong, C.C. Finglas; Oonagh Scannell with Fr. Furlong's dog Bruno; Johnny Maher's son; George Kennedy; and Mrs. Johnny Maher

Pictured from left : Bill Lonergan, George Kennedy, Oonagh Hammond, J.R. Currie, another lady pilot, Ivan Hammond, The Wilson sisters

Next stop London: Dublin's Lord Mayor, Alfie Byrne, travelling on the inaugural Dublin-Bristol-London flight, is greeted by the Lord Mayor of Bristol and local dignitaries, 1936

The first Aer Lingus commercial flight

The first Aer Lingus commercial flight took off from Baldonnel Aerodrome to Bristol with five passengers at 9am on May 27th, 1936. Aer Lingus continued to operate from Baldonnel until Collinstown (later Dublin Airport) opened its first flight on January 19th, 1940. The inaugural flight from Collinstown, took off from a specially prepared grass runway and flew the Dublin to Liverpool route.

Aer Lingus was incorporated under the Companies Act on May 22nd, 1936. The first passenger flight followed five days later, on May 27th, from Dublin to Bristol. At that time Aer Lingus had just one aircraft, a de Havilland Dragon 84 (five seater), and one pilot, Captain O.E. Armstrong. The aircraft was named the 'Iolar', i.e., 'The Eagle', and five passengers were: Mrs. Sean O'hUadhaigh; Mr. W. H. Morton (a director of Aer Lingus); a newly married couple, Mr. and Mrs. Fitzherbert; and Dr. Timothy J. O'Driscoll, who at the time was principal officer of the Civil Aviation Division, Department of Industry and Commerce and later played a key role in the development of the transatlantic routes. He served as Ambassador to the Netherlands and became first chairman of Coras Trachtala, the Irish export board. Dr. O'Driscoll, a Corkman, was director general of Bord Failte Eireann for a period and for a time was also executive director of the European Travel Commission. He became a director of Aer Lingus.

EI-ABI Iolar in flight

An early advertisement for the newly formed company of Aer Lingus, Irish Sea Airways

The first Aer Lingus flight to London took place on September 14th, 1936, with the Lord Mayor of Dublin, Alfie Byrne, officiating and linking up with the Lord Mayor of Bristol en route. The first directors of the company were: Sean hUadhaigh; Percy Reyñolds; J.J. O'Leary, who were members of the Irish Aero Club; W.J. Morton, general manager of the Great Southern Railways; and T. J. Flynn, assistant secretary in the Department of Industry and Commerce, Aviation Branch.

A short time later the Bristol stop was eliminated and Aer Lingus flew directly to London, using a 10 seater, DH 86 Express. Seasonal services were opened to the Isle of Man in 1937. The Isle of Man service was operated by Captain Ivan Hammond. A third pilot, Cap 'Darby' Kennedy, was later added to the payroll.

In the first six months, Ivan was not paid a salary but got three pounds a week subsistence allowance and flying pay. Flying pay at that time was one pound for a co-pilot on a London flight and seven and sixpence an hour on charter flights. It was not until April 1938 that he began to be paid a salary and flew full time as a pilot with Aer Lingus.

The Aer Lingus flying company at the time went under the name Irish Sea Airways. Advertising was very important to get the new airlines off the ground.

EI-ABI D.H. 84 Dragon 2, Reg'd. 26/5/36, Aer Lingus Teoranta

C/no, 6076, ex G-ACPY

This machine was the first aircraft owned by Aer Lingus and was delivered from its former owners, Railway Air Services, in Irish marks on 26/5/36, prior to the commencement of Aer Lingus services on the following day the fleet name was 'Iolar'. In 1938, the Dragon was replaced by a Rapide. It was ferried to the U.K. on 16/2/38 and cancelled from the register 19/2/38. It was restored as G-ACPY and flew on airline routes in the U.K. until shot down by German aircraft between Scilly Isles and Lands End on 3/6/41 in the the ownership of Great Western and Southern Airlines.

Aerlingus, Teóranta.
Aerṗort Áṫa Cliaṫ, Baile Doṁnaill. 178
DUBLIN AIRPORT, BALDONNEL.
Ainm (Name) ...
Ó (From) ...
Go (To) Dublin ... Luaċ (Fare) £ ...
Áiteanna Tuirlingṫe ar ar aontuiġeaḋ (Agreed Stopping Places) ...
Maiṫ go dtí (Valid until) 25.5.37
Tugṫa amaċ ag (Issued by) ...
(At) Dublin
Uimhir (Number) Seirbhís (Service)
Dáta (Date)
Dáta a tugṫa amaċ (Date of Issue) 25.5.37
Ticéad bagáiste Uimhir (Baggage Ticket No.)
Fá na Coingeallaċa Ioṁċarta Lastall.
(Subject to Conditions of Carriage on Back).

A photocopy of one of the early passenger tickets of Aer Lingus, Irish Sea Airways. The ticket is dated May 25th, 1937. Aer Lingus photo

EI-ABI early photograph taken at Baldonnel Aerodrome. EI-ABI inaugurated the first Aer Lingus flight from Dublin to Bristol on May 27th, 1936. Photo courtesy of Tommy Craddach

De Havilland D.H 84 Dragon in flight

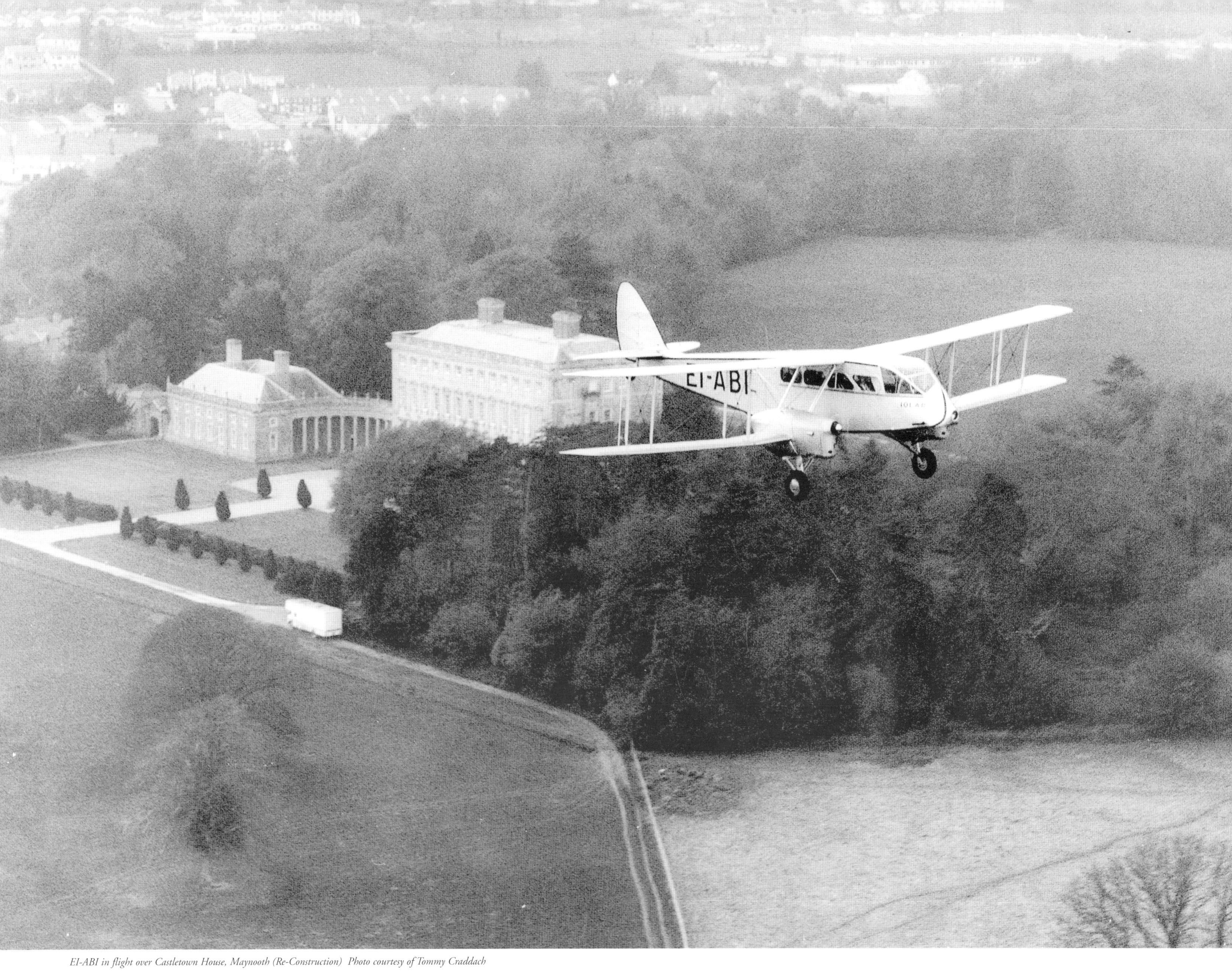

EI-ABI in flight over Castletown House, Maynooth (Re-Construction) Photo courtesy of Tommy Craddach

EI-ABK D.H. 86A, Reg'd 16/9/36, Aer Lingus Teoranta

C/no. 2338, ex-G-ADVJ

Aer Lingus, second aircraft, fleet name 'Eire', purchased from Blackpool & West Coast Air Services and later converted to D.H. 86B standard. Remained in service until the delivery of DG-3 aircraft post-war. Sold in the U.K. as G-ADVJ in October 1946 and scrapped in August 1952.

EI-ABK: an early photograph taken at Baldonnel Aerodrome. Aer Lingus photo

EI-ABP D.H. 89 A Dragon Rapide, Reg'd 24/2/38, Aer Lingus Teoranta

C/no. 6341, ex G-AENO

Fleet name 'Iolar 11', replacing the original 'Iolar', Dragon EI-ABI. Cancelled on 10/2 after sale abroad as VH-ADE. Impressed for the RAF as A33-7, but later restored. Crashed at Cape Sidmouth on 27/1/44.

D.H. 89A Dragon Rapide 'Iolar II' passengers disembarking, possibly Baldonnel

The nose portion of Iolar II

Captain P.W. (Darby) Kennedy, Weston Aerodrome. Weston photo

Weston Aerodrome was established in November 1938, when Captain Kennedy and his wife, Joan, first began to operate a flying school and later an aerial taxi company from there. In November 1988, a committee, established by Tom Keating, ran a suitable 50th birthday celebration.

In attendance was the President, Dr. Patrick Hillery, senior politicians and business men. The VIPs included the Minister for Transport and Tourism, Mr. John Wilson; the chief executive of Aer Lingus, Dr. David Kennedy; and his successor, Mr. Cathal Mullan; the chief executive of Ryanair, Mr. P. J. McGoldrick; and the President of the Irish Aviation Council, Mr. Tom Farrington, who made presentations to Captain Kennedy to mark his contribution to Irish aviation. Monsignor Michael Ledwith, the president of St. Patrick's College, Maynooth, blessed the new hangar. It was officially opened by Dr. Hillery.

Also present on the day was a line up of 1930s vintage aircraft, including the Aer Lingus Dragon (formerly owned by Captain Kennedy and sold to him in 1967 by the State airline), a Tiger Moth, a Piper Super Cruiser, several Piper Cubs and a Stampe SV-4. The President and several other VIPs went on an aerial tour of the city in the Dragon. When Kildonan Aerodrome ceased operations in 1938. The Dublin Aero Club moved to the new Weston Aerodrome.

The First Air Lingus Hostesses

J.F Dempsey and colleagues say farewell to the last Aer Lingus DC3 1964, EI-ACE

EI-ABT D.H. 86B Reg'd, 14/10/38, Aer Lingus Teoranta C/no. 2336, ex G-ADOH

The Sasana EI-ABT DH86B was sold to the U.K. in November 1946 and restored as G-ADUH. It was damaged beyond repair in a ground collision with Autocrat 11-ABC at Bahrein, late in May 1951.

These were the early aircraft of Aer Lingus. They were not unlike the aircraft that we were used to. They had a little more sophistication, perhaps, but the human scale was still there. Shortly after Ivan joined the company, two Lockheed 14s were added to the fleet. They were the first aircraft Ivan had flown which reflected the technical advances in aeronautics - the earlier aircraft were all made of wood and fabric.

Ivan had entered service at Aer Lingus in August 1937 when the airline was but one year old. He flew as a second pilot until 1938 when he was promoted to captain, flying de Havilland 89s from Dublin to the Isle of Man. But the groundwork had been done at the Kildonan Aerodrome, which he joined in 1934. He obtained his first licence, the 'A' licence in November of the same year. It was then that he decided to undertake further studies and began a course in technical aviation. He made many flights throughout the country at this time in de Havilland Moths, the Klemm Swallow and similar aircraft. At the end of the war, Aer Lingus had one DC3 and two DH86s. The Rapide had gone by that time, a good little aircraft and perhaps the fastest of that type in these islands at that time. It had been specially prepared to take part in the King's Cup Air Race and had a speed of about 140 m.p.h. - as fast as the 86s. In 1946, Ivan became a senior pilot and in 1949, a first class senior pilot.

During the war, the planes flew with the windows blacked and without guiding or landing lights and virtually without any radio contact

During his years with Aer Lingus, Ivan flew a whole range of aircraft: DH84s, DH86s, DH89s, Lockheed 14s, DC3s, Vickers Vikings, Lockheed Constellations, Bristol Wayfarers, Vickers Viscounts and F. 27 Friendships. When constellations came in after the war, he flew them on the London and Rome routes. He flew the Rome inaugural flight with Sean Lemass, the then Minister for Industry and Commerce, and G.M. Jerry Dempsey, on board. He flew all the company's European routes, including Great Britain, Denmark, Holland, Belgium, France, Spain, Portugal, Germany, Switzerland and Italy. He piloted the first Aer Lingus flights from Dublin to Rome, Dusseldorf, Birmingham and Lisbon and was captain of the first flight from Dublin to London after the Second World War. A short time after the beginning of the war, Ivan piloted the first service flight to Liverpool and kept the service open during the whole of the duration of the war. During the war, the planes flew with the windows blacked and without guiding or landing lights and virtually without any radio contact. On one occasion, the plane which Ivan was flying was attacked over the River Mersey by an armed merchant boat and his resourcefulness enabled him to arrive safely at his destination. Of all the aircraft he flew, Ivan's favourite was the BAC One-Eleven.

In those days the equipment was still very basic. One of the duties of the co-pilot on the DH86s. was to lower and raise the trailing radio aerial which hung anything from 70 to 200 feet below the aircraft. Flight planning was virtually non-existent. The pilot got a written meteorological forecast. There were no charts. Voice communications were on the medium frequency and this was used for navigation also. Pilots used to tune in to marine radio beacons which they timed with a stop watch to enable them to pinpoint their location. Even at a later stage when direction finders were first incorporated into the aircraft, the loop had to be hand operated by the radio officer. Flying conditions in those days were pretty grim. The pilot had no way of avoiding bad weather, except not to fly at all. If you flew, you had to fly through it. The aircraft flew mostly between two and five thousand feet, compared with today's jets which can go to 37,000 feet. There was no cockpit heating. In cold weather the pilot had to wear an overcoat and fur boots. Aer Lingus had only three pilots: Darby Kennedy, Noel McAuley and Ivan. They used to borrow a co-pilot occasionally from the Air Corps. All three pilots were interchangeable. They flew as both captain or co-pilot and it was not unusual to do two return London trips and a Shannon flight in one day. A London journey then took from two and a half to three hours each way. During one month, Ivan clocked up 140 hours' flying time which is about twice as much as pilots do now.

On his retirement Ivan said: "I wish I was starting all over again." Not the words of one who was tired of flying. Where did he acquire this attitude? I put it down to the early days in a fine aerodrome in Kildonan, Finglas, where we did everything for the love of flying.

Auster in flight

Ivan was the longest serving pilot with Aer Lingus. He dedicated his life to the service of flying. He was the first pilot in the history of Irish aviation to fly a million miles and by the year 1963 he had flown more than 16,000 hours and over 2,630,000 miles. It became a tradition at Aer Lingus because of the deference shown to Ivan that he would make the first flight of the year out of Dublin Airport and it lasted for more than 20 years.

Ivan always wanted to be a pilot. He did not look on flying as just a job. It was something that he enjoyed in spite of the difficulties of flying, particularly in the pioneering days. On his retirement Ivan said: "I wish I was starting all over again." Not the words of one who was tired of flying. Where did he acquire this attitude? I put it down to the early days in a fine aerodrome in Kildonan, Finglas, where we did everything for the love of flying.

Perhaps a symbol of the close ties which existed between the Hammond Family and Aer Lingus is the fact that the house which is now used as a training centre - Castlemoate House - was once the family home of Ivan's family.

Both Ivan and myself maintained our interest in the clubs associated with flying. One of the very pleasurable occasions which I can recall was the naming of An Dreolin, the first aircraft of the City of Dublin Aero Club. I was delighted to be asked to officially name this new aircraft. It was a £500 Auter with dual controls and a 90 h.p. engine. The ceremony took place at Collinstown. I also took a keen interest in gliding and was a member of the Irish National Gliding Club and also their honorary treasurer. I can recall Ivan taking part in a deputation in April 1946 on behalf of the newly formed Irish Aviation Club, the controlling body for private flying in Ireland. The deputation, was received by the Department of Industry and Commerce. The other members were: S. O'hUadhaigh, chairman; Mr. J. Carroll; D. Green; M. A. Quillman; J. B. Lalor; and C. F. Bruton. Flying is in our family's blood and our daughter Olga followed Ivan into Aer Lingus.

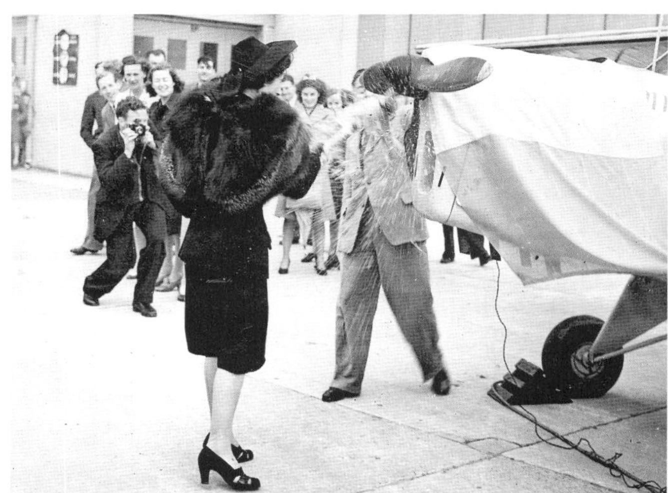

Oonagh Hammond on the occasion of the naming of An Dreolin, the first aircraft of The City of Dublin Aero Club, an Auster, at Collinstown Airport, Dublin

In foreground Auster 'An Dreolin'

Portrait photograph of Olga Hammond, daughter of Ivan and Oonagh Hammond, who was an air hostess with Aer Lingus and BOAC

The late Captain Ivan Hammond, pictured in his Aer Lingus uniform at Collinstown, Dublin

Coincidence at Fiumicino Airport, Rome. An Aer Lingus BAC-ONE Eleven jet arrived just as a BOAC Boeing 707 was disembarking passengers. Captain of the Aer Lingus plane was Ivan Hammond who was pleasantly surprised to find that the attractive BOAC air hostess smilingly saying goodbye to her passengers was his daughter Olga. Father and daughter hail from Dublin and their chance encounter was one in a million for their work takes them to different corners of the world. She was heading for New Delhi. He was on his way to Zurich. Rome is certainly the gateway of the world and in true Irish style the Hammonds swopped stories over a cup of tea before flying off again on their trips around the world

Taoiseach Eamon DeValera boarding a Lockheed Constellation accompanied by John Leydon, Chairman of Aer Lingus and Oscar Traynor Department of Transport

Oonagh Hammond; Denis Green; Séan O' hUaighaidh; Mrs. O' hUaighaidh; and Kay Green

Ivan Hammond Pictured during the first airmail flight to the Isle of Man

Aer Lingus commuter plane in flight

SAAB 340B, one of four Aer Lingus Commuter aircraft

Gerry Carroll, General Manager, Seán Ó hUadhaigh, Chairman, and J.F. Dempsey, Secretary/Accountant in 1940

Dublin Airport, Collinstown, Co. Dublin.

Captain J. C. Kelly Rogers, 1905-1986

Captain J.C.Kelly-Rogers was born in Dun Laoghaire, County Dublin. He served as a Cadet and later as a Second Mate in HMS navy operating between Britain and Australia. In 1927 he joined the RAF and as a Pilot Officer operated flying boats and seaplanes on a worldwide scale. In 1937 he joined Imperial Airways (later to become BOAC, and afterwards British Airways), first as First Officer on the four-engined flying boats, later as Commanding Officer on BOAC's routes from Britain to South Africa and Australia and then as their North Atlantic Chief Pilot. In 1938 he pioneered re-fuelling tests with seaplanes. He was awarded and OBE in 1941 for his contribution to British Civil Aviation. Kelly-Rogers joined Aer Lingus in 1947 as Technical Manager and in 1948 was appointed Assistant General Manager, Technical. He became Deputy General Manager in 1952, a position which he held until he retired in March 1965.

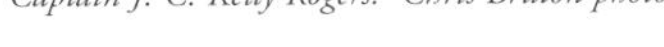

Captain J. C. Kelly Rogers. Chris Bruton photo

The first transatlantic service from Foynes was inaugurated on August 6th, 1939. Also present at the opening were John Dulanty, Irish High Commissioner in London; Eamon De Valera; John Leydon, secretary, Department of External Affairs; Timothy J. O'Driscoll, head of the Civil Aviation Section of the Department of Industry and Commerce; and Captain J. C. Kelly-Rogers.

A graceful sight! Pan Am Boeing 314 18603 'Yankee Clipper' trailing spray in 1939

The first regular passenger service arrived at Foynes on July 8th, 1939. The British Service (British Overseas Airways Corporation, successor to Imperial Airways) opened with Captain J. C. Kelly-Rogers piloting the flying-boat, Caribou. Kelly-Rogers, who was born in Dublin, flew Winston Churchill, Britain's war-time Prime Minister, on his flights across the Atlantic. Afterwards he became deputy general manager of Aer Lingus.

In February 1947, Aer Lingus secured the services of Captain J. C. Kelly-Rogers, who at this time was in charge of BOAC's operations out of Montreal. He played a major role in building up the technical developments of Aer Lingus. He had a worldwide reputation in aviation. He was later to become deputy-general manager of Aer Lingus. Captain Kelly-Roger's prowess as a pilot is well known.

The imperial flying-boat 'Caribou' attended to by Shell personnel

The meticulous servicing of the flying-boat 'Caledonia'

July 20th, 1938: the 'Mayo' composite is prepared for take off at Foynes

Taoiseach Eamon De Valera was on hand to welcome 'Clipper III' making history, west to east. He is seen here talking to Captain Harold Gray and crew

Taoiseach Eamon De Valera greeting the crew of the Caledonia on their Atlantic crossing from Foynes. 1937.

Short 'Empire' Boat

Short "Empire" Boat

BOAC B.314 - The Bristol

Chapter Fifteen

Kildonan 1933-1936:

A memory

by Sr. Katherine Bayley-Butler

Sr. Katherine Bayley-Butler in her youth

Chapter 15

Kildonan - 1933-1936, A Memory by Katherine Bayley-Butler

In the early 1930s Finglas was a small village consisting mainly of one hilly street with some little houses and shops, a church and a school. A left hand turn at the top of the street led to a muddy or dusty road, depending on the weather, little better than a country lane that brought one to Cappagh Hospital. Continuing on the main road, one passed Flood's public house, Parkes' garage, a few clusters of cottages with vegetable gardens, then along by the road flanked by fields and hedges until about a mile out on the left a house named Kildonan came into view, the property of people named Fitzpatrick. A path by the side of this led to a field with a hangar, some aircraft, a clubhouse, a petrol pump and a windsock - Kildonan Aerodrome.

At the start of the decade, Hugh Cahill, owner of the Iona garage at Cross Guns Bridge, Glasnevin, had joined the Irish Aero Club operating at Baldonnel. At that time there were only three private aircraft carrying Irish registration marks and of course there was no commercial airline. The sight of one of these or of one of the few planes belonging to the Free State Army Air Corps was an event. People stopped in the streets or ran out into their gardens, craning their necks to catch a glimpse of "these magnificent men in their flying machines".

Hugh Cahill, together with another keen amateur aviator, J. C. Malone, went over to Croydon where Cahill purchased a DeSoutter Mark II aircraft which was flown to Dublin and registered EI-AAD. This was to become the first Irish commercial machine with the title 'Iona National Air Taxis and Flying School' painted on its fuselage. He also bought a de Havilland Gypsy Moth and some similar type aircraft, the Moth being used for instruction at the club.

DeSoutter II VH-BQE ex EI-AAD and VH-UEE : Ireland's first commercial aircraft

By August 1930, all was in readiness to begin with taxi work, joy flights and instruction. As the pioneer of aerial photography in Ireland, John Horgan was a founder member, his speciality providing another area of business.

John Horgan, pioneer of aerial photography in Ireland

Novelty assignments were to follow, such as banner towing and later still, dropping a ball to start Gaelic football matches at Croke Park and Cusack Park, Mullingar, where the ball was dropped to start the first game of the day - in 1932 - between Cavan and Monaghan. Kerry and Dublin played in the second match, according to Pearse Cahill. The machine which dropped the ball on that day bore an English registration, G-ABDE.

Anthony Fokker

Dropping the football to start a Gaelic football match at Cusack Park, Mullingar

In 1931, Hugh Cahill purchased the site near Finglas and here - at Kildonan - was Ireland's first commercial aerodome, with a competent pilot, Mr. M. F. Coogan, in charge. He was formerly an officer in the Free State Army Air Corps. An early employee was Captain O.E. Armstrong, later to become the first Aer Lingus pilot and another was John Robert Currie, a young Southampton born engineer who was to gain fame as the designer of the Currie Wot Aircraft, a single-seater biplane first built in 1937.

Fokker D. VII in flight

Captain O. E. Armstrong, pilot of the Iona aircraft Gypsy Moth EI - AAP, which flew mail from Galway to Baldonnel to link up with the giant Fokker monoplane owned by the Dutch Airline KLM, which flew to Berlin

John Robert Currie (centre), designer of the Currie Wot Aircraft, a single seater bi-plane, built in 1937. Also pictured are Mick Brady (left), engineer, and Dermot Duffy. Weston photo, Dublin

In 1931, Hugh Cahill sold the DeSoutter which thereafter had a chequered career, being for a time in the service of a small Tasmanian company, the Tasmanian Aerial Services. This was actually the start of the giant airline, Ansett-Australian Airways. Under her new registration, VH-UEE, later "christened" Miss Flinders, she was flown on a wide variety of missions in Australia until she was retired in 1958. However, after lying for years unheeded in a hangar somewhere in Sydney, in 1962 when a new terminal building was being planned at Launceston Airport, Tasmania, it was suggested that the plane, a pioneer of flight in the land of the Southern Cross, be displayed as a museum piece. Here she has been since October 29th, 1966 when the new building was opened.

Liam Byrne, in his book 'The History of Aviation in Ireland', has this to say: "... the popularity of aviation in Ireland was very much in evidence as thousands of curious citizens made their way to Baldonnel to view a giant Fokker monoplane owned by the Dutch airline, KLM. It was a cold and dismal autumn morning with heavy rain clouds hanging low and threatening over the east coast. Shortly after 7.30 a.m., the distant rumble of a small aircraft could be heard. In minutes, the silhouette of a Fox Moth owned by Iona appeared in the sky. It was slowly making its way towards Baldonnel from the west and moments later it touched down on the grass runway and taxied across the airfield until it drew alongside the giant Fokker. Captain O. E. Armstrong, pilot of the Iona aircraft, climbed from the cockpit of the Moth registered EI-AAP and extended his hand to Captain Scholte, the Dutch pilot. Armstrong had left Galway earlier that morning, his aircraft loaded with mailbags which were then transferred to the Fokker. This was the inaugural mail and passenger service between Dublin and Berlin and Hugh Cahill's most ambitious undertaking to date.

This was the inaugural mail and passenger service between Dublin and Berlin and Hugh Cahill's most ambitious undertaking to date

As a matter of fact, this was not the first airmail from Ireland, though the first to the continent. In 1924 and again in 1928, mail was flown from Belfast to Liverpool and in August 1929 from Galway via Baldonnel and Sealand to Croydon. One interesting air taxi service must be mentioned. In 1932, after the Eucharistic Congress, the Mayor of New York was flown by Iona to Southampton to catch a liner there. A very popular effort which brought aviation to the people was begun by Alan Cobham in 1931 in England. His brain child was an air circus which would bring to the men and women in the street "the excitement, thrills and pleasure of seeing the best pilots in the world perform outstanding feats in the best aircraft in the world. He also planned to give joy-rides at a very moderate price, thereby enabling tens of thousands of ordinary folk who could not otherwise afford to sample it, the experience of flying for themselves". (Hist. of Aviation in I).

Hugh Cahill, also anxious to put Ireland on the aviation map, invited Cobham to Dublin. He accepted but did not confine his displays to the capital, giving them in Belfast, Derry, Portlaoise, Waterford, Tralee, Galway, Castlebar, Cork, Wexford and Kilkenny to the delight of huge crowds. His aircraft included, besides an air liner from Imperial Airways, London, one of the world's first helicopters, then called autogiro.

After the flypast of all participating aircraft, there were joy-rides for the spectators and then the performance started in earnest with all sorts of stunts or aerobatics, to give them their correct title. Looping, spinning, inverted flying and wing walking were some of the visual treats and to add a humorous touch, flour bombing.

During one of his visits to Dublin, possibly in the summer of 1933, among the admiring crowd were two teenage girls whose ambition since childhood was to become airborne. When the time for the joy-rides was announced, there came with it an unexpected obstacle. Anybody under 21 years of age had to have a form filled in by a parent or guardian. Rules and regulations of necessity had to be broken if ambitions were to be realised and so the dauntless pair - Marjory Bayley-Butler and Denise Beattie - without a word joined the queue, paid their money and got their first flight - a thrilling experience as they clung to one another screaming with delicious terror.

In the same year, Hugh Cahill's Iona National Airways faded out to be replaced by Everson Flying Services, the title deriving from a combination of the new owners' names, Lady Kathleen Nelson and Mr. George Everett.

On a sunny June evening the following year, the two teenagers were on their way once more to Kildonan where they had discovered joy-flights were available at the cost of 10/- for 15 minutes. My friend Denise Beattie, from Dublin, was at that time staying with my family in Howth.

As we walked along the road from Finglas Village, we noticed a small machine coming in to land. Running we were able to reach the field as it touched down. Out jumped a man from the front cockpit and then, to our amazement, he was joined by a girl who appeared no older than ourselves who'd been having a flying lesson. Her name was Oonagh Scannell and on entering the clubhouse we met another pupil, Ivan Hammond, who would later marry Oonagh and later still would become chief pilot at Aer Lingus.

We asked for our flight or 'flip' and requested that we go over Howth. I cannot recall who the pilot was on that occasion but the machine was the Fox Moth EI-AAP with a small cabin that seated three. Within minutes we were over home and coming down lower and lower until we were less than 50 feet above the ground. Round and round we circled, climbed and dived while the family waved excitedly, as did the sisters in the nearby convent, little guessing who it was. Later we learnt that this behaviour was a risk not merely to life but to pocket, for if we were spotted low flying we could face a fine of £5.

Back home that night we were greeted with remarks such as: "Oh, you missed it: There was an aeroplane flying ever so low - we thought it was going to land - what a pity you weren't here." Our reply was obvious, to the amazement of all.

EI-AAP D.H.83 Fox Moth, Reg'd. 20.7.32, Iona National Airways

c/no. 4003. New aircraft, 2/12/33, C. Nelson, 22/3//35, Dublin Air Ferries

Used for charter operations in turn by Iona National Airways, Everson Flying Services and Dublin Air Ferries, until ferried to England on 31/8/38. Cancelled on 18/9/38 and late registered in the U.K. as G-AFKI. Impress for the RAF on 31/8/41 no RAF serial number allocated. Final fate unconfirmed, but presumed scrapped.

EI-AAP at Baldonnel with members of the Irish Army Air Corps

A/c EI-AAP with R.L. Capt. O. E. Armstrong in the cockpit. Also pictured are John Horgan, photographer; Mrs. Horgan with their child; and a student pilot

September 4th saw us back at Kildonan where we met another pilot, Fred Griffith, who was from New Zealand. As we were booking our flight he said: "Why don't you join the club and then you could have lessons at no extra cost?" We promptly paid our £2 subscription and became the proud possessors of a log book each, then borrowing a helmet and goggles, had our first lesson with John Currie, gaining what was called air experience. By the next time we came out we managed to scrape enough money between us to buy our own helmet and goggles which we shared. The machine in which we were to have many lessons over the next nine months was a de Havilland Gypsy Moth, originally registered G-ABBV, to which registration she returned after her sojourn in Kildonan was ended. While with us she bore the letters EI-AAK, or AK as we affectionately called her. She was a single-engined red and silver biplane with dual controls for instruction. Her engine was of 85 horse power. She was so light that she could be pushed along the ground when the tail plane was lifted and so sensitive that a little bump was felt during hot weather when she flew from one surface to another, as for example over a ploughed field, across a river or road. Both cockpits were open. In one way, the machines of flight were very simple in those days. In the cockpit, a switch turned on the engine but as there was no self-starter the propeller had to be swung by hand to bring the engine to life. Then the throttle, a small handle on the left, was pushed forward to rev up, chocks were wedged against the wheels to prevent movement. To prepare for take-off these were taken away and with the help of the rudder worked by the feet and the stick, the plane was taxied into the wind. Another handle low on the left was used to raise the tail and facilitate take-off. This was popularly called the 'cheese cutter' - correct name, tail trimming apparatus.

In the cockpit, a switch turned on the engine but as there was no self-starter the propeller had to be swung by hand to bring the engine to life. Then the throttle, a small handle on the left, was pushed forward to rev up, chocks were wedged against the wheels to prevent movement

So, to take-off, the throttle was opened, stick pushed forward, tail lifted and then when sufficient speed had been gained a gentle easing back of the stick lifted her. There were certain speeds for climbing, cruising and landing and the air speed indicator on the dashboard and another between the wings gave the required information. Apart from the height indicator and fuel gauge, spirit level, rev counter and compass (which beginners did not use anyway), there was no other source of information available, no contact with the ground, no voice from the aerodrome guiding, warning and so on. Once up and at the height desired, one learned first how to fly straight and level. Communication with the instructor in the front cockpit was by a speaking tube plugged into one's earphones. Because of the dual control, every movement of his stick and rudder were felt by the pupil on his or hers and so the feeling for flight was developed.

The instructions given at the start were really very simple. The first was: "Keep your nose on the horizon." This meant of course the nose of the machine and ensured level flight. One automatically eases it forwards with increased speed and loss of height. The former must have been my fault for Fred Griffith not merely told me over and over again to keep up flying speed but on January 20th, 1935 wrote these words at the back of my log book: "Keep up the flying speed - it isn't the drop that hurts but the sudden stop at the end of it." Loss of speed would result in a stall with the machine out of control and that of course would be the finish, unless one were so high as to have the opportunity of regaining speed as the plane fell. At another time, the voice over the headphones would warn: "Hold her, hold her! Don't let her go!" when one's descent was too rapid and so my friend Denise wrote in the front of my log book: "Take fast hold of instruction, let her not go, keep her for she is thy life." (Proverbs 4.13.)

Fred W. Griffith, chief pilot with Everson Flying Services. Weston photo

Another homely piece of advice was: "Rudder and stick together," in order to secure a proper banking turn. As might be expected, landing was the most difficult operation. One had to learn how to judge just when the engine should be cut off and the plane allowed to glide earthwards, circling and banking and possibly slide-slipping when one was more proficient, until it was the right moment to approach the field some feet to spare above the hedge and land within the area available and this not a large one either. Two mistakes could be made here, either of which would result in a crash: to undershoot, meaning the touchdown would come before the field was reached and to overshoot, when it would come beyond the boundary hedge. Once the trouble was spotted, the remedy was simple: open the throttle and do another circuit making a fresh approach. The ideal landing was of course a three-point one, where wheels and tailskid touched down together. While under instruction pupils made circuits of the airfield as much as possible for the more take-offs and landings one got in, the better. The usual time for a lesson was 15 minutes duration but sometimes a keen instructor, if he were also generous, would throw in an extra few minutes at no additional cost. Every morning first thing, all machines were given test flights and an early arrival might be taken up as a passenger, free of charge of course as there was a risk involved. The pilot would put the aircraft though her paces, "throwing her about a bit" was the phrase used and so one might be lucky enough to experience looping, spinning, slow rolling or flip rolling and another stunt called 'falling leaf', all very breath-taking.

Another sport was 'shooting up' which meant flying very low over the house of some friend or relation. This was even more dangerous, owing to the risk of crashing on a roof and killing someone. One such disaster happened in 1934 when a man named Arthur Russell flew very low over his own home, 'Clarendon', 46 Terenure Road East, succeeded in hitting a tree, crashed and was killed

Occasionally, someone going for a flight over the city or cross country might welcome a passenger, especially an envious teenager whose purse was smaller than her desires. In those days, the general regulation was that flight above a city should be at such a height as to enable the pilot in case of engine failure to glide to an open field and make a forced landing. For Dublin at that time, the height was 500 feet. Despite this regulation, there were some dare-devils who delighted in a forbidden sport called 'hedge-hopping' which was just as the name implies. To hedge hop, one power dived at a hedge or tree and then, at the last minute, hopefully, as the undercarriage was almost brushing the foliage, a quick movement of the stick lifted the plane up and over, to continue skimming the surface of the next field, about six feet off the ground to the next hedge and then up over that one and so on.

Another sport was 'shooting up', which meant flying very low over the house of some friend or relation. This was even more dangerous, owing to the risk of crashing on a roof and killing someone. One such disaster happened in 1934 when a man named Arthur Russell flew very low over his own home, 'Clarendon', 46 Terenure Road East, succeeded in hitting a tree, crashed and was killed. His passenger, Sgt. Canavan, had to remain some time in hospital due to injuries received. There is a reference to this in a magazine called Aviation (Vol. 1, No. 1, January 1935) edited by Col. Charles Russell, brother to the unlucky Arthur. The same magazine has an interesting reference to the chief instructor of Everson Flying Services. It reads (under the heading 'A Good Flight'): "Aeroplanes enjoyed a field day following the British Royal Wedding (Princess Marina and the Duke of Kent). Newspapers and film companies chartered them on all sides for the speedy transport of photographs and news films. Perhaps the finest achievement was that of Everson Flying Services, Kildonan, for the story of which we are indebted to the Irish Times whose pictures he was carrying. Leaving Heston for Dublin in a Fox Moth, at about 1.30 he landed safely in difficult conditions at Speke Aerodrome, Liverpool, after more than one and a half hours of virtually 'blind flying'. He took off again shortly, realising that the approach of night would render his landing at Dublin even more difficult, but he brought the machine down safely at his destination Kildonan, at 4.40 pm."

This was not the first occasion that newspapers used Kildonan. In 1933, Captain Armstrong had crashed landed in a fog there on returning from Aintree with pictures of the Grand National - the first to be published in an Irish newspaper on the morning after the race. (The Iona Story', Flarepath, May-June 1964) In February 1935, there was reorganisation at Kildonan, the company being taken over by Lady Mary Heath and her husband, Mr. G. A. R. Williams, who became directors. They renamed it Dublin Air Ferries. An article entitled 'Ireland Finds her Wings in a Decade of Aviation History' by Michael Haslam which appeared during 1980 in the Irish Independent, giving a good potted biography of Lady Heath:

"Sophie Mary Pierce was born in Newcastle West, Co. Limerick, in 1897 and was the first woman to hold the British Ministry's 'B' or commercial licence which she got in 1926, the same year she set up a world altitude-record for light aircraft at 17,000 feet. The year 1928 brought her greatest achievements.

First solo is surely the chief event in a pilot's life and at Kildonan this was surrounded by a conspiracy of silence, so far as the victim was concerned. By grapevine word would get round if he/she made a few good landings, he/she would be allowed to go up alone

Happily all goes well and -AK glides smoothly towards the earth while you make a few banking turns right and left to lose height. Then the ground comes close to you, closer and closer and at last you ease the stick back and, wonder of wonders, the wheels and tail skid touch down together and you have made a three-point landing.

She made the first solo and light aeroplane flight from Capetown to Cairo and set up a further world altitude record for light planes at 23,000 feet. She had acted as second pilot to the young Dutch airline KLM in Amsterdam and flew on all of their rapidly expanding European routes. In 1929, while on a lecture tour in the United States, she decided to enter for the National Air Race at Cleveland, Ohio, but while competing she crashed through a factory roof at more than 100 mph and received extensive injuries."

By the time she took over Kildonan, she was in pretty bad shape, partly due to the result of this accident which left her with steel plates in her skull. Many and varied were the stories with which she regaled us, beginning with her romances and in this area she was an expert having been married three times. Her first husband was a Captain Elliott Lynn; her second Sir James Heath, who she told us, financed her flights; and her third was Jack Williams. He was not only a skilled pilot but also a keen horse rider and apparently once when jumping in a competition his horse was startled by movements from a lady in a bright red dress. He lost and furiously made his way towards this lady who had spoilt his chances and thus encountered Mary Heath. I do not know if this story is true or false, all I say is that I heard it. While at Kildonan she founded the Junior Aviation Club to encourage the interest of teenagers in flying and give them some of the basic principles of flight. During the summer months on Friday evenings there were practical demonstrations and quizzes.

For those really keen on aviation the crowded clubhouse held little attraction. Better by far to be out in the hangar with the engineers Bell, Ghosh (from India) or Mick Brady, who was to die at a young age. Here, clad in gloriously dirty dungarees, it was possible to be given an unskilled job to do, such as putting dope on the fabric of the wings. The hangar was dark and draughty but it was full of fascinating smells - oil, petrol, paint, glue and, of course, the dope itself. First solo is surely the chief event in a pilot's life and at Kildonan this was surrounded by a conspiracy of silence, so far as the victim was concerned. By grapevine word would get round if he/she made a few good landings, he/she would be allowed go up alone. Suppose for a moment you were that victim, this is what you would have experienced.

At a word from Mr. Williams you would pick up your helmet and goggles and with no one (apparently) paying attention, you would make for -AK. (From autumn 1935, EI-ABE was substituted for this machine.) Once aboard there was the usual routine and then when the engine was ticking over you would taxi into the wind and wait for the voice from the front cockpit to tell you to take off. Up and round and down you went, perhaps three times and then as you waited again for take-off the voice said: "Wait a moment, I've dropped my glove" and the figure in the front bent down as if retrieving something that had fallen. In reality, he was removing the stick from his cockpit and before you were aware of what was happening, he was standing on the grass beside you waving you off... and off you went, very wobbly indeed as the weight now missing from the machine made it difficult to control as she gathered speed. The far hedge drew nearer and nearer but thankfully you cleared it easily and climbed steadily almost forgetting there was no instructor to correct your mistakes until you looked down and saw him far below. You saw too, from the hangar and clubhouse, everyone else emerge to watch you - they had known all the time! The circuit complete you checked your height and the landmark above. You would throttle back the engine and prepare to descend, saying a prayer if you were wise for at this juncture almost anything could happen. Perhaps Fred Griffith's words would cause a moment's unease: "It isn't the drop that hurts but the sudden stop at the end of it."

Happily all goes well and -AK glides smoothly towards the earth while you make a few banking turns right and left to lose height. Then the ground comes close to you, closer and closer and at last you ease the stick back and, wonder of wonders, the wheels and tail skid touch down together and you have made a three-point landing. Congratulations and drinking of health are the order of the day and also some phone calls to family and friends announcing the glad tidings: "I've gone solo !" For me that day was April 14th, 1935.

A cutting taken from the magazine Aviation for May 1935, kindly sent to me by Mr. Pearse Cahill, has some interesting items of information about Kildonan under the title:, 'Dublin Air Ferries Ltd.'

I quote: "During the month March 19th to April 19th, 1935, the company has had 63 hours, 20 minutes' flying. There would have been eight more hours in the air had one machine not been undergoing a top overhaul. The unpleasant weather also had an effect on the flying. During the month, seven first soloists were sent off into the air and all did extremely well. The first record time was put up by Mr. Culleton of Galway, who went off alone after 7 hours 45 minutes, but a few days later this was beaten by Miss Beattie, who went solo after 7 hours 20 minutes. This record was again beaten by another soloist, Mr. Mick Brady, assistant ground engineer at the aerodrome. He took six and a half hours for his solo." Other names are given in the following order: myself, Mr. B. Little, Mr. L. U. Smith and Mr. E. J. Gleeson, a new member who was joined by other newcomers, Mr. B. Regan, Misses Kathleen and Nora Wilson and their brother Claude.

"A deaf and dumb pupil, Mr. Peacock, who is learning to fly, is showing great aptitude and is nearly ready for his first solo. He has to be trained entirely by signs, as he knows no deaf and dumb hand language."

For the 'A' licence - on the practical side - one had to climb to a certain height, glide down and land on a 'spot', a barograph in the cockpit recording the steadiness of the climb and descent. The only clue regarding possible altitude is an entry in my logbook - dated May 11th, 1935 - which records a height of 7,000 ft (the only time a specific altitude is mentioned) but this was done in a machine with an engine of 105 horsepower, a Gypsy II, so I feel that this would be a far greater height than the less powerful Gypsy I could attain. Figure-of-eight turns had to be practiced. Two places were selected, say a church and a clump of trees and at a certain height a number of turns had to be made around these, the barograph registering whether the required height was maintained or not. All this preparation for the test was done in EI-ABE. After three hours solo application could be made for the licence and then followed a medical examination. All was in order, so on 14th January, 1936, Mr. Williams and I flew to Baldonnel for the great occasion. Finbarr O'Cathain is the only one of the examiners whose name I recall, but Mr. Myles Carr adds those of P. Hassett, B. Keane, T. Hanly and W. Delamere. Fortunately, they asked me very simple questions or maybe they just helped me through knowing that in my future career I'd not be a menace to myself or anybody else. The licence reached me on January 16th.

Marjory Bayley Butler RSC (Sr. Katherine) with her friend, Denise Beattie, at Kildonan. Denise is standing in the cockpit of EI-AAK

In the clubhouse at Kildonan (from right): Kevin Sheridan, George Morris, Fred Griffith, Mick Brady, Harry Graham

The clubhouse at Kildonan 1/5/38. (from left): Harry Graham, Bill Nolan and John Duggan

Outside the clubhouse at Kildonan - standing (from left):George Kennedy, Miss Wilson, Bill Lonergan. Seated (from right): Mick Brady, Oonagh Scannell, Fred Griffith, Ivan Hammond and Kevin Sheridan - George Weston photo

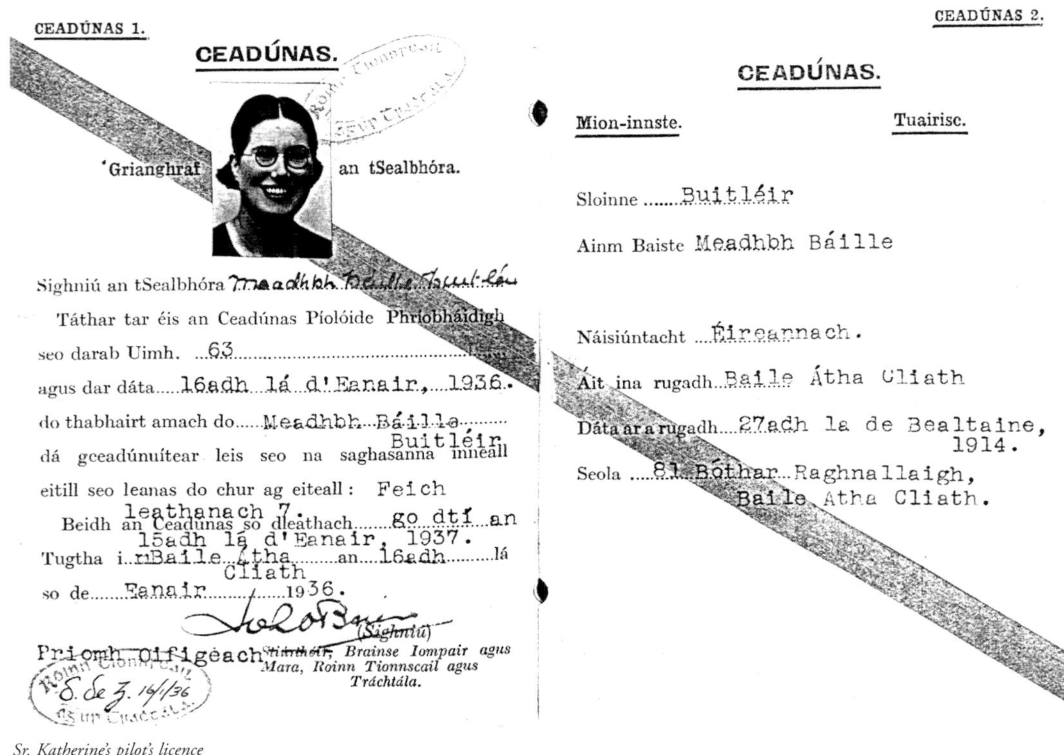

CEADÚNAS 1.

CEADÚNAS.

Grianghraf an tSealbhóra.

Sighniú an tSealbhóra Meadhbh Báille Buitléir

Táthar tar éis an Ceadúnas Píolóide Phríobháidigh seo darab Uimh. 63 agus dar dáta 16adh lá d'Eanair, 1936. do thabhairt amach do Meadhbh Báille Buitléir dá gceadúnuítear leis seo na saghasanna inneall eitill seo leanas do chur ag eiteall: Feich leathanach 7.

Beidh an Ceadúnas so dleathach go dtí an 15adh lá d'Eanair, 1937.

Tugtha i mBaile Átha Cliath an 16adh lá so de Eanair 1936.

(Sighniú)

Príomh Oifigeach, Brainse Iompair agus Mara, Roinn Tionnscail agus Tráchtála.

CEADÚNAS 2.

CEADÚNAS.

Mion-innste. Tuairisc.

Sloinne Buitléir

Ainm Baiste Meadhbh Báille

Náisiúntacht Éireannach.

Áit ina rugadh Baile Átha Cliath

Dáta ar a rugadh 27adh la de Bealtaine, 1914.

Seola 81 Bóthar Raghnallaigh, Baile Átha Cliath.

Sr. Katherine's pilot's licence

My flight of terror

It was a beautiful crisp sunny day in mid-January 1936, Thursday 16th, to be exact. Beneath a cloudless sky, the early morning frost had vanished leaving the grass of the airfield a brilliant green. Just the day for flying I thought, putting on my leather coat and taking my helmet and goggles from the shelf in the clubhouse cloakroom.

Among the staff at Kildonan were three engineers: George Bell from Lancashire; Mick Brady; Dublin and Prativa Ghosh from India. Bell was also an instructor and Mick a student pilot. There were many club members, one of them being Denise Beattie, my special friend who joined the same day as I did, and Oonagh Scannell, engaged to Ivan Hammond, then working for his 'B' and later to be chief pilot with Aer Lingus. One unusual member was Father Furlong, a local priest, who always brought his red setter, Bruno, with him when he flew.

Now, to return to January 16th, my precious license reached me two days previously and so wings could be spread and they were going to be. Even though knowledge of the compass was not required for one's first test it would be possible to fly quite a distance beyond the city, or indeed any direction, provided that with head over the edge of the cockpit, I could find my way by sight.

The two engineers, Mick Brady and Prativa Ghosh, had the aircraft, EI-ABE, out on the grass runway, a little red and silver coloured bird, ready, waiting, her engine sweetly ticking over. Ghosh was also a special friend of mine and as we walked over to the plane, he asked: "Where do you want to go?" "Over Howth," I replied. "Don't do that," he said quietly, "keep to the other side." A small argument ensued as we moved nearer to -BE. (We always called the machines by their two final registration letters.) Ghosh was gentle, ever so gentle, but very firm and would give me no reason, which really annoyed me. I never could stand men bossing me,

EI-ABE D.H.60G Moth, Reg'd. 1/3/35, Lady Heath, c/no. 1048, ex G-AASY, 20/2/37, Dublin Air Ferries
Delivered to Ireland as G-AASY on 21/12/34. Cancelled on 7/2/38 upon re-sale as G-AASY. Impressed for the RAF as AW128 and later to an instructional airframe as 4490M.
F. two-tone, upper half emerald green, lower, light green, fin and rudder, same colours. Wings and tail-plane, silver-doped. M. same colours as F., but in reverse order to background colour. i.e., half and half.

but I had to give way or not fly at all. Accepting my half-promise to keep to the south, he let me go. It was too nice a day for bad humour, so in the cockpit as I adjusted the safety harness he wished me "Happy Landings!", then with a smile and a wave I was ready for my adventure. First came my careful take-off, doing all I had been taught by my instructor, heels on the floor, feet poised lightly above the rudder bar, right hand on the stick between my knees. To the left were two handles, the lower worked the 'cheese-cutter' or 'tailtrimming' apparatus, which helped raise the plane. Above this was the throttle which when opened (moved forward), caused -BE to taxi, even faster across the grass. Then a gentle easing back of the stick and we were airborne, climbing steadily. The cheese-cutter moved back and a little pressure on the left rudder and a movement of the stick to the left and we did a nice turn over the airfield, seeing Ghosh below, some more climbing then, up to about 500 feet and we were really off. In the cockpit, a dial showed our height, another our airspeed, one wing having a second airspeed indicator and finally a spirit bubble helped in keeping the plane even, neither wingtip dropping. To maintain level flight at the desired height the rule was: "Keep her nose on the horizon," which of course I would endeavour to do.

Within minutes, the city lay below and then came Ballsbridge, Merrion, Blackrock and finally Dun Laoghaire. Revelling in this first flight, my very first one away from Kildonan all on my own, I rejoiced in the freedom of it all. Across the sea stretched the peninsula of Howth from Sutton to the Baily Lighthouse, gleaming white, beckoning, inviting. But, no, I couldn't go there oh, no, definitely not, yet it looked so delightful. I dallied with temptation and succumbed - who'd know, anyway? Over the bay I soared. So far, so good, but drawing close to the land I noticed a small strip of mist, so thin as to be almost see-through. To fly beneath it might bring me down too low, and height like flying speed, must be kept up. To fly above

ERSON FLYING SERVICES.
MEMBERSHIP CARD.
68
ber's Sig. H. Bayley Butler

Membership card

Anyway, very shakily I flew alongside the fog, seeing the city ahead, past the Pillar, then Glasnevin Cemetery, the green fields of Finglas, (in the country at that time), Cappagh Hospital on my left, and, to the right our tiny airfield, with Kildonan in large letters on the hangar roof and the little windsock, our only landing guide, fluttering in the breeze. Still shocked, I was shaking uncontrollably and to make matters worse a few members were standing outside the clubhouse watching for me, so long overdue

it seemed unnecessary as it was so sparse. Of course I could have gone alongside it, but no, nothing would do me but to go through it, thinking it would only be a second or two until I'd safely emerge. How wrong I was! Now came my first experience of blind flying and I mean really blind - no instruments to guide me, no voice on the radar directing me, nothing! I was totally and literally blind. The thick grey wall of fog was impenetrable. Turning left, right, flying higher, lower, all was to no avail and after a time panic set in. Screaming and screaming, my voice rose above the sound of the engine as I shouted to God to help me - there was no one else and I was never so dreadfully alone. Years before a line out of 'Peter Pan' by J.M. Barrie struck me and remained in my memory: "To die will be an awfully big adventure," well, here I was in the middle of a "big adventure" and not a bit impressed!

After what seemed like ages, suddenly, there was land below me, The fog had cleared, so I thought and I found myself on my side only about 50 feet off the ground zooming over Barren Hill. Terror had made me forget to keep a check on the height and to fly "straight and level" as all beginners are taught. Thankfully I began to climb, only to get back into the fog again. Several more minutes elapsed, seeming like hours and then I found myself out over the sea, in the clear air, sky so blue and the water sparkling in the sunshine and not a trace of land. Cautiously turning round I saw the Baily Lighthouse behind me - I had been going in the direction of Holyhead! What puzzles me still is how Ghosh knew to warn me - weather reports were not as common then as now and even today while "fog patches" might be mentioned, there would hardly be the detail "over Howth!" Possibly some sort of sixth sense. I don't know. Anyway, very shakily I flew alongside the fog, seeing the city ahead, past the Pillar, then Glasnevin Cemetery, the green fields of Finglas, in the country at that time, Cappagh Hospital on my left, and, to the right, our tiny airfield with Kildonan in large letters on the hangar roof and the little windsock, our only landing guide, fluttering in the breeze. Still shocked, I was shaking uncontrollably, and, to make matters worse, a few members were standing outside the clubhouse watching for me, so long overdue.

They certainly got their money's worth for my landing was atrocious. To begin with, I came in too high over the boundary fence and what I should have done was to open the throttle, climb up a bit and make a fresh approach. What I actually did was to let the aircraft drop on the ground, making a pancake landing and of course it bounced up into the air and continued bouncing until it came to a stop. Nearly shaken to bits I just sat back in the cockpit unable to move. Ghosh, full of concern came running over the grass. When he reached me and saw I was uninjured he just said softly: "So you went to Howth after all?" I nodded dumbly.

De Havilland Moth: The De Havilland Moth biplane was the world's first really practicable light aeroplane. It was cheap (originally only £885), reliable, light (only 775lb empty), easy to fly and could be operated from small airfields. First flown by Captain Geoffrey De Havilland in February 1925, it was widely adopted by clubs and private owners. Despite its low power and frail construction, a number of notable long-distance flights were achieved. The most famous Moth was Amy Johnson's Jason, which flew her in 1930 from England to Australia in 19 and a half days. In 1931 Francis Chichester flew in his Gypsy Moth from England to Japan.

These words taken from the magazine, Aviation, make a fitting conclusion to this section:

"Unto the stars and the Milky Way;

The sky above and the earth below;

Seeking the light of another day

And the dawn of a future new."

(P.A.S.)

Four days later, it was all over, for on Monday January 20th, my "future new" dawned, as a very different way of life opened out before me. Kildonan and the many happy landings there became and still are just a very precious memory.

On Monday January 20th, Katherine Butler entered the Order of the Religious Sisters of Charity.

EI-AAC, D.H.60 Moth, Reg'd. 11.4.29, O.G. Esmonde

c/no. 1000. New aircraft, 26/2/37, Dublin Air Ferries. Cancelled from the register on 5/4/37. Stored until ferried to England, 1/9/38, later registered as G-AFKA. Impressed for the RAF as DG582 and became an instructional airframe as 2592M. Struck off RAF charge on 16/11/45.

Original colour scheme: Fuselage (F.), light blue & silver, flying-surfaces (F/S.), silver-doped. From 1937 onwards, F. dark blue, N.B. This A/c. was always a 60G. Moth and was fully operational throughout 1937 and 1938 - up to September.

Sr. Katherine relaxes on the wing of D.H. Moth EI-AAC at Kildonan

My flight of a lifetime

The story of my first flight had a happy ending. -BE was only slightly damaged and I recovered after a short time. Nothing more was said about Howth and no questions were asked in the clubhouse. Lunch over, I was sent up again to prove my nerve was not lost. Friday, Saturday and Sunday there were various flights, including one to the Curragh which I co-piloted. Late Sunday afternoon there were goodbyes all round and I left the hangar for the last time, setting off for home, knowing that never again would I see Kildonan or have a flight in a Gypsy Moth.

Late Sunday afternoon there were goodbyes all round and I left the hangar for the last time, setting off for home, knowing that never again would I see Kildonan or have a flight in a Gypsy Moth

The following evening, Monday January 20th, 1936, I took off on a new 'flight' when my family brought me to the convent at Milltown which I was entering. Thinking back over it now, I can see some interesting similarities, as well as some contrasts, between becoming an air pilot and a sky pilot. (This term is normally used for priests but it suits our purpose here.) To begin with, in both there was a definite 'call' which just had to be answered and for which there seemed to be no reasonable explanation. People just got smitten by the 'flying bug' and flight became their life. A vocation, or call to the convent, is also inexplicable and so strong that nothing else in life can satisfy one but to respond to it and say "Yes" to God.

To go on with, there was a period of several years' duration, a training time, not in the "principles and practice" of flight, but in the religious life. It too was a life lived in close companionship with others, all learners like myself and at varying stages, but there was nothing of the clubhouse atmosphere about it! Definitely not! Yet we were a happy crowd and I can look back over half a century and recall the fun and laughter, as well as the sad and weepy moments, for the wrench of parting from home can be felt for a very long time.

De Havilland Gypsy Moth in flight.

Going solo is an important event in a would-be pilot's life when the instructor deems the pupil fit to take-off, fly (around the aerodrome) and land in safety. At a certain stage in noviceship training, a comparable event takes place when she spends some months in another convent sharing in the apostolate of the sisters there. Her responsibility is limited, she is still only a learner, but as with the solo flier, this period is very important. She gets a taste of what her future life will be like - does she still feel she is called to it and can the community discern in her the makings of a future Sister of Charity?

All going well, the next parallel in the training of our two pilots would be the 'A' licence for one and First Profession for the other. These are very big steps and bring with them increased responsibility as well as a protracted period of further training and study for the 'B' licence for one and for her future apostolate for the other. Social work, child care, health care and education are the four main areas, but each of these has numerous small branches so there is something to suit everyone, some place where God will call her to serve His people in need. Apostolates are as varied as the sisters themselves. Apart from what she may be doing, a sister's course of study may be dictated by where she will be working, for as well as convents here, in England, Scotland and California, we are in Zambia, Nigeria, Venezuela and Ethiopia, so the culture and language of one or another of these countries must be studied.

What happened in those far-off days in preparation for the 'B' licence, I've not got an idea. My entrance put a stop to that. But I do know that the training was very exacting, the course a very wide one, for this licence was a passport to a career in aviation. Final profession could be looked on as the passport to the sister's apostolate, the real take-off for her flight of a lifetime. From all this, it might seem that the reason for becoming a sister is the apostolate that is paramount in her life ! By no means ! What she is doing is of little importance compared with what she is - a person given completely to God. What she does then follows as a natural consequence.

Having said so much about the 'organisational' aspect, let us now come to the 'spiritual' side of both flights - nothing to do with training, examinations, qualifications and so on. First came the calls, mentioned already, the one to fly when I was an early 'teenager', and the one to the convent several years later. In both cases, the first approaches were made secretly for fear of parental displeasure. Flying lessons, with approval, began around the age of 18, but the convent door did not open for me until I was 21. Here, there was a good deal of opposition, but in the end my vocation was accepted with peace, if not with joy, both of which were experienced by me in my response to the two calls.

One early fear was that I'd be unable to cope, that I'd be given an apostolate I'd find difficult which would not appeal personally. (I was! Teaching!) There was always the fear I might not be allowed to continue, deemed unsuitable for some reason and of course there was ever the tremendous challenge of obedience

There is another side to all this, that of challenge, a major part of which would be the overcoming of fear. Flying was a risky business, especially long ago with our very primitive planes. Each time I went up I was scared - feelings were really mixed - for there was always the possibility that I might not walk away afterwards! In religious life too, risks abounded, each with its own fear, each the result of a challenge faced and to be overcome. For instance, one early fear was that I'd be unable to cope, that I'd be given an apostolate I'd find difficult and which would not appeal personally. (I was! Teaching!) There was always the fear I might not be allowed to continue, deemed unsuitable for some reason and of course there was ever the tremendous challenge of obedience.

Obviously, the greatest risk of all was taken the day I went in the door of Mount St Anne's, Milltown, hoping to give myself totally to Christ - fears of the future not with standing. Raw newcomer that I was, I understood enough to realise that His demands could be great, there would be a price to pay for life with Him. Would I be able to pay it? I really needn't have worried for I gradually, oh so very slowly, learnt that with every challenge there comes a grace to help and once I did my poor little bit He would take over the rest. He brought me through 40 years of the classroom and that was quite something. Just as the engine keeps the plane aloft and moving, so prayer could be likened to the engine of the inner life - should it stop, all would be lost. However, the engine needs to be kept in good running order, cared for and even be taken apart from time to time to check its airworthiness, so a flight engineer is an absolutely necessary person and there is no need to say who fulfils this function. So the flight of life goes on, sometimes very pleasantly, blue sky above, green fields below, all bathed in sunshine with happy landings in various places. At other times there is turbulence, strong winds, chill damp air swirling round the open cockpit and quite frequently with visibility reduced to zero, not a glimpse of anything that could offer comfort or consolation, such as beautiful scenery. There is not even the realisation that the Flight Engineer was concerned about me, so sorely tossed about and troubled, as I struggled to keep on course.

So the flight of life goes on, sometimes very pleasantly, blue sky above, green fields below, all bathed in sunshine with happy landings in various places

One of the great trials in religious life, as also in other ways of life, is that of disillusionment. We, each of us, cling to our own ideas, ideals, aspirations, convictions about God - and one by one we find them shattered. It really is painful! But disillusionment is a very essential part of growing up in God, of moving from spiritual infancy into the real world, a world of flesh and blood, of living people with all their human frailty - and each of us is the same!

We began by being full of illusions, false notions and they must go. If we are not disillusioned, we live forever in a dream world. In our 'flight of a lifetime', one of our illusions is that God is not merely the Engineer, but our Co-pilot, ready to take-over when the flight gets too difficult for us. To misquote Robert Browning: "God's in my cockpit, all's well with my flight" - and of course this is just not so. Help and guidance are given me, but I must do the flying. The decisions, good or bad, are mine and my responsibility. How very demeaning it would be were God to act otherwise! Having given me my mental equipment, provided me with adequate training, is it likely He would override my free will, take over my flying lest I make an error or maybe even crash. Unthinkable! So, welcome be the disillusions!

The years pass, so very rapidly and the final approach draws near. Flying speed has been kept up, the Engineer has always seen to that, but the little aircraft herself has become somewhat shabby - paintwork faded, fusilage a bit dented, wings patched. None of this really matters, for she has begun her descent in preparation for the last and happiest of all landings

Most people have heard of the stick which plays an essential part in flight. By means of it the plane climbs, descends and with the rudder turns the machine. But many may not ever have heard that the original word was JOYstick - and this of course would symbolise the delight and happiness of a life given to God, the hundredfold promised to all who follow Christ. So, despite the inevitable suffering, there is a certain peace and contentment.

The years pass, so very rapidly and the final approach draws near. Flying speed has been kept up, the Engineer has always seen to that, but the little aircraft herself has become somewhat shabby - paintwork faded, fuselage a bit dented, wings patched (these were made of fabric stretched tightly over wooden frames). None of this really matters, for she has begun her descent in preparation for the last and happiest of all landings.

In the words of an Irish poet, Patrick Kavanagh.

"Only those who have flown home to God have flown at all."

Katherine Butler RSC

Sr. Katherine at the Bremen commemorative plaque at Baldonnel's Casement Aerodrome together with Brig. Gen. Brian McMahon D.S.M. and Pearse Cahill

Sr. Katherine Bayley Butler

Chapter Sixteen

Chapter

Kildonan - Brief reminiscences by Chris Bruton

Chapter 16

Kildonan - Brief Reminiscences

by Chris Bruton

With fear and trepidation, some school friends and I cycled there and on looking in saw at close quarters real aeroplanes that flew

I cannot say for certain at what stage I first became, for want of a better word, converted to aviation. I was, from an early age, fascinated by things mechanical - trains, cars and boats - but at some time a particular preference for aeronautics began to evidence itself. This developed into Christmas gift subscriptions to 'Flight' or the 'Aeroplane', the latter then edited by a rabidly anti-Irish but efficient authority on aeronautics, C.G. Grey. I am referring to the early 1930s, when a number of significant developments in aviation were happening or about to happen here in Ireland.

The amount of flying in the country in those far off days was practically nil. There were, from time to time, Atlantic flights, our own Fitzmaurice and the Bremen, or the protracted stay of Kingsford Smith and his merry men. Outside the Army Air Corps at Baldonnel, with largely First World War vintage aircraft, there was little to tempt the flying palate of the native would-be aviators. Although change was coming, it was doing so with remarkable reluctance compared with other countries - Imperial Airways was spreading to the far reaches of the British Empire; Air France to the Orient; Lufthansa was building a name for itself in central Europe; while Swiss Air was quietly but most efficiently spreading its wings outside its mountain fastness. But at home, with the exception of a demonstration mail flight from Galway to Berlin, spearheaded by Col. Charles Russell, Irish Army Air Corps (retired), all was quiet.

Then, out of the blue (excuse the pun), there came a Dublin garage proprietor from Cross Guns Bridge who leased some fields about one mile north of the then sleepy village of Finglas and started an air taxi service. His name was Hugh Cahill - the father of Pearse Cahill of Iona - who had a couple of DeSoutter monoplanes. With fear and trepidation, some school friends and I cycled there, and on looking in, saw at close quarters real aeroplanes that flew. Among the handful present was a famous Irish 'aviatrix', as women pilots were then called, Lady Mary Heath. She was most anxious to promote an interest in aviation in Ireland, particularly among the youth, and so formed the Irish Junior Aviation Club, out of which ultimately developed The Model Aeronautics Council of Ireland, the Irish Aviation Council and the Limerick Flying Club.

About this time there appeared one Johnnie Maher. He was genial, enthusiastic and always helpful. He was attached to the Air Corps of Baldonnel. His advice and organising ability was readily available to all, in particular to the Junior Club. He had seen service with the RAF in the latter part of World War 1, had experience on the R33 and R34 Dirigible - the British answer to the Zeppelin. One of these great airships flew the Atlantic in 1919. He formed the first Irish Gliding Club (at Baldonnel), did experimental work on parachutes, joined the Irish Army Air Corps at its inception and later became the first chief engineer of Aer Lingus on its formation in 1936, typically coining the phrase, "they kept all their spares in a biscuit tin".

But back to Kildonan. We teenagers became well known there and helped to move planes about, fuel them with a hand pump and make ourselves generally useful. In that way, we became familiar with many interesting machines of the day. Lady Nelson was a frequent caller in her sturdy, powerful high wing Stinson. A low winged twin of advanced design called a Monospar ran a regular service to Galway. Fr. Furlong had a wire braced Aeronca (nowadays it would be described as an 'ultralight'), and I have seen Lily Dillon fly in from Fermoy in her much travelled Swallow. The instructor and engineer was J.R. Currie, who later enjoyed

The entrance gates to Kildonan are still there and there are roads in the vicinity called after it, but I feel there should be a plaque. When you next pass along the Derry/Ashbourne Road, raise your hat to the pioneers of Kildonan

fame as the designer of the Currie 'Wot'. Ivan Hammond, later a senior Aer Lingus pilot, married Oonagh Scannell who had learned to fly at Kildonan and it should be mentioned that the fair sex were well represented at Kildonan. Another famous person one might meet there was the famous bowler-hatted, pin striped Sir Alan Cobham and his air circuses.

Those were the days! The development of Collinstown - Dublin Airport to you, because of its proximity, eventually closed Kildonan. The entrance gates are still there and there are roads in the vicinity called after it, but I feel there should be a plaque or the like to remind later generations of a private development, the first of its kind in Ireland, that hastened the development of an industry of which we can be proud. When you next pass along the Derry/Ashbourne Road, raise your hat to the pioneers of Kildonan.

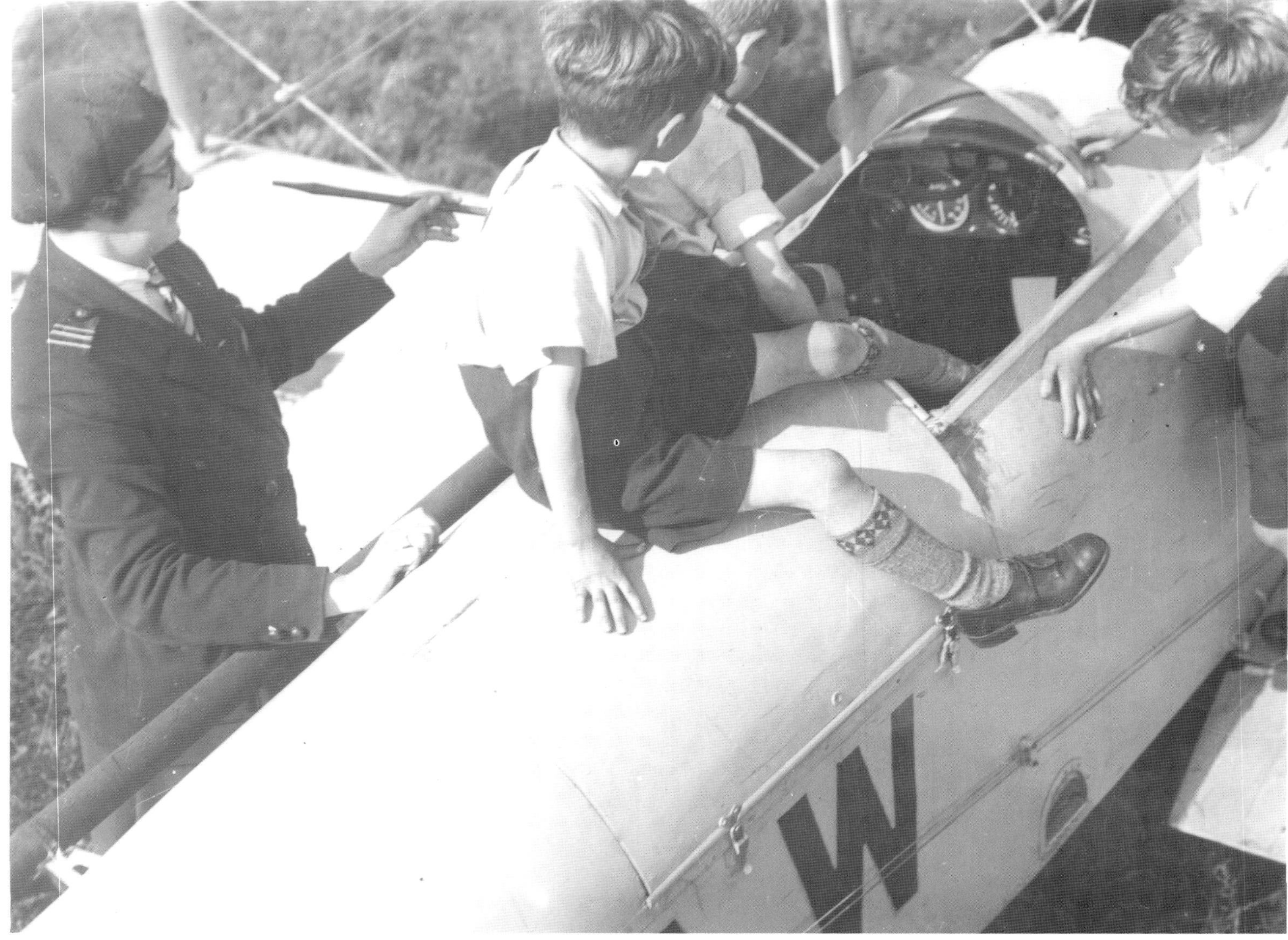

The late Lady Heath giving instructions flying instructions on flying instruments to young pilots of the future of Kildonan Aerodrome

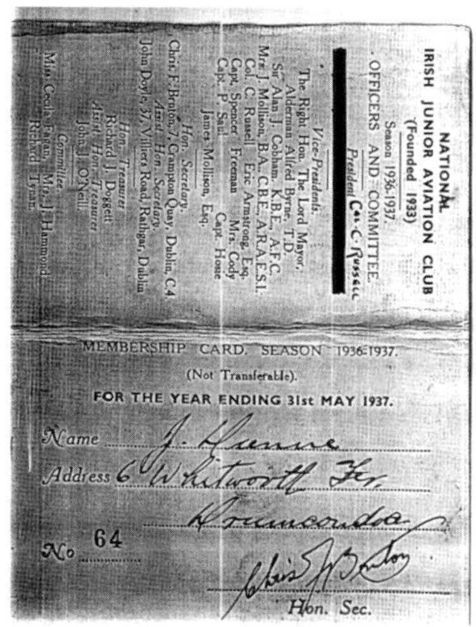

NATIONAL
IRISH JUNIOR AVIATION CLUB
(Founded 1933)
Season 1936-1937.
OFFICERS AND COMMITTEE.
President Col. C. Russell

Vice-Presidents.
The Right Hon. The Lord Mayor,
Alderman Alfred Byrne, T.D.
Sir Alan J. Cobham, K.B.E., A.F.C.
Mrs. J. Mollison, B.A., C.B.E., A.R.Ae.S.I.
Col. C. Russell Eric Armstrong, Esq.
Capt. Spencer Freeman Mrs. Cody
Capt. P. Saul Capt. Hoste
James Mollison, Esq.

Hon. Secretary.
Chris. F. Bruton, 7, Grampton Quay, Dublin, C.4.
Assist. Hon. Secretary.
John Doyle, 37, Villiers Road, Rathgar, Dublin.

Hon. Treasurer.
Richard J. Doggett
Assist. Hon. Treasurer
John J. O'Neill

Committee.
Miss Cecilia Fagan, Mrs. J. Hammond
Richard Tynan

MEMBERSHIP CARD. SEASON 1936-1937.
(Not Transferable).
FOR THE YEAR ENDING 31st MAY 1937.

Name ....
Address ....
No. 64
.... Hon. Sec.

Membership card

Irish Junior Aviation Club at the Theatre Royal, 1939 for the showing of the film 'Tail-Spin', they brought along their models for publicity. At this point it was possible to identify only a small number in the photo. Hopefully the response to this publication will make it possible to do so.
Front row: 1st man on left, R. J. Doggett, 4th left, Des McDonagh, 6th Left, Charlie Horton.
Second Row: Striped cardigan, Margaret O'Connor, Third row: 3rd left Mohan Lokk, 6th from left Maher, very top of photo J. J. O'Neill. Evening Mail

Members of the Irish Junior Aviation Club - Phoenix Park

Chapter Seventeen

Kildonan People

Mr O E Armstrong, chief pilot of Iona National Airways Ltd., Dublin

Mr. O Grattan Esmonde, president of the Irish Aero Club

Chapter 17

Kildonan People

by Captain John Duggan

Captain Oliver Eric (Paddy) Armstrong:

Captain Oliver Eric (Paddy) Armstrong was a major contributor to the development of aviation in Britain and in the Irish Free State. He was also the first Aer Lingus pilot and in 1936 flew the Iolar from Bristol to complete the first Aer Lingus flight. Captain Armstrong was born in Terenure, Dublin on March 19th, 1903 and was educated in the Diocesan Intermediate School, Dublin. He enlisted with the Royal Air Force in 1919 and served in Egypt, Iraq and India.

He became a sergeant pilot in 1927, he obtained a discharge from the RAF in 1931 and joined Iona National Airways Ltd. at Kildonan where he became chief pilot. He planned the pioneering air mail test flight from Galway to Berlin via Baldonnel with Col. Russell and Hugh Cahill in 1932, piloting the first leg (Galway-Dublin). Col . Russell flew the second stage (Baldonnel - Berlin) with Royal Dutch KLM pilot J.B. Scholte and O.E. Armstrong. The plane for this occasion was a triple engined Fokker F12.

O.E. Armstrong also set up a company, Western (Irish) Airlines, which operated regular air mail flights from the west of Ireland to Dublin and organised special flights from Cork to Killarney for American Tourists. In 1933, Armstrong crash landed at Kildonan in fog on his return from Aintree Grand National with pictures for the Irish Independent.

At the time of his death, F. Dempsey, general manager of Aer Lingus, paid this tribute to him: "Those of us who were with Aer Lingus in those early formative years will always remember with gratitude the part that Captain Armstrong played when in fact he was our only pilot until joined by Captain J.B. Hammond"

Armstrong flew the first ever Irish International air service established by Independent Newspapers to fly the Evening Herald from Dublin to Galway. He had an address at No. 55 Brighton Road Rathgar, Dublin. After a period with West Coast Air Services he joined Aer Lingus in 1936 and became chief pilot of the new airline.

When World War Two broke out he tried to enlist again in the RAF but at the age of 42 he was too old. Instead, he joined the Air Transport Auxiliary and was stationed in Belfast ferrying aircraft in all kinds of weather to bases all over Britain, flying during this period about 100 different types of aircraft. After the war he flew for Morton Air Services and Cambrian Airways, and later for Don Everall (Aviation) Ltd, flying charter flights and scheduled services to varied destinations including the Isle of Wight, Jersey Palma, Perpignam. He became commercial manager of Don Everall. O.E. Armstrong died in 1959 in Birmingham at the age of 56 years. At the time of his death, F. Dempsey, general manager of Aer Lingus, paid this tribute to him: "Those of us who were with Aer Lingus in those early formative years will always remember with gratitude the part that Captain Armstrong played when in fact he was our only pilot until joined by Captain J.B. Hammond."

O.E. Armstrong registered a separate company, under the name Aran, a Galway company, to operate air mail flights from Oranmore airfield to Dublin. My photographs of the Monospar are the first of these flights. Only Lady Heath and myself were on the airfield when the Monospar landed after this first flight. Armstrong was operating in an individual capacity as well as being part of the Iona operation, per se. Through Armstrong, Iona became the first operator of air mail services in Ireland, with a service from Galway to Dublin. This differs from earlier attempts, which had been entirely, individual or once off, demonstration-type flights.

James Milo St. John-Kearney

James Milo St. John-Kearney was Born in Dalkey, Co. Dublin on February 17th, 1896. Educated at Blackrock College, Dublin and at the National University Dublin. Served with the Royal Inniskillin Fusiliers, 1914-17. Royal Flying Corps and R.A.F., 1917-19; joined the Irish Aero Club and took the first 'A' licence test held in Ireland. Founder member of the Kuala Lumpur Flying Club, 1930-31. 'B' licence 1932. St. John Kearney, together with Arthur Westcott Pitt and Captain Eric Stewart, formed a company, Irish Air Lines which provided joy-riding flights, air displays and air taxi services. Waterford was the base for this company's operations. After it closed down at the end of the summer 1932, J. M. St. John Kearney joined Iona National Airways Ltd. as a pilot. When Iona National Airways Ltd. ceased flying, Kearney went to Malaya. He later returned to the Irish Aero Club and became the club's chief flying instructor. Clubs: Irish Aero Club, Royal Singapore Flying Club. He had an address in Dublin at 118, Lower Baggot Street.

James Milo St. John Kearney with Lady Glider of Scott's, air display in the Phoenix Park

The Hon. William Francis Forbes - Master of Sempill

Holder of the Air Force Cross, Fellow of the Royal Aeronautical Society, was deputy chairman of the Council of London Chamber of Commerce. Member of standing committee of Civil Aviation Section of the London Chamber of Commerce, director of National Flying Services; vice-president International Commission for the study of Motorless Flight; member of the Advisory Committee of the Science Museum. Member of the Advisory Committee for Aeronautics, Hull University. Born Devonport, 1893. Took an active interest in aeronautics since 1912. He served in the Royal Naval Air Service, the Royal Flying Corps and the R.A.F. during the War, retiring at the end of 1919. He held key technical positions in all services and acted as official representative on Advisory Committee for Aeronautics, later Aeronautical Research Committee) and other technical committees. Special mission to the U.S.A. in 1918. In 1921, he headed a mission of 30 to Japan to organise, equip and train the Imperial Japanese Naval Air Service; and in 1926, he visited Greece at the request of the Greek Government to advise on the reorganisation of the Greek Naval Air Service. He concentrated his attention on commercial and sporting development in aviation. He was chairman of the Royal Aeronautical Society, 1926-1928 and president, 1928, 1929 and 1930. He was involved in many aero clubs, including Athenaeum, M.C.C. and Junior United Service.

Sempill had arguably done more for the development of civil aviation than any other person at the time

It was a very big occasion when the Master of Sempill touched down in his Puss Moth at Kildonan Aerodrome in the early afternoon of Thursday January 19th, 1933. He came as the guest of the Institute of the Motor Trade. During his visit, he was made a member of the Irish Aero Club. He thanked Dr. Furlong of the Irish Aero Club for this honour. Sempill had arguably done more for the development of civil aviation than any other person at the time.

A lot of the people at Kildonan were just members and friends while on the flying field. The war scattered us all and in fact we never met again as a group. While most of the people mentioned were associated with Kildonan, other people prominently associated with aviation during the Kildonan years are also mentioned. It is impossible to think of Kildonan in isolation. There was the constant interplay between members of the Irish Aero Club, members at Kildonan and the Irish Army Air Corps. In many instances, there was dual membership of the Irish Aero Club who were flying at Baldonnel and of the Dublin Aero Club, who flew at Kildonan.

Sir Alan John Cobham

Knight Commander of the Order of the British Empire (cr. 1926), Air Force Cross. Aviation consultant; Life director of Alan Cobham Aviation Ltd; Born London on May 6th, 1894. Served in the Royal Flying Corps, 1917-1918. Started civilian flying, 1919, joy riding and commercial aerial photography; joined de Havilland Aircraft Co., 1921; toured Europe, North Africa and Southern Europe in 1922. Awarded Britannia Trophy, 1923 and 1924. Flew from London to Capetown and back in 1925 (not solo). Flew in India. Flew to Australia and back in 1926. Won the King's Cup in 1924. Won International Traffic Competition at Gothenburg, 1923. Started Municipal Aerodrome campaign in 1927. Toured Africa in 'Singapore' flying boat 23,000 miles, 1927-1928. Publications: 'Skyways', 'My Flight to the Cape and Back', 'With Cobham to Australia and Back', 'Twenty Thousand Miles in a Flying Boat'. He also produced travel films 'With Cobham to the Cape and Back' and 'With Cobham Round Africa'. Clubs: R.A.F., R. Aero.

Lieutenant Andrew Cecil Woods

Lieutenant Andy Woods

Andy Woods was born in Dublin on November 22nd, 1909 and was educated at the Catholic University School, Dublin and lived at 131, Morehampton Road, Donnybrook, Dublin. When he was only 19 years of age, he flew from Baldonnel to Croyden. Andy was a natural pilot. During the Cosgrave regime, Andy tried to join the Army Air Corps and he was turned down twice because his father was deemed to have I.R.A. sympathies. He had fought with De Valera at Boland's Mill. Subsequently, when De Valera came to power, in 1932, Andy, who was then a qualified pilot, got direct entry to Baldonnel in 1933. When Andy came across to Kildonan in his uniform, all present in the clubhouse nearly fell out of their seats. Andy first qualified as a pilot with the Irish Aero Club. Like myself he was one of the earliest members at Kildonan. Andy Woods, Pitt and Miller formed a barnstorming group and operated a lot from Tramore Strand. Andy was flying a Bluebird, when he crashed and was badly injured. As a matter of fact he broke both ankles and was hobbling around Kildonan and the Aero Club for about eight months on crutches and then on sticks. As a result he was out of flying for the best part of a year. Andy Woods was an early member of the Irish Aero Club. He was an outstanding pilot. When Kildonan opened up, like myself, he joined Kildonan as well. He spent 32 years in the Air Corps, up to retirement. He was in the fighter squadron. Some of the other members of the Air Corps differed greatly in background. These men, including Captain Oscar Heron, Sweeney and Mulcahy, were years before Andy Woods. They had served in the R.A.F. before the Irish Army Air Corps had been set up. They had served in the Royal Flying Corps. When these men came back to Ireland, they were qualified pilots with war experience. Fitzmaurice, on the other hand, who gained fame as the navigator on the Bremen flight, did not have this kind of experience. He had been in the trenches, as a sergeant, without flying training during the war years. Fitzmaurice's experience of flying was virtually nil compared with the men just mentioned. He had flown mail planes, a war-time plane, which gave him limited experience. Fitzmaurice was not chosen for the Bremen flight because of his experience. He had the least experience of the senior pilots in the Air Corps at the time of the Bremen flight, the first non-stop crossing of the Atlantic from east to west. Sweeney, Mulcahy, Oscar Heron, Fred Crosley and Col. Russell had all got war-time experience. Fitzmaurice, was able to recommend himself for the Bremen flight, because he was commanding officer of the Air Corps at the time. Fitzmaurice, in my opinion and in the opinion of many others, including Army Air Corps officers, was a glory seeker, with no small opinion of himself. He was in a position at the time to recommend himself for the Bremen flight. The selection was not based on merit, or the experience of prospective candidates. Andy Woods lived at 17 Butterfield Crescent, Rathfarnham, Dublin and at 131 Morehampton Road, Donnybrook Dublin.

Kathleen and Nora Wilson

Kathleen and Nora Wilson

Sisters Kathleen and Nora Wilson were friends of mine. As yet they had not joined any club but it so happened that, they approached me, in that they said that they would like to learn to fly. These two sisters lived in Shankill, Co. Dublin. Coincidentally, Lady Heath approached mother because we were family friends, asking her to ask me if I knew of anyone who should like to fly, as she now had her machine at Baldonnel. Immediately, I thought of the Wilsons and I introduced them. Those two sisters became the first two pupils that Lady Heath had instructed there. They took their first lessons at Baldonnel and had most of their flying training completed before Lady Heath moved over to Kildonan. They did not pursue flying afterwards. Kathleen married and went out to the Far East, probably Singapore. Nora continued her flying at Kildonan, right up to the last days of Dublin Air Ferries Ltd. She finished with flying after that.

Cyril and Dorothy Catchpole

Dorothy Catchpole was involved with her brother Cyril at Kildonan. Cyril was a ground engineer there for a time, then went to England and joined Imperial Airways as a ground engineer. Dorothy was learning to fly, right up to the end of Dublin Air Ferries and was an active member of the Dublin Aero Club. She joined her brother in London. Dorothy did not take out a licence at Kildonan.

Second from left, Bill Nolan

Bill Nolan

Bill Nolan's home was in Dalkey, Co. Dublin. He was a good pilot and flew frequently at Kildonan.

Denise Beattie

Denise Beattie

Denise was a member at Kildonan during the Everson Flying Services days. She was a close friend of Sr. Katherine, whose name was then Marjory Bayley-Butler.

George Morris

George Morris

George Morris was a native of Finglas. He was the steward and cook at Kildonan and lived at the clubhouse. George went on afterwards to become a porter with Aer Lingus.

Hugh Cahill

My earliest recollection of Hugh Cahill dates from the formation of Iona National Airways and my connection with that company as a member of the Dublin Aero Club, which Hugh Cahill started in conjunction with his flying school and special charter operations. Hugh made a number of charter flights deserving special mention. One of these was to Paris, on which the DeSoutter Mark II was used. This was a cabin machine, EI-AAD. Another special charter flight took passengers to Bristol, London, Cardiff, Cork and then back to Kildonan. This was all in the one day. It was quite a notable feat for any aircraft of the day. Another idea which Hugh Cahill had was to connect Dublin with the Atlantic liners which operated from Galway. The idea was to collect the mail from the incoming Atlantic liners, fly them to Dublin from Dublin to London, with either a stop at Bristol or Manchester, and eventually on to Berlin. This would effectively join the continent of Europe with the United States of America, with regard to mail. Hugh Cahill had thought of this very advanced form of mail service, but the Government was not interested and would not back Hugh Cahill. Without Government backing, it fell through. Hugh Cahill founded the Dublin Aero Club, not to be confused with the Irish Aero Club. The latter was based at Baldonnel, the headquarters of the Irish Army Air Corps, later to be named Casement Aerodrome.

Lady Katherine Nelson

Little is known about Lady Nelson, or of her husband Mr. George Everett. But, certainly, she was a competent pilot and business woman. She had some rather large machines not normally flown by women at that time. These aircraft were privately owned. One of these was a Stinson Reliant Junior, a big machine for the day. In 1933, Lady Nelson took over Kildonan Aerodrome. The company which she operated was called Everson Flying Services, Ltd.

Captain Eric Stewart

Captain Eric Stewart was an instructor with Everson Flying Services Ltd. He flew a number of cross-channel charter flights for the company. He was a former sergeant pilot with the Royal Air Force. A very good pilot, he had been on the scene at Kildonan from the days of Iona National Airways Ltd. right up to the days of Dublin Air Ferries. He was a 'Camel Pilot' flying the Sopwith Camel airplanes during the First World War. Captain Eric Stewart was a New Zealander with a fine record of flying on the Basra-Baghdad-Cairo section of the Indian Air Mail route. He had also previously flown with the Royal Air Force and with Imperial Airways. He became chief pilot of the newly formed Irish Aviation Company in 1931 which leased a DeSoutter Mark I registered G-AAPY and obtained permission to use Collinstown Aerodrome where the DeSoutter was based. This company decided to concentrate on the operation of internal air services within Ireland, speeding up the delivery of mail, newspapers and freight. The company had a contract with the Daily Mail, whereby the edition printed in Manchester arrived in Sligo before the Irish papers printed in Dublin arrived there. The first flight bringing this service to Sligo took place on July 10th, 1931. The Irish Aviation Company ceased operations in November 1931 and Captain Eric Stewart, with an address at Drumcondra, took up employment as a pilot with Iona National Airways Ltd. at Kildonan Aerodrome. Captain Stewart spent only a short time with Iona, after which he, together with Arthur Westcott Pitt and J. M. St. John Kearney, formed another company, Irish Air Lines, which provided joy-riding flights, air displays and air taxi services. With a base in Waterford, Irish Air Lines had three aircraft, two Avro 504s - EI-AAM and EI-AAN - and a Blackburn Bluebird EI-AAO.

EI-AAM, Avro 504K, Reg'd. 15/3/32, Irish Air Lines, c/no. - ex H9833, G-AAYH

Bought for pleasure flying operations from Irish Air Lines' base at Waterford. Fate unknown although one of Irish Air Lines' aircraft crashed at Tramore Strand, Waterford, on 19/8/32

EI-AAN, Avro 504K, Reg'd. 23/7/32, Irish Air Lines, c/no. - ex J8371, G-ABAP

Fate unknown, but see EI-AAM, above.

EI-AAO, Blackburn Bluebird IV, Reg'd. 20/5/32, A. W. Pitt, c/no. SB.249, ex G-ABJA

Owned by A. Westcott Pitt, who was managing director of Irish Air Lines. Written-off in crash at Tramore Strand, Waterford, on 31/7/32.

Right through the summer of 1932, 'barnstorming' tours were carried out by Irish Air Lines and during the Eucharistic Congress in June 1932, which was held in the Phoenix Park, Dublin. They conducted sight-seeing tours of Dublin and its environs, using Collinstown as a temporary base, according to some commentators. The Bluebird which crashed at Tramore on July 31st, 1932 and the two Avros were taken out of service at the end of the summer of 1932, following which Irish Air Lines ceased trading.

George Kennedy

George Kennedy

George was a very active member at Kildonan and a good pilot. He went to England at the start of the war and was one of the older and more experienced members at Kildonan. His association with the aerodrome went back to the early days of Iona National Airways Ltd.

Bill Lonergan

Bill Lonergan

During the emergency years, as far as I know, Bill was with Aer Lingus as meteorological officer in the tower, for some considerable time. He was a very good pilot and a very active member at Kildonan, where he had been from the earliest days. He lived at Infirmary Road.

Fr. Furlong was never seen without his red setter dog, Bruno, who accompanied him on all his flights

Father Furlong

Fr. Furlong

Fr. Furlong, a curate in the parish of Finglas, who was part owner of a Japanese Aeronca machine, was extremely interested in flying and travelled extensively throughout the country. Apparently, he had been a chaplain with the R.A.F. in the First World War, where he suffered shellshock. This stayed with him for the rest of his life. He later became parish priest of Glencullen, Co. Kildare. Fr. Furlong was never seen without his red setter dog, Bruno, who accompanied him on all his flights.

Father Furlong demonstrated more than anyone else the fact that Kildonan Aerodrome had the strongest links with Finglas and did not exist in a kind of vacuum. He had served as a chaplain in the R.A.F. before he moved to Finglas and it was there that he developed his interest in flying. Fr. Furlong was part owner of an Aeronca, a Japanese monoplane with enclosed cabin. Lady Heath apparently was also part owner of the Aeronca. When it arrived from Hansworth to Kildonan, it was the first time that one been seen in Ireland. The news of Llewellyn's flight to Capetown in an Aeronca was still in the papers. The Aeronca monoplane was a light craft, with enclosed cabin-cockpit and transparent roof. Its landing speed was lower than the moths. It was good for instruction because of the lower landing speed and also because the seating was side by side, rather than fore-and-aft which meant that the pupil could see as well as hear what the instructor was demonstrating. The Aeronca, however, was a difficult aircraft to handle and there was the danger of stalling in the hands of the less experienced. Fr. Furlong, in his own quiet way, made a significant contribution to the encouragement of civil aviation in the Irish Free State. He was enthusiastic and steadfast providing training and fostering the love of flying. He himself flew the length and breadth of the country.

J. C. Malone

J. C. Malone was a committee member of the Irish Aero Club. He learned to fly with the Irish Aero Club at Baldonnel and he also flew at Kildonan. He built a Pou du Ciel (Flying Flea), a tiny French designed craft invented by M. Henri Mignet. It was found to be inherently dangerous to fly and was accordingly banned.

Oonagh Scannell Hammond

Oonagh Scannell (Hammond) and Ivan Hammond

Oonagh, like her husband Ivan, got their pilot's licence at Kildonan, having trained at that aerodrome. Oonagh was at Kildonan at the same time as her friends, Marjory Bayley-Butler and Denise Beattie. It was her husband, Ivan Hammond, who kept up the flying and by mutual agreement, Oonagh did not pursue her career as a pilot. Ivan eventually became chief pilot of Aer Lingus.

Mick Brady

Michael J. Brady

Michael, or Mick as he was called by his friends, was born on August 8th, 1913. His address was 44 Lower Dodder Road, Rathfarnham, Dublin. He was a ground engineer at Kildonan. Other ground engineers included Mr. O'Riordan and Cyril Catchpole. He became the holder of Irish Free State private pilot's licence No. 50 and a British licence, enabling him to fly all types of light aircraft, privately owned and registered in Great Britain and Northern Ireland. He worked with Iona National Airways Ltd., Everson Flying Services and Dublin Air Ferries, all at Kildonan, and also at Brooklands Civil Aviation School, Sywell and at R.A.F.,

Peterborough. The planes he flew included: D.H.86A, D.H.82, Tiger Moth, Miles Hawk, Hawker Hart, Audax, Fury and Avro Cadet. The period in question was 1931 to 1938, and his main flying was between 1933 and 1938.

First on left, Harry Graham

Harry Graham

Harry was educated at St. Columba's College Dublin. He was elected secretary of the Dublin Aero Club during the Everson Flying Services days. He was a top salesman and ultimately manager of Underwood Elliott and Fisher, a typewriter company, which was located at Clare Street. Just before the war, Harry moved to Glasgow. Tony Millea was then elected secretary of the Dublin Aero Club. Harry's wife also had taken an active part in an assistant secretary capacity, keeping records, though not as a flying member. One of Harry's colleagues was Mr. Kingstown, who was a club member at Kildonan.

Harry was a friend of mine. There was a scheme for people who were already licenced pilots in Britain, whereby if one joined the Civil Air Guard, which flew initially all Tiger Moths, one got all one's flying free, as well as all of one's flying gear. In return one did coastal patrol. This was before the war. People who joined the scheme flew at weekends. It was only a matter of months before the war would break out and everyone knew that it was inevitable. Everything was on a war footing.

On the outbreak of war, Harry joined the fleet air corps, because members of the Civil Air Guard, on joining, gave an undertaking that in the event of hostilities they would join some unit of the army. In the fleet air corps, he was an instructor on link trainers. He made some very important additions to the link trainer system. His station was HMS Daedalus, which was located possibly in the Southampton region. Having made the important improvements to the link trainer system, he then went on to heavy bombers. Harry survived the war and received the honours appropriate to his significant accomplishments. Eventually, he went to live with his brother who was a Canon at Abbeytown, Co. Roscommon.

Captain Jack Williams

Captain Jack Williams

Captain Jack Williams was Lady Heath's third husband. It would appear that she met Jack either when she was in the West Indies or in the United States. Jack had served with the United States Air Force and flew with them. It is quite likely they met in 1929, while Lady Heath was on her American lecture tour. His father was Sir Joshua Williams, governor of Antigua in the West Indies. As far as I know Jack returned to the West Indies after Kildonan closed.

Lady Heath

Lady Heath was taking part in the Ohio State Races in 1929. It would appear that her machine, a parasol Lockheed monoplane, was the firm favourite to win. She was still climbing and she had just cleared some buildings when she crashed, sustaining very severe head injuries. Her life was in great danger and she finished up having a silver plate in her skull. There were rumours that her aircraft had been tampered with. It was an attempt, I believe, to hobble her as a winner, to eliminate her as a winner. How long she spent in hospital I cannot say, but she was back in Ireland in 1931. Lady Heath was a charming person, a delightful person and everyone thought very highly of her. She continued to fly afterwards and was a superb pilot.

Lily Dillon

Lily Dillon

Lily Dillon was born in Listowel, Co. Kerry, in the Irish Free State and obtained her Irish 'A' licence in 1934, having learned to fly at Fermoy. Her instructor was E. J. Dease. Lily Dillon flew a whole range of aircraft, including D. H. Moth, Hornet, Aeronca, B.A. Swallow and Percival Vega Gull. She flew not only in the British Isles, but also in various parts of Europe and North Africa.

Lily Dillon had an address at 28 Glenuse Rd., Blackheath, London S.E. 3. Her own aircraft was registered EI-ABD, a B. A. Klemm Swallow, a monoplane with a Pobjoy Cataract 2 engine and a seating capacity for two.

Lily Dillon was a very prominent pilot from 1934 to 1939. She won the Ladies' Cup and a £50 prize in the Oasis Rally in 1937 and took part in the King's Cup in 1937. She was on the British team in 1937 when they won the Prize of the Nations in Paris and also in 1938. She took part in many European rallies, Deauville four times, Budapest, Esch, Luxembourg, Brussells and Dinard. These were in addition to all the more local rallies and displays, including the Phoenix Park, Newtownards, Ulster Rally, Carlisle, York, Eastbourne and Rochester.

When she took part in the prestigious King's Cup in 1937, she was one of two Irish competitors. Her aircraft, on this occasion, was a Percival Vega Gull. The other Irish competitor was also the oldest man in the race, 63 year old Galway man Brigadier-General A.C. Lewin, C.B.C.M.G., piloting a Miles Whitney Straight.

She has also the distinction of having been the first person to land a plane on the Aran Islands in March 1935.

EI-ABD, Klemm L.25C-1A Swallow, Reg'd. 22/3/35, E.J. Dease

c/no. 28, ex G-ACZK, 29/1/36, Miss L. Dillon

On the outbreak of war in 1939 this aircraft was in the U.K. and was later impressed for R.A.F. service, still wearing Irish marks. Cancelled from the Irish register on an unknown date "after warnings to the owner". Last heard of at RAF Henlow in January 1947.

Arthur White

He was, in flying terms, absolutely wild and I have never known any other pilot to get lost so quickly after leaving the aerodrome or so frequently

Arthur White was one of two brothers, the other was Michael. They were of Jewish nationality with a chain of well known Dublin shoe shops, known as the Standard Shoe Company. One of the last of their shops was in South Ann Street, adjoining Grafton Street. Arthur learned to fly with the Irish Aero Club at Baldonnel and then, like several others, he joined Kildonan. He was most active, from the time of Everson Flying Services on. He was, in flying terms, absolutely wild and I have never known any other pilot to get lost so quickly after leaving the aerodrome or so frequently. He would take off and 10 minutes later or less you would get a phone call! Jack Williams would take the call and Arthur would say something like: "I am down somewhere, in a farmer's field and I think it is somewhere on the left hand side of the road near Ashbourne." That was all the information that Arthur could give as he would have been completely lost. At the early stages, he had not acquired a good sense of direction in the air. This meant that one member and in several cases it fell to me, had to take off and look for Arthur.

In one particular case, he did in fact only get beyond Ashbourne, near Slane. Jack Williams took the message and came out to me and I was sitting outside the clubhouse. He said: "John, that bloody fellow Arthur has got lost, would you mind going out and looking for him." He had only left the aerodrome 15 minutes earlier. Jack was concerned for both pilot and machine and also at the fact that a second person's time was wasted. The extraordinary thing about it was that Arthur was quite good as a pilot, as evidenced by the fact that he carried off all these landings successfully. I cannot recall him damaging a machine. In any case, I went looking for Arthur and located him in a very small field. Sometimes you can get into a field but cannot get out of it, especially if there are high trees or fences around the perimeter, or if there are electrical cables and pylons.

Arthur had this habit of getting lost all over the place, which irritated Jack Williams very much

Arthur had landed in the field successfully and was parked right up against the hedge. I thought that as Arthur had got in, I also could get in. I had the great advantage of having been instructed initially by Captain Fred Crosley who had war-time experience. One thing that all the war pilots knew was how to side slip a manoeuvre where you sliced through the air sideways and at the last minute you straightened out and touched down. By these means you could kill your height without travelling the normal distance. So I threw the machine into a side slip, immediately I crossed the hedge and landed in the field. Then I set about getting Arthur out of the field first. What I did was to get Arthur to rev up the machine while I held it back. This was the only way I could retard the machine as there were no air brakes or wheel brakes. I hung on to the tail while Arthur got up revs and then jumped clear. Arthur got away. I had said to Arthur: " As soon as you take off circle above me, until I get to your level." This would be roughly about 800 feet. Arthur was then to follow me. It was a cloudy afternoon so that even at that height, we were in cloud. We went into some low cloud which we could not avoid and when I came out the other side, there was no sight of him. I had to go into circles around, waiting and waiting, only to find him heading off in some other direction, east towards the sea, instead of south towards Kildonan. I had to chase after Arthur and round him up again. Arthur could not at that time steer a straight course. Arthur had this habit of getting lost all over the place, which irritated Jack Williams very much. It virtually forced a landing in each case. There was always the risk of an accident to the aircraft. However, in spite of all this, he never had an accident.

One other day, I was outside the aerodrome talking to Jack Williams. Arthur had taken off some time beforehand and when he arrived over the hangar, he attempted a loop which apparently he had not been taught to the extent of being able to attempt it on his own. He did not gain enough speed in his dive before pulling up to go over the top. The result was that he stalled upside down, although for a very short time, sufficient for the machine to hang there. Petrol poured out of the centre section tank through the overflow, with the result that it fell onto the hot exhaust pipe.

He did not gain enough speed in his dive before pulling up to go over the top. The result was that he stalled upside down, although for a very short time, sufficient for the machine to hang there. Petrol poured out of the centre section tank through the overflow, with the result that it fell onto the hot exhaust pipe. We could see the vapour momentarily, white in appearance. We all thought that it would explode and that would be the end of Arthur and the machine

We could see the vapour momentarily, white in appearance. We all thought that it would explode and that would be the end of Arthur and the machine. It was the mercy of God that it did not go up. Arthur just flopped out of the loop, almost upside down. Jack was furious and when Arthur landed, although he had got a very bad fright himself. He gave him a hell of a telling off there and then. He was so mad that Arthur was banned for six months and literally ordered him off the aerodrome. Arthur, who was quite an independent person, took himself off and bought his own machine, EI-AAU, a Gypsy and a very fine one. It had the inverted Gypsy engine III, Gypsy Major. He bought it from the Irish Aero Club. Then about three or four weeks later, on a summer's evening, we heard a machine coming very fast from the direction of Baldonnel and also very low.

Then right over the trees came Arthur, who pulled way up into a rocket loop, right over the aerodrome to show us that he could do it. He demonstrated a perfect loop and then blew off, having shot up the place as it were. He did not fly at Kildonan after that. When it came to the war, Arthur joined the Royal Air Force and he survived. He had developed into a good pilot in spite of his lack of a good sense of direction in the early days. After the war, he settled down to live in London.

Ex-RAF Sergeant Pilot Toy

He was an English man who was taken on as an instructor by Dublin Air Ferries Ltd. He did not stay long at Kildonan. He crashed the Fox Moth in Galway, making "a good job of it" and it had to be brought back by train. This took the Fox Moth out of commission for some months. The accident occurred during a landing on a charter flight.

Jackie Smalldridge

Jackie was an old friend and his family were friends of ours. I knew Jackie Smalldridge all of his life. He was of a well to do family. He did not have any flying experience but was drawn to Kildonan by virtue of our acquaintance. He had the idea of making a film. Jackie was a very good cine camera-man and had been to the United States, bringing back just about the finest cine equipment that you could get. The brand name was Bausch and Lomb, I recall. He brought back the whole lot - camera, developing equipment and a projector. We decided that we would make a film but we would do it surreptitiously. Even though I knew Lady Heath, or Sophie as we called her, might not object, her husband Jack Williams surely would. He would be concerned for a number of reasons and it involved a certain degree of danger for Jackie who would occupy the front cockpit of the machine. In order to take cine film, you would have let down the flap of the cockpit and lean out or as I suggested and with suitable adjustments to the harness, to put one foot out on the wing root and the other in the cockpit on the seat. This would mean that he would have to wear a safety belt. I devised an extension to the normal safety harness which I made out of a horse's body belt. This was fixed around Jackie's waist, with a ring which attached individually by a single webbed strap to the normal harness anchor point in the cockpit. This allowed Jackie to stand up in the cockpit, put one arm around the inter-plane struts and grip his camera again with both hands, with his right foot firmly planted on the wing roof. In this way he could photograph between the flying and the landing wires, the inter-plane wires. Thus we set off with no particular programme.

Initially, we went up the coast to just beyond Drogheda, Dundalk and almost to the border in fact. We photographed Newgrange, the Naul, all the towns and coastal areas on the way up, then turning inland.

We photographed Tara, Clongowes College, Slane, the Bog of Allen, Carlow-Kilkenny, Kildare Newbridge, after which we came back to the Dublin area. We covered Dublin quite extensively. On one evening, and a lovely evening it was too, we went out to meet the mail boat and photographed that. Then we flew down to the Sloblands in Wexford, where we dropped to almost tree-top height, to take the birds and the Sloblands. The geese immediately took off and this made quite a magnificent shot. Jackie's elder brother, Sammy, was commodore of one of the Dun Laoghaire yacht clubs and he asked Jackie if we would take him on film meeting his squadron somewhere off Howth on the following Sunday. He gave us a time of three o'clock for the rendezvous. This was agreed. In the heel of the hunt, either they started off earlier or had more favourable wind so that they appeared to be nearly half way to the Isle of Man when we caught up on them. The result was that we were going six miles out over sea in a land plane which would not float for more than five minutes if you had to come down.

We had rehearsed getting out of the wing before our film making by going across to the Bull Island and landing there. Consequently, neither Lady Heath nor Jack Williams knew what was going on. When we landed at Dollymount, Jackie would practice getting in and out of the cockpit, in order to perfect the technique.

I was forced to go down in a glide over the sea, which definitely spelled the end of the pair of us. The only chance would be that one of the yachts might have reached us before the plane would sink

I had worked it out with Jackie beforehand that once we sighted the squadron, I would go down in a gliding turn, to either right or left, according to what the conditions were and that he would get out. Usually it would be to the right. Although it was a risky business and Jackie was in the full blast of about 150 m.p.h., he was at this stage quite proficient at it. In a dive the speed would be appreciably higher. This is why I felt that the taking of the film would not have been approved by Jack Williams. He would have seen immediately what the dangers were and he was very cautious with regard to the aircraft. He would see potentially something going wrong, like Jackie falling out of the machine altogether. Here was the squadron, far out to the sea, and I did not like it because I couldn't swim. Anyhow, they were nicely grouped together at the time and I went down into a dive. We went over at 6,000ft and when I went down in a right hand gliding turn, the engine throttled back. We were just getting them nicely and you can see this on the film when suddenly there was a hell of a kick, like a boot in the backside, and I immediately thought that Jackie had fouled the control with the seat. He was still connected with the speaking tube to me. I picked up the mouthpiece immediately and said: "Jackie, have you maladjusted anything in the cockpit?" We had been subjected to quite a violent bang. Jackie looked over his shoulder.

He looked into the cockpit and replied: "No, everything is as it should be, my foot on the seat, away from the controls." I replied: "Jackie, get back in the cockpit because we are in trouble." Jackie got in and closed up the flap and the revs dropped away altogether. I could not get the engine to run at flying speed at all. I was forced to go down in a glide over the sea, which definitely spelled the end of the pair of us. The only chance would be that one of the yachts might have reached us before the plane would sink. Neither of us had life-belts. We had not thought about it at the time. Suddenly, however, the engine picked up again. I should mention that the film shows first of all the effects of the violent jerk, which throws Jackie's camera off target, and what you see is suddenly sky and then water, sky and water and then blank as though Jackie points the camera up to the wing or something. You can see this in the film, as well as the violent vibration. Anyway, Jackie was now back in the cockpit. I, of course, immediately turned for home. But we went back in trepidation, with alternatively, the engine picking up, followed by a drop in revs, a loss of height and the same repeated all over again. Every time the engine picked up, I went for height so that we gained a few hundred feet, the engine would start playing up again and I would have to go into a glide to maintain flying speed. Then again, luckily, it would pick up. The rev counter was going down to zero and then up to 20,000 revs per minute.

You see me starting off including the entire run, taking off over the clubhouse and around in a circuit and just as I come around over Cappagh Hospital and then over Fitzpatrick's house, the engine cut out suddenly and this time quite dead

With this almost fatal fluctuation, I kept my eye on Dollymount Strand, a really safe place to put down. Howth was a bit dangerous, except possibly landing on a golf course. In the heel of the hunt, by climbing and gliding, climbing and gliding, we actually proceeded on beyond Dollymount and miraculously reached none other than Glasnevin, which looked, to say the least of it, too inviting. And I do remember, poor Jackie - who is a long time gone now - looked over the side and said to me: "What are all those white dots down there?" I replied, soberly: "Jackie, they are gravestones." His humorous remark showed that Jackie possibly did not realise the full gravity of the situation. Well, we were actually down to 400ft when we crossed the Merville Dairy tower and we could actually see Kildonan but I felt that I was not actually going to reach it. I was looking around for a landing place when, suddenly, the engine came to our rescue again and just at the very last minute, she picked up and we made a safe landing.

Jackie said when we landed that as this was the last day of filming and we had not got a picture of myself flying an aircraft, it would be a pity if such a shot were not included. I agreed to give it a go, because at this point the engine was ticking over sweetly, without any cadences. Now, this was a very foolish decision on my part and could have had serious repurcussions if I had been anywhere except Kildonan. So I asked Jackie to go out about 50 yards or more and go down on his knee so that he could take a low shot. I taxied back for take off. I told Jackie that when he heard me open up the engine, to start rolling the camera. Jackie does this quite perfectly in the film. You see me starting off including the entire run, taking off over the clubhouse and around in a circuit and just as I come around over Cappagh Hospital and then over Fitzpatrick's house, the engine cut out suddenly and this time quite dead. Consequently, I come in a little bit too high to make a forced landing on my own aerodrome, which is quite a unique experience.

In the film you can even see the propeller come to a stop and this time there was no question of starting the engine. Again, I brought my skill of side slipping to good use and side slipped over the trees at Fitzpatrick's and was able to make a perfect touchdown. That was the last part of the flying film. The machine was wheeled into the hangar. We took all the members in the flying field that day, including Lady Heath, in a group but Jack Williams was not there. The prominent members of Kildonan, with the exception of Jack, were all there. That ended the filming. By agreement, in exchange for flying lessons which I was giving to Jackie, the film was my property and I took charge of it. It was processed by Kodak in Grafton Street and they thought very highly of it. They borrowed the film four times in order to show it in their own private studio. They had a studio and shop near Bewley's. Then Sammy, Jackie's elder brother, said that he would like to show it to the yacht club members because we had good footage of the squadron out at sea. Now this was some years later and in the meantime all the club members at Kildonan had seen the film. They all came out to my home, on invitation, to see it. Anyway, I loaned the film to Sammy to show at the yacht club. He very carefully locked up the film in his locker. Well, it was stolen - that would on recollection be about 1949 or 1950. It has not been seen since. In those days, the thought never occurred to me to have a duplicate made of the film and I did not think of it at the time as a very historic film. Now it is and such a film should be made available, not hidden away.

To my knowledge, this was the first aerial film made in the Irish Free State. It was also the first aerial film of Dublin City which was covered in some detail. The film took nine flights to complete, over a period of 10 weeks. Four different aircraft of the Kildonan fleet were used in its making. The film had a running time of 45 minutes. I piloted the plane on each occasion and Mr. E. J. Smallridge did the filming. It was made in the spring and early summer of 1938.

Edward Anthony Millea (Tony):

Tony Millea was secretary of the Dublin Aero Club when it moved to Weston Park Aerodrome, Leixlip, following the closure of Kildonan Aerodrome.

Tony's wife's name was Phyllis, They had two sons, Edward and John, and three daughters, Gwen, Noreen and Mary.

The Millea family lived first at 26 Parkgate Street and moved to 'Liseux', 21 Conyngham Road, Phoenix Park. Tony obtained his licence at Kildonan in 1936 and flew various aircraft, including Puss Moth, Gypsy Moth, Aeronca, Avro Cadet and B.A. Swallow. His instructor was G.W. Williams of Dublin Air Ferries. After the war broke out Tony became an aircraft inspector in England.

Tony Millea was a personal friend of mine. He learned to fly with the Yorkshire Flying Club. He was working for Wimpey, the building firm, as a costing clerk. Tony was a very active member of the Dublin Aero Club and was elected secretary shortly before the Second World War. His wife also took an active part in the Dublin Aero Club, but not as a flying member.

Tony Millea, who was at Kildonan from June 11th, 1933 until the time of its closure

Phyllis Millea, wife of Tony Millea, who was an active member of the Dublin Aero Club at Kildonan and later at Weston Park Aerodrome, Leixlip

Oliver Bertram Morrogh Ryan was killed on active service on July 26th, 1941, having been through Dunkirk and the Battle of Britain

Oliver Bertram Morrogh Ryan

Oliver Bertram Morrogh Ryan, born March 28th, 1919, at Dunboyne Castle Co. Meath, learned to fly at Kildonan Aerodrome. He became a flight lieutenant in the R.A.F. He was killed on active service on July 26th, 1941, having been through Dunkirk and the Battle of Britain. Before the war, he had spent time in Vienna, where he did some flying and aerial photography. After Vienna, he was apprenticed to the de Havilland Company at Stag Lane, London and while there joined the reserve of the R.A.F. The Air Ministry offered him a commission which he accepted. A letter written by Oliver's mother, Laura Morrogh Ryan, stated that he was shot twice in the Battle of Britain and had she recalled six or eight Messerschmitts to his credit, "and was for a time occupied in some very secret scientific work to do with the Spitfire Planes".

The Morrogh Ryan family presented a cup for a competition which bore their name (The Morrogh Ryan Cup). It was won on this occasion by a Mr. J. Nolan.

The Morrogh Ryan Cup is presented to Mr. J. Nolan by Laura Morrogh Ryan

Gloster Gladiator in Norwegian Air Force markings

De Havilland Leopard Moth

De Havilland Tiger Moth G-AYIT

De Havilland Puss Moth G-ABLS

Miles Magister P6382 (G-AJDR)

Denis M. Greene

Denis Greene was born in 1916 and became a solicitor. His instructors at Kildonan Aerodrome, where he learned to fly, were O.E. Armstrong and F.W. Griffith. He obtained his 'A' licence, Irish, on the March 19th, 1935; his English 'A' licence, on June 15th, 1936; and his Irish 'B' Licence on September 15th, 1943. The family's business address was 11 Wellington Quay and the company was Roger Greene and Sons, Solicitors. Denis was a member of Dublin Aero Club at Kildonan until the end of 1935 and in January 1936, he joined the Irish Aero Club. He was elected to the council of the Irish Aero Club. Denis was closely associated with the promotion of a number of air displays which toured Ireland under the auspices of the Irish Aero Club. After its dissolution, he continued flying both in the privately-owned aircraft then available and the aircraft owned by Captain P. W. Kennedy, until the total ban on flying was imposed on the outbreak of the Second World War. On April 7th, 1942, Denis joined the Air Transport Auxiliary and served with this organisation as a ferry pilot until June 9th, 1943. His pilot's rating with this organisation authorised him to fly all types of single-engined aircraft and all types of light twin-engined aircraft. The nature of the duties of ferry-pilots were such that all pilots had to be prepared to fly on immediate notice any type of aircraft covered by their rating. This frequently necessitated flying types of aircraft of which the pilots had absolutely no prior experience. The training courses undergone by ferry pilots was specifically designed to make them competent to handle all types of aircraft. In 1943, Denis Greene joined the Irish Aviation Club and soon thereafter was co-opted onto the Executive Committee, on which he continued to serve. In 1944, he inaugurated a pilot's course in the club designed to give intending pilots a very comprehensive training. For the year ending March 31st, 1945, he served as assistant honourary secretary of the Irish Aviation Club. On April 1st, 1945, he was appointed chairman of the Flying Technical Sub-Committee of the Irish Aviation Club. The following were types of aircraft flown by him:

Airspeed Oxford
Hawker Hector
AvroAnson
Hawker Hind
Avro Tutor
Hawker Hurricane
B.A. Swallow

Klemm Swallow
Boulton & Paul Defiant
Miles Hawk
D.H.Puss Moth
Miles Magister
D.H.Hornet Moth
Miles Martinet

D.H.Tiger Moth
Miles Master
D.H. '60' Moth
N.A. Harvard
Fairchild 24
Percival Proctor
Gloster Gladiator

Spartan 3 Seater
Hawker Audax
Supermarine Spitfire
Hawker Hart
Westland Lysander
Whitney Straight

De Havilland Tiger Moth EI-AHC

Captain T. L. Young

Captain T. L. Young, a veteran of the war of Independence and later Camp Commandant at Rathduff in the Divisional Manoeuvres of August 1942, had between times joined Iona National Airways Ltd. as operations manager in 1931.

As ground organiser at Kildonan, he recorded over 4,000 people as having made joy flights organised by Iona National Airways Ltd., at various locations, including Skerries, Athy and the Curragh.

John Noel Duggan

John Noel Duggan

John Noel Duggan was born in Rathgar, Dublin on December 24th, 1913. He was a member of the Irish Aero Club at Baldonnel Aerodrome from 1926 to 1934. He was a pilot graduate of the Dublin Aero Club (Dublin Air Ferries Ltd.) Kildonan Aerodrome, and holder of pilot's licence No. 74, granted at Dublin on November 18th, 1937. His instructors were Lady Heath and R.J. Williams. He went solo at Kildonan after six and three quarter hours instruction. He was a member of the Dublin Aero Club from 1938-1941 as its organising secretary of the D.A.C. from 1938-1941. He had been one of the organisers of flying events held at Kildonan Aerodrome. In company with H.W. Graham and E.A. Millea, he re-formed the Dublin Aero Club at Weston Park, Leixlip Co. Kildare in 1939.

In addition, John Duggan had a considerable number of flying hours as co-pilot on the following types of aircraft: Armstrong-Whitworth Whitley Bombers, Short Sunderland Flying Boat.

John Duggan served in the Defence Forces (A.A. Artillery and Cavalry Corps) and later in England on important work under the Ministry of Aircraft production (M.A.P.) and with British Overseas Airways Corp. at Shannon Airport, Foynes.

Mr. Fred Griffith

Mr. Fred Griffith

Fred Griffith was chief pilot at Everson Flying Services Ltd., the company which operated at Kildonan Aerodrome from 1933 to 1935. He was injured while flying from Croydon, London to Marseilles, south of Avignon at Remy-de-Province in October 1935. Griffith, who spent much of his early youth in New Zealand, flew many notable flights, including an aircraft specially chartered by the Irish Times which brought photos from London of the wedding of the Duke and Duchess of Kent to Dublin. This was the only machine to leave Heston Airport, London that day because of the dense fog. Another flight which he piloted brought the photos of the Royal Jubilee celebrations to Dublin. Both were in the same year, 1934. Fred Griffith was recognised as one of the best commercial pilots flying from Croydon Airport at the time.

Chris Bruton

Chris Bruton was secretary of the National Irish Junior Aviation Club. He was prominent in the organisation of the various clubs and councils which succeeded the National Irish Junior Aviation Club and its successors, the Irish Junior Aviation Club and the Irish Aviation Club. He was active in the setting up of branches of Irish Aviation Club throughout the provinces, including, Limerick, Galway and Kildare. Between 1936 and 1940, the Irish Aviation Club organised an excellent series of lectures by the best speakers on the subject of aviation of the day, including Captain Dowds, Captain Kelly-Rogers and Dudley Hiscox.

Sr. Katherine

Born Marjory Bayley-Butler, Sr. Katherine was a daughter of Professor Bayley-Butler of the Zoology Department, University College Dublin. She graduated in Botany and Zoology in September 1935. Marjory - tall, happy, extrovert and single minded - entered religion shortly after obtaining her pilot's licence at Kildonan.

Members of the National Irish Junior Aviation Club who attended the Annual Meeting in the Manison House, Dublin, on the 5th June 1936. Front row: 2nd from left Chris Bruton, Second row: 1st left John Doyle, 4th from left John J. Dunne. The Irish Press, Saturday, June 6, 1936

The Flying Nun - A poem by Brenda Roche

You all know Sr. Katherine, she is so meek and mild
She may have even taught you when you were just a child
About the origin of the human race
And the attributes of social grace
Well last month her fellow sisters were aghast
When she revealed her secret from the past
Of how, against odds which were immense,
This brave woman gained her first pilot's licence
About fifty years or so ago
Against the advice of those who should know
With one engine and the Grace of God
She flew over Howth on her todd
And when the fog was thick and heavy
She kept her cool and her hand steady
With only a counter, indicator and spirit level
She defied the elements and the Devil
Then with Nelson's Pillar in her sights
She turned left for her homeward flight
With rosaries, hymns and a big Amen
She landed safe and sound in Kildonan
Now the newspapers made her a feature
Then all the stations tried to reach her
For interviews, testimony and revelation
Which were then broadcast live to the nation
On Women Today she went down a bomb
Now B.B.C. Radio 4 want her on
To add some excitement and culture
To their otherwise rather highbrow vulture
With her knowledge and revision
Next step's got to be television
Perhaps a serial they may have in view
The Thornbirds, Dynasty and Dallas to outdo
So if you see a black spot across the sun
Don't worry, it's probably our flying nun
As with Amy, Amelia and those heroines of days gone by
She's gonna fly 'till she reaches that last heaven in the sky
And if St. Peter's at the Gate
Lets hope that he is wide awake
For he'll need some spanners, pliers and things
To help her, at last, to fold those metal wings.

Chapter Eighteen

Chapter

Lady Heath - The Silver Lining - A Tribute by the Author

Lady Heath. Photo by Chris F. Bruton

Lady Heath on her trip to the United States, before her near fatal accident at the Cleveland Ohio air races

Chapter 18

Lady Heath - The Silver Lining

It was a bright sunny morning at the end of June 1935. The sun was on its climb through the skies at the early hour of five and came streaming into Lady Heath's bedroom. The dazzling brightness of the morning and the dawn chorus of the birds could not be resisted. The symphony of birdsong was deafening and demanded attention. Lady Heath was not angry with the feathered winged wonders of the sky. She felt a strong affinity towards them, the masters of flight. She was their understudy. Human engineers could not match their gift of flight with all its intricacies. It would be a nice morning she thought to savour the ambiance of the little idyllic village of Finglas and the surrounding area. Finglas and its quaint beauty held a special fascination for Lady Heath. Having leisurely strolled through the countryside she would take her silver bird, 'The Silver Lining' to flights real and of fancy over the Royal Kingdom of Meath.

Her husband Jack was one with her in her morning plan and they both hurried themselves so that they would arrive at Finglas Bridge by taxi at the early hour of six o'clock. The narrow bridge spanned the River Tolka. Its setting was a thing of real beauty, unspoiled, romantic and serene. The woodland foliage was saturated by the long rays of the morning sun which had earlier crept into the wood touching the tree trunks with a golden glow. The woodland grass was wet with the morning dew, reluctant to give way to the new day. They paused at length at the bridge, looking down into the clear waters of the Tolka, which was joined by the little stream, 'the Fionn Ghlaise', from which Finglas gets its name. The river reflected the azure sky above. Here and there, in the shaded areas, they could see brown trout dangling horizontally in the waters, sometimes real, sometimes imaginary. Almost in unison their eyes scanned the branches of the trees along the river which fanned out into a vast canopy of woodland which covered both banks of the river. The wooded area on the north side of the river was known as Finglas Wood. Not a leaf quivered in the stillness of the brittle morning air. But it was the giant Mill Wheel on the Tolka, man's artefact, in an otherwise almost totally natural setting, that gave the scene its picturesque character. Tolka Lodge House high up on the left bank of the river, formed a fitting backdrop, on a large site which was studded with mature oak trees. Wildlife was everywhere apparent. Nocturnal animals, like badgers, foxes and owls, had long since gone to ground before the morning rays of the sun had crept over the horizon's foggy air. Squirrels dashed and scampered around on their morning forages, a kestrel hung high in the sky, dazzling its terrified immanent prey, while individual seagulls wheeled about effortlessly in the higher echelons of the sky, in the slow motion of a timeless space. Lady Heath and her husband Jack were genuinely overawed by the fantasy that nature had created for them. It was theirs totally. Not another soul had emerged from sleep's sweet trance.

They would have liked to have lingered at Tolka Bridge, but they must slowly wend their way to another wonder, an oasis of flying machines in the fertile lands of Finglas. Kildonan Aerodrome was their destination.

Some years previously, while on a lecture tour of the United States of America, when she had reached the dizzy heights of success as an aviatrix, Lady Heath had been the centre of attraction. But while taking part in the Ohio Air races in Cleveland, her plane plunged to near disaster. It was an accident that shattered mind and body. As her aircraft plunged to earth, the thoughts of her achievements flashed through her mind and then there was nothingness. Everything was blotted out. Forever after that near fatal accident, she wondered whether she would ever fully recover from the shock and terror of those awful moments. Why had fate dealt her such a cruel blow? Why had death not taken her? She would always wonder why! She tried to banish the thought that there had been human interference and that her plane had been tampered with. She knew that there were many others who were strongly of this opinion. One way or the other now, she would always feel

Some years previously, while on a lecture tour of the United States of America, when she had reached the dizzy heights of success as an aviatrix, Lady Heath had been the centre of attraction. But while taking part in the Ohio Air races in Cleveland, her plane plunged to near disaster. It was an accident that shattered mind and body

She tried to banish the thought that there had been human interference and that her plane had been tampered with

Lady Heath often thought back of her great achievements of the late 1920s. Then she had been the toast of the aviation world. The adulation was great in Great Britain and the United States in particular. After her epic flight from Capetown to London, her name was etched forevermore on the parchment reserved for the names of aviation greats

physically and psychologically scarred. Like a wounded fawn that seeks refuge in the deep recesses of the woods, she would often now retreat into the crevices of self-pity, where nobody could help her and where she felt utterly alone and abandoned. But she would always keep a brave face and hide these feelings and moments of depression that silently and insidiously crept through her being. She had work to do and made very significant contributions to the development of civil aviation in Ireland. Perhaps time, the great healer, would resolve the tangle of mind and body and restore her fully to her former self. In the deep dark hours of depression, no bird sings. It was the very confidence that was natural in her nature that made her optimistic. She never despaired and named her aircraft, The Silver Lining, to remind her to look for the rays of sunshine. After her near fatal plane crash, Lady Heath underwent brain surgery. Medicine had failed to heal the in-built psychological scars, the inward hurt to dignity, to pride and to self-confidence. How deceptive was the outward appearance of being fully healed? The silver lining of underlying confidence that had always been natural to her, could, she felt, dispel the clouds of uncertainty.

But on the day in question the clouds had lifted and she felt buoyed up by happy memories of the past, by the natural beauty of Finglas and by the moral support of her partner Jack Williams who was so supportive.

She asked herself could she ever settle down in a place like Finglas, with roots as deep as the giant oak trees that hung in canopy over her. Finglas was a good place to be, but she had always been drawn to the bright lights of city life and loved the adulation that she had enjoyed after her successes in flight, when she became the toast of the aviation world. She longed for that experience to be repeated. She longed to climb to the pinnacle again.

Lady Heath often thought back of her great achievements of the late 1920s when she had been the toast of the aviation world. The adulation was great in Great Britain and the United States in particular. After her epic flight from Capetown to London, her name was etched forevermore on the parchment reserved for the names of aviation greats.

Mrs. W. D. Elliott-Lynn, a former world high jump champion. She plays lawn tennis, golf, hockey and lacrosse. Lady Heath dispatch rider British Transport Unit during the First World War

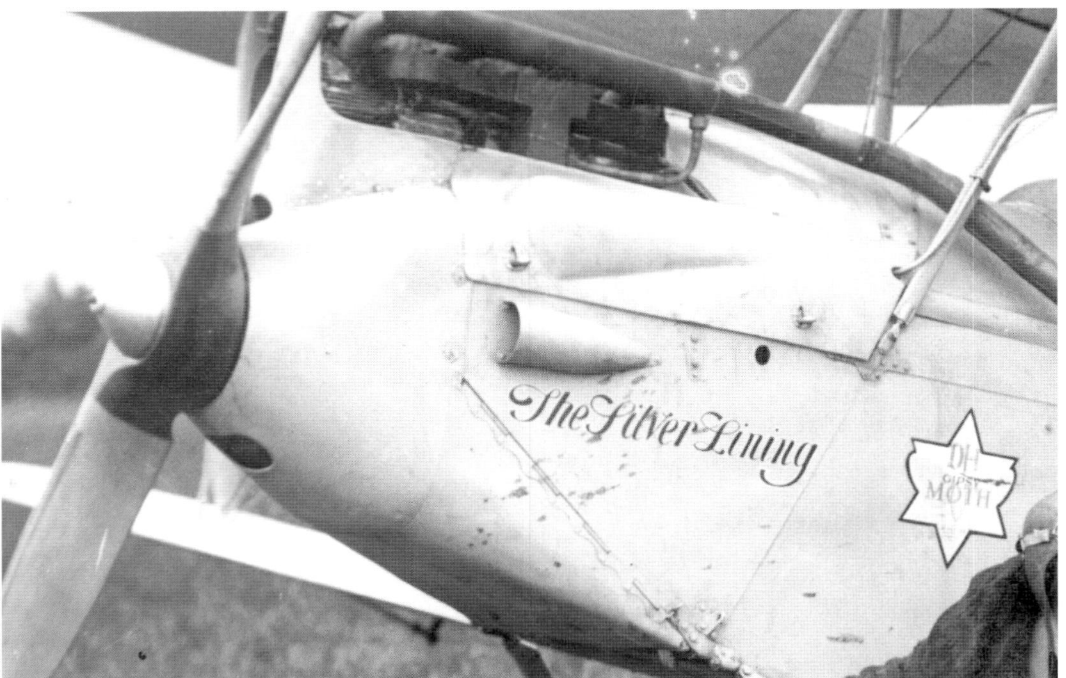

The Silver Lining De Havilland Moth

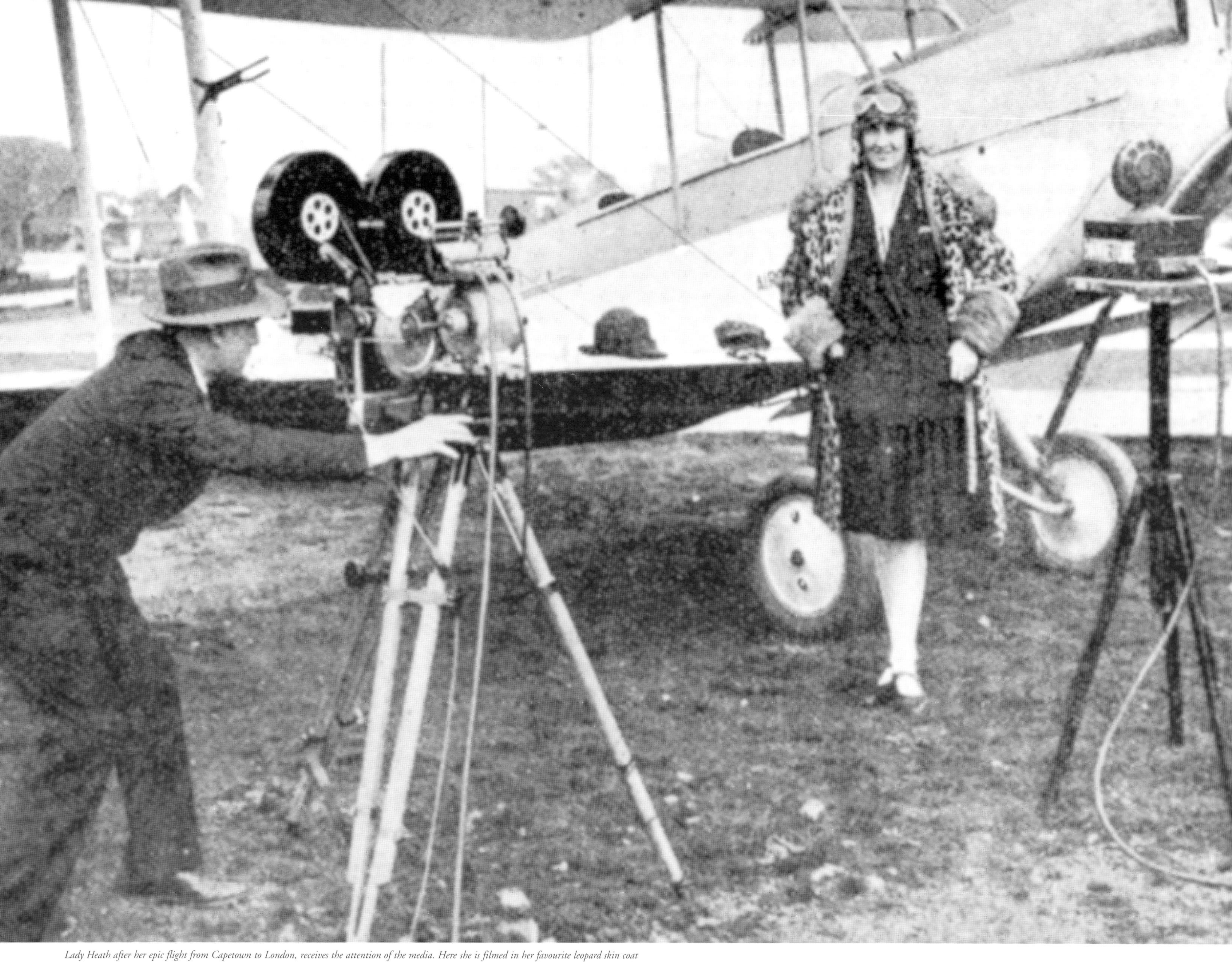

Lady Heath after her epic flight from Capetown to London, receives the attention of the media. Here she is filmed in her favourite leopard skin coat

The Derhams were a Roman Catholic family and great friends of the Craigies who were Church of Ireland. In Finglas, religion was and is now, no barrier to friendship

The sound of the wood-pigeons dominated the symphony of sound. It was eerie, loud and persistent cooing, hidden high up in the beech, oak and ash trees. Their sound was a discordant one out of tune as a dominant seventh on the musical scale. Pigeons were the ultimate navigators of the world, needing no instruments to guide them, other than the stars in the sky and their general affinity with earth and universe.

As they neared the gates of Merville Dairy, the scene suddenly changed. A massive steed, pulling a milk float, emerged from the open gate, the float laden with a myriad of silver white bottles, the horse manicured to the last and dressed in shining harness. The float was brightly painted and spotless. The milkman shouted to the huge beast in language that only it could comprehend. The milkman's white starch coat completed the picture, it was the essence of spotlessness. Soon another horse and float emerged, then another and another, almost identical except for the differing shades of brown to black of the animal's skin. Each and all were beautifully turned out, strong and healthy animals drawing floats made by the craftsmen from Mountjoy Square. The harnesses glistened like a bayonets in the dazzling sunshine. One line went north and the other went south, like armies dressed for battle, moving relentlessly towards enemy lines. But these were peaceful times, contrasting with the same journey northwards, which was made by Cromwell and his roundheads centuries before when the villagers scattered in fear, petrified by the reputation of his savagery. The stream of floats seemed endless and Lady Heath stopped her count at 50.

The Finglas road, which some minutes before had been as quiet as a nun, was suddenly alive with activity. Other horse-drawn vehicles began to appear, intermingling with the dairy's regiment. It was Tuesday morning, when the 'hay mangers' brought the hay to the Smithfield market in double carts, drawn by two horses, with the driver almost lost in the huge stack of hay. Then there were 'Scotch Carts', loaded up with pyramids of potatoes, cabbages or turnips. The dislodging of one would probably cause an avalanche. The odd 'Punchen' and high sided grain cart stood out in contrast to the rest. A drove of cattle came next, on their way to the cattle market leaving their mark on the dusty road. Further up the hill, as they moved closer to Finglas Village, a half dozen hunting horses emerged out of a tree-lined laneway on their morning canter. The tall slender, well-groomed, disciplined noble steeds moved in unison up the hill in front of them. They had come from St. Helena's, the family home of the Craigies, a fine house which stood on 200 acres of rich land. The team of horses was led by Rachel and Florence Craigie, the daughters of Jack who owned Merville Dairy. The Craigies often visited Kildonan Aerodrome and Hugh Cahill, the founder of Kildonan, serviced the new lorries which the dairy had now acquired to collect the milk from outlying farms. The vehicles were serviced at Hugh's Iona Garage, at Cross Guns Bridge. The Craigies were also involved in the cattle auctioneering business from their premises at 37 Prussia Street. They bred some very successful race horses, including Sillogue Prince, Splash, LastLink, Lime Juice and Florina. They also hunted fox and deer with the Fingal Harriers and the Ward Union Staghounds.

In ancient times, the Finglas Fair surpassed all others in popularity and acquired the description of 'The Donnybrook of the North'. Right through the 1930s, the horse sustained Merville and guaranteed steady employment to hundreds of Finglas people. The close association of horse and people runs right though history and displays itself in a different form in recent times with the phenomenon of the horses owned by residents of the local authority suburban house, with obvious limitations and resulting problems of care and containment. Travellers who had a tradition of halting at St. Patrick's Well alongside the village sold their goods and rested their horses before moving on.

Just above St. Helena's, on the left-hand side, they could see Farnham House, a fine building set in a well-landscaped site with formal grounds. To the east and on the opposite side of the main north/south road. stood Rosehill House. It was home to another wealthy family, the Derhams, an imposing building on raised ground.

Home was where the hangar was and the hangar was at Kildonan, Finglas. The real feeling of home could be found in the whine of an aircraft engine, the smell of burnt fuel, the comraderie of flying friends. Her special home was in the sky. Today, she had only one ambition, to fly The Silver Lining. Hugh Cahill had chosen the perfect place for an aerodrome

The Derhams were a Roman Catholic family and great friends of the Craigies who were Church of Ireland. In Finglas, religion was, and is now, no barrier to friendship. Rosehill House dominated the landscape and looked down on the Lower Flood's public house and the parochial hall, the centre of the social life of the area.

Next on the same side as St.Helena's was the ruins of St. Canice's Abbey and the Celtic cross of Nethercross, looking out of the graveyard in which the abbey stood. Close by was St. Patrick's Well and King William's Ramparts. Then they passed the new St. Canice's Roman Catholic Church, opened in 1922, the post office and the Upper Flood's, all on their right. The Widow O'Donnell's was on their left. Then into view came a building which fascinated them. It was known as Gofton Hall and years before as Eagle Lodge. It was a fine Georgian house with beautiful gardens of flowers, shrubs, garden furniture and trees, set in perfectly manicured lawns. Immediately north of the village was Ashgrove House and then the welcome site of Parkes' Garage, with its immaculately dressed chauffeurs and shining black taxis. They would avail of the services of one of these to complete the last leg of their journey to the aerodrome.

When they reached Kildonan, they alighted from the taxi and proceeded to the hangar. As they approached it, their steps quickened, imperceptibly, but steadily. Lady Heath felt her heart beat quicker as she felt irresistibly drawn to her plane, The Silver Lining. Home was where the hangar was and the hangar was at Kildonan, Finglas. The real feeling of home could be found in the whine of an aircraft engine, the smell of burnt fuel, the comraderie of flying friends. Her special home was in the sky. Today, she had only one ambition, to fly The Silver Lining. Hugh Cahill had chosen the perfect place for an aerodrome.

She breathed the pure morning air deep into her lungs. It was so good to be alive. It was a flyer's day. She felt the green grass under her shoes, a sweet sensation. The open hangar stared out on the airfield, on the surrounding plains and on a vast expanse of sky devoid of any cloud. They pushed The Silver Lining out of the hangar area and with one turn of the propeller, Lady Heath spun the engine into life. She allowed the aircraft ample time for the engine to warm up. When Jack Williams removed the chocks from the wheels, it was a clear signal for Lady Heath to begin her take off. The little craft began slowly, then gathered speed as it raced along the smooth green carpet that was Kildonan. Having attained take-off speed the wheels parted company with the earth. The engine cowling rose smoothly up towards the horizon, pointing at the single cirrus-streaked sky. For a few moments she stared fixedly at the blue sky beyond the pitched up nose and invisible propeller. The wings cut through the deep blue sward of the sky. Now and then, she strained her eyes, searching meticulously into the dazzling brightness of the sun for any aircraft that might be concealed within its glare. She could feel the unique uplifting feeling, that magical sensation all over, like a gull savouring the soft summer eddies along the cliff edge. She loved the free fresh wind in her face. It was as if the soaring wings of the little craft had suddenly filled with air, like the sails of a ship. Lady Heath craned her neck over the side of the cockpit and watched the grassy take-off ground of the airfield sliding back towards the leading edge of the left lower wing. The far boundary of the airfield slowly disappeared under the wing. It seemed as if by rising in the air, she had suddenly become a god, shaking off the human chrysalis. Lady Heath, as usual, had made the perfect take-off. She searched the sky for other aircraft but there were none to be seen. Her little craft had been absorbed into the friendly sky. The world aloft was pure brilliance. Her soft featured face and pale blue wide-pupiled eyes, behind wizard goggles, were absolutely still, lost in total concentration. Visibility was brittle-sharp and unlimited, while the sound of the engine filled the blue domed sky. Her ears were finely tuned to the music of the wires as her steady speed held a single prolonged note on the continuum of sound. She felt secure and content in the great aloneness, cushioned from reality, in the ambiance of the Eternal.

She was queen of all she surveyed. Feelings of great power, strength, peace and tranquillity welled up in her soul

Flying today was an end in itself. She longed to fly where no one could reach her. She could hear the birdsong of the morning over the engine's roar. Far below was a vast patchwork of fields spread out, clean and toy-like. The wings crawled slowly across the miniature landscape. She could see a white blanket of birds floating beneath. Her favourite season was the autumn when the trees were burnt gold and red in the last splendour of the growing year. But today, verdant green was the colour which saturated almost the entire ecology of the landscape below. Her thoughts turned momentarily to the differences in the seasons. What once she revelled in, but now frightened her, was the blaring gale of the slipstream on a cold winter's day. Her silver-plated head could no longer stand the freezing blast of the airflow, like an icy avalanche hurling hailstones against her injured brain, pounding the leather helmet that she wore. On such days, the wild hurting howl of the airflow and the whine, snarl, growl or bullying roar of the engine brought back frightening memories of that awful day, when like a leaf, caught up in a storm, she was dashed against earth's jagged crust.

Lady Heath and The Silver Lining were now as one, soaring eagle like The Silver Lining flew effortlessly over the vast plain of Moynalta, her silver plumage glistening in the sunshine, contrasting with the sky which was now all blue except for a few short cirrus streaks, here and there. She was queen of all she surveyed. Feelings of great power, strength, peace and tranquillity welled up in her soul. She longed to fly to the high rocky mountains, the stark mountainous regions of the world, the inaccessible haunts inhabited only by golden eagles, the true rulers of the sky. Their flight is unsurpassed in power, grace and precision, perfect aerial acrobats, commanding vast territories. There she would dwell with the masters of the air, amid cliffs and rocky precipices. There she would find a true resting place and dwell amid eternal solitude. Life's wanderings would be over. Once she had watched at length these magnificent birds of prey, handsome creatures shaped for speed, with sharp talons, beaks of vice-grip and fierce eyes. Their deceptively leisurely, well-directed flight sustained by powerful wing-beats, now soaring, now gliding, full of the poetry of motion. Hovering, wheeling, swooping, then suddenly that dashing flight from dizzy heights with unerring aim to seize helpless prey. Today Lady Heath felt the freedom of the great creatures she contemplated.

She knew the qualities that were needed for success in the air - grim determination, the eye of an eagle, the hands of a surgeon, nerves of steel, eternal vigilance, meticulous care and for long distance flight, the knowledge of an engineer

Flying was all about freedom; freedom of movement, freedom of thought, freedom of feeling, freedom of expression, freedom from the chains and limitations of earthly existence. But strangely, the freedom of escape from earthly things merged into the longed for unity with the aircraft she loved and flew. Lady Heath was as one with the machine, her arms were the wings, her fingertips the ailerons and elevators. She had settled into the natural rhythm of flight. Routinely, at intervals as regular as clockwork, she searched the sky for aircraft or any signals or changes in the elements. A careful pilot does not put her trust in a minute-old look-out.

Flying was also about feelings. Lady Heath remembered the jittery elation of her first flight. Now, instinct, courage and experience served her well. She had developed over the years an ice-cool temperament for flying. But even the pilot of ice-cool appearance could experience all the feelings on the continuum-tension, terror, cool calm action and relief and all within the shortest space of time.

Lady Heath listened to the music in the wires and to the healthy sound of The Silver Lining's engine. She looked for landmarks on the ground and checked her altitude, keeping the nose of the aircraft level with the horizon. All was well. She knew the qualities that were needed for success in the air-grim determination, the eye of an eagle, the hands of a surgeon, nerves of steel, eternal vigilance, meticulous care and for long distance flight, the knowledge of an engineer. She had demonstrated them all in an eminent way in her epic solo flight from Capetown in South Africa to Cairo and then on to London in 1928.

This golden age of flying of the Lady Heath era is gone forever. New technology, labelled buttons and insulation have destroyed the triple symbiosis of pilot, aircraft and the elements. Man has forgotten how to fly with the wind, the sky and all the senses tuned into the elements

This flight had forever placed her in the human stars of the sky, indelibly printed in the annals of world aviation. Little did she know that her achievements would never be surpassed by an Irish aviator. But Lady Heath was humble to a fault about her achievements. Her main ambition now was to make a significant contribution to the development of civil aviation in the Irish Free State.

This golden age of flying of the Lady Heath era is gone forever. New technology, labelled buttons and insulation have destroyed the triple symbiosis of pilot, aircraft and the elements. Man has forgotten how to fly with the wind, the sky and all the senses tuned into the elements. The senses were of prime importance, the sense of judgement, speed sense, sense of height and sense of error. Knowledge of the sky and the wind and the weather were of the utmost. In those days you did not fly above the storm - you flew through it or did not fly at all. Today, the romance of flight has been designed out of flying. After the golden years of the 1930s, flying would never be the same.

When Lady Heath looked down, she could see the River Boyne below, a running pageant of Irish history. A two mile stretch of this river, west of the City of Drogheda called Brugh na Boinne, is a cemetery of stone age kings. Its focal points are the tumili of Dowth, Newgrange and Knowth. These artefacts crowned the ridge of the River Boyne. There were dozens of mounds and megaliths in the area. The River Boyne was always sacred, named after Boann, wife of the chief of the ancient gods known as Tuatha de Danann or people of Danu. Not far away, Lady Heath could see the two remarkable monastic sites of Monasterboice, with round tower and high crosses, followed closely by Mellifont Abbey. Not long afterwards, her tiny aircraft was over the Hill of Tara, once the home of the High Kings of Ireland. This was the Royal Kingdom of Meath and Lady Heath felt at home with kindred spirits of ancient times who centuries before had been laid to rest in these holy places. But she was not spirit only. Her aircraft had the limitations of man's creation so she must begin to re-trace her flight to the safe haven of Kildonan and share her thoughts with her colleagues of flight. Slowly, Lady Heath flew her tiny craft along the return route she knew so well. Soon in what seemed like half the time it had taken her on the outward flight, she was back, near the airfield with her favourite landmark, Dunsoghly Castle in her sights. She was nearly home. Her homing instinct was as strong as that of a long-lost pigeon. Her helmeted head glanced left, noting a distant wood as a landmark. She banked sharply, wheeling the biplane into a steep right turn, her head, twisting this way and that, searching the sky for other aircraft. The shadows of strutts and wires flickered across her face as the wing traversed round the horizon. Throughout the whole flight, the aircraft had flown straight and level.

Freedom had escaped her again. She knew well that flight was a momentary escape from the eternal custody of the earth. The wings that a moment ago were tameless, swift and proud as the eagle's, were metal and wood once again, inert and heavy as the deepest anchor in the ocean

Now gently, like a dying eagle, it dipped and flew towards the airfield. The cross shaped machine had sunk into what had been the patchwork of the countryside. From the cockpit of The Silver Lining, she could now see the branches of the trees, the shape of the stones, the difference in colour of the grass. Then even lower she flew, almost dusting the leaves with blue exhaust, the shadows of aircraft and pilot riding close to the ground, which crept under the wings leading edge. The warm sunburnt sunlit ground and the hangar quickly expanded in the frame of the centre section struts. She throttled down allowing enough revs to prevent the aircraft from stalling. The plane nosed groundward. The wings strained to the firmer cushion of earthbound air. The wheels reached for solid ground.

She felt the wheels of the undercarriage take hold of the earth. The Silver Lining made one stiff-legged little bounce then settled, finished its landing roll and taxied towards the hangar. Jack Williams, Lady Heath's husband, was out waiting for her. He stood watching the machine as it taxied towards him. When it came up close, it swung round for parking. He could see Lady Heath clearly in the cockpit. She waved at him and smiled. When she cut the engine, the propeller slowed, swished back and forth between two compressions and stopped dead. She relaxed in her seat and adjusted her ears to the silence. It was not the silence of emptiness, the silence of doubt, the silence of fear, but the silence of deep-seated tranquillity. Her eardrums

Ground engineers J.R. Currie and Mick Brady were waiting in the corrugated walled hangar to check out The Silver Lining and make it ready for its next flight. Lady Heath had more trust in the engineering expertise and meticulous care of these men than she had in human nature itself. They were two of the high priests of engine and aircraft tuning and maintenance

felt woolly. Freedom had escaped her again. She knew well that flight was a momentary escape from the eternal custody of the earth. The wings that a moment ago were tameless, swift and proud as the eagle's, were metal and wood once again, inert and heavy as the deepest anchor in the ocean.

She wriggled around in the cockpit, pulling off her helmet and draping it over the windscreen. She then climbed out onto the lower wing and onto the ground, pulling off her gloves and pushing back her hair with her right hand. Ground engineers J.R. Currie and Mick Brady were waiting in the corrugated walled hangar to check out The Silver Lining and make it ready for its next flight. Lady Heath had more trust in the engineering expertise and meticulous care of these men than she had in human nature itself. They were two of the high priests of engine and aircraft tuning and maintenance. They were held in high esteem by all who flew at Kildonan. Theirs was the hymn of purring pistons. This air of confidence and trust prevailed at Kildonan from the moment Hugh Cahill had set foot on the airfield to the time when the hangar closed behind the last exiting aircraft. As a result not one single life was lost.

Lady Heath visits the Lockheed factory in the United States prior to her participation in the Ohio State races, Cleveland

EI-AAW, D.H.60G Moth, Reg'd. 29/5/34, Lady Heath c/no. 1849, ex ZS-ADB, G-ACBU

This aircraft had been based at Baldonnel in British marks from at least August 1933 and was used for charter work by Everson Flying Services. Crashed and destroyed by fire at Stone, Staffordshire on 26/11/35, en route Dublin - Speke - Croydon.

Personal A/c. of the late Lady Sophie Heath. Colour scheme as G-ACBU silver-doped overall, the front colour being very slightly darker than the F/Ss. As EI-AAW, same as for EI-AAE, above. The name, The Silver Lining, was deleted.

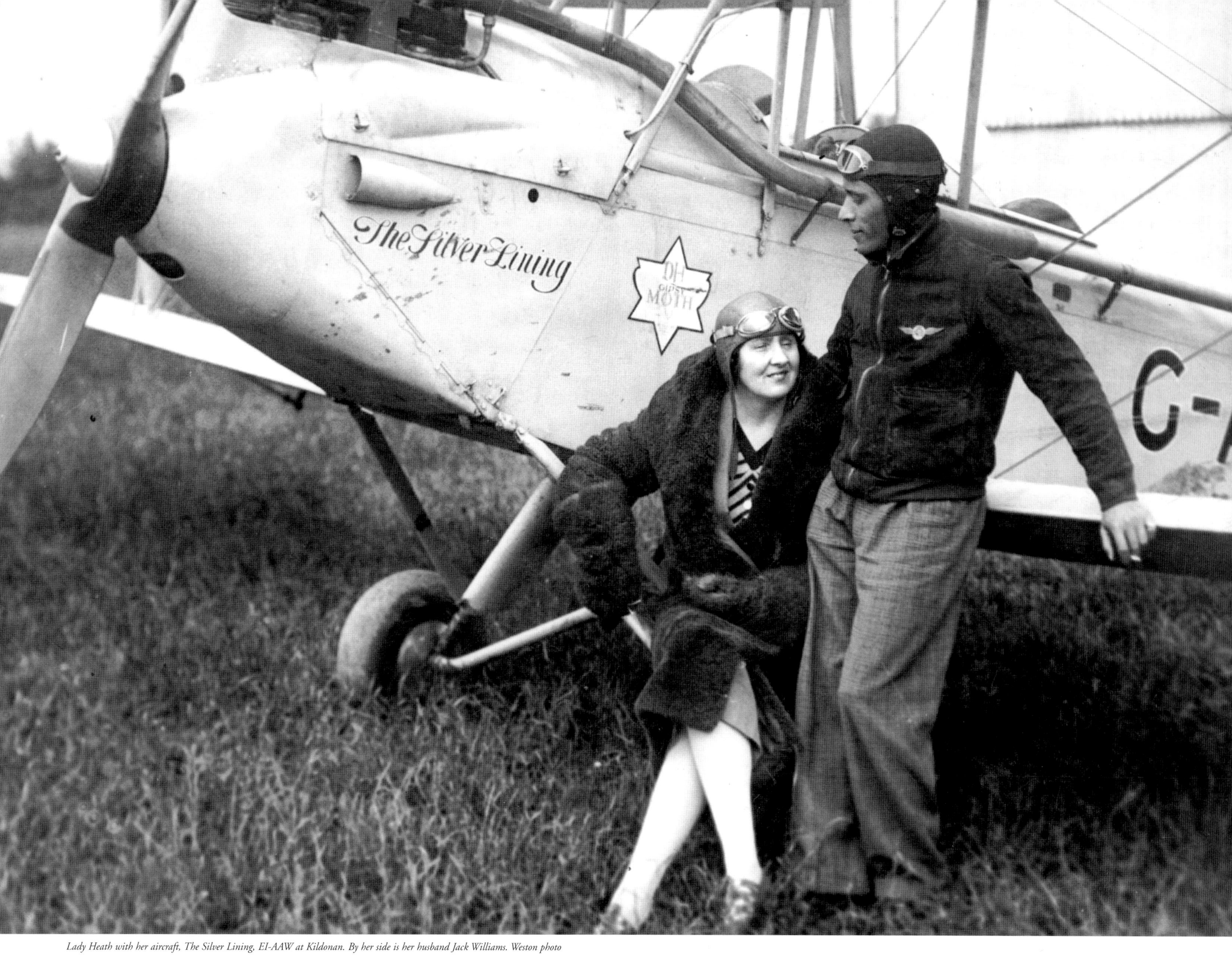

Lady Heath with her aircraft, The Silver Lining, EI-AAW at Kildonan. By her side is her husband Jack Williams. Weston photo

Mrs. Elliot Lynn, at the first French competition for private aeroplanes held in August 1926 at Orly, putting her De Havilland Moth, through the official measuring gauge.

Lady Heath at Tullabawn Strand

Chapter Nineteen

Lady Heath - Ireland's greatest aviator/aviatrix

Portrait of Sophie Peirce by Sir John Lavery. Circa 1918

Chapter 19

Lady Heath - Ireland's greatest aviator/aviatrix

Childhood

Sophie Mary Pierce was born on the November 10th, 1896 and baptised on November 26th. She was born at Knockaderry House, Newcastle West, Limerick and baptised by J. Vance, rector of Newcastle West. She was reared by her aunts in her grandfather's house in the Square, Newcastle West.

Lady Heath's family and relations

Dr. George Pierce's house at the south west corner of the Square, Newcastle West, Limerick, circa 1890. Sophie Pierce grew up in this house looked after by her aunts and her grandfather, Dr. George Pierce. The property was acquired by the Munster & Leinster Bank after the 1914-18 war. They demolished the house and constructed the present bank premises which opened for business on May 7th, 1924

Sophie Pierce's paternal grandfather was Dr. George Pierce, who was a brilliant doctor with his practice in Newcastle West. Her father Jackie Pierce inherited Knockaderry House and farm from his maternal grandfather, Tom Evans. Her mother's maiden name was Kate Teresa Doolan, who came from Co. Kerry. Her parents had married on May 29th, 1895. The marriage was blessed with a daughter, christened Sophie Pierce. Sophie was reared by her aunts Cis and Annie in the home of Dr. George Pierce in Newcastle West. Miss Creagh Langford of Ardagh, near Newcastle West, a kinswoman of Sophie's, has a fine portrait of her by Sir John Lavery.

Sophie had several changes of name in later life. On the occasion of her first marriage, Sophie Pierce Evans became Mrs. Elliott-Lynn. However, it is as Lady Heath that she is best known, a title she attained when she married Sir James Heath in October 1927 following the death of her first husband. She joined the British Transport Unit during the 1914/1918 war and was a rider.

Elliott-Lynn

Elliott-Lynn, at the time of his marriage to Sophie Pierce, was serving in the Royal Engineers. They married shortly after the war and they both went to live and farm coffee plantations in Kenya, East Africa. The pair had met and fallen in love while Elliott-Lynn was home on vacation from East Africa and visiting friends in Ireland.

Education

When Lady Heath committed herself to a career in flying, she was 22 years of age. For her education, she attended St. Margaret's Hall School in Dublin. She had completed a degree in Agricultural Science, at University College, Dublin. She then began lecturing at the University of Aberdeen in Scotland.

Sophie Pierce in the uniform of the British Transport Unit which she joined towards the end of the 1914/1918 war

Sophie Pierce, with her first husband, Major William Davies Elliott-Lynn whom she married in 1919

Her early life and achievements, Lady Heath's remarkable versatility

In his introduction to 'East African Nights', a book of poetry by Sophie C. Elliott-Lynn (Lady Heath), published in 1925, Captain F. Russell-Roberts M.C. wrote: "Mrs. Elliott-Lynn's versatility is remarkable. She finds time to write verse between her travels and her coffee planting, her public service over here and her athletics. Representing England in the Olympic Games and putting up worlds athletic records serves to keep her fit for strenuous African Safaris. An expert motorist, she had three years of war service overseas during which time the frontispiece portrait by Sir John Lavery was painted."

Lady Heath - the poet

Lady Heath wrote poems of love, love of people, love of nature and love of Africa. Her poems written in East Africa capture the character and atmosphere of life there and her personal feelings and experiences. The collection of poetry shows a sensitivity, tuned into the beauty of nature. They also show a deep appreciation of the lives of others in their varied roles, in the African continent, as well as her adaptability and inherent optimism.

Elliott-Lynn (Sophie Peirce) in Kenya C.1920

'Left After' by Lady Heath (Mrs. Elliott-Lynn)

The moon is curved and thin tonight
Above Pangani river.
And very still the waters lie
Without a crest or quiver.
If love has smiled and gone away
I think one ought to find
That there are other things in life
As lovely, left behind.
I only have the dawn wing left
Upon Bishuri's height,
The crimson sunset and the blue
Starlit, of early night.
And there are other lovelier things,
The spring, the hills, the sea.
What matter it if love be gone,
If these be left to me.

PANGANI, December 11th, 1923.

On May 30th, 1925, Lady Heath, made the case to the Pedagogic Conference of the Olympic Congress, Prague, for the inclusion of women into the Olympic Games

'Disaster' by Lady Heath (Mrs. Elliott Lynn)

The coffee fails, the coffee wilts and dies.
Droughts in the land, born of the brazen skies.
The stunted corn is brown and cannot bear,
Hungry for moisture from the burnt-out air.
Long lines of beans lie shrivelled, yielding nil,
Idle the waterwheel is standing still.
And sickness ravages the oxen teams
Nothing is left to us beside our dreams.
What does it matter if the gombes (cattle) die,
What if the roof fall in and all crops lie,
Producing nothing! Life is always grand,
If we can face the future hand in hand.
KISUMU

This book came with the highest commendations and was an inspiration to existing and prospective women athletes of the day. In the field of athletics, as was the case later in the sphere of aviation, Lady Heath, reached out and touched the stars

Lady Heath - world champion athlete

Today, world champion athletes are revered and feted. In Lady Heath, we had a true world champion. Her world record was the culmination of years of dedication to the cause of women's athletics. On May 30th, 1925, Lady Heath, then Mrs. Elliott-Lynn, made the case to the Pedagogic Conference of the Olympic Congress, Prague, for the inclusion of women into the Olympic Games. Her submission had already been approved by the Medical Sub-Commission, appointed by the Olympic Congress of which she was a member. She co-operated with Major Marchant of the English Women's Amateur Athletic Association in 1922. At the time there was one club and about 20 girls participating. By 1925, this had mushroomed into 500 clubs and over 25,000 girls participating in athletics.

Elliott-Lynn became vice-president of the Amateur Athletic Association of England. Her own club was 'The Ladies' Atheneum Club, London West One'. In 1923, Elliott-Lynn broke the world record for the high jump, with a jump of 4ft. 11ins. It was August 6th that she became world champion for this event. On August 23rd, 1923, she became the British javelin champion. Her book 'Athletics for Women and Girls', provided very valuable information on training, technique and achievements of the great athletes of the day, for all track and field events. This book came with the highest commendations and was an inspiration to existing and prospective women athletes of the day. In the field of athletics, as was the case later in the sphere of aviation, Lady Heath reached out and touched the stars.

Mrs Elliott-Lynn's, advice on training and keep-fit was eagerly sought. She was also proficient in tennis, golf, hockey and lacrosse.

Sophie Peirce, 1923, surrounded by her athletic trophies

Mrs. Elliott-Lynn, first woman member of the London Light Aeroplane Club, receiving instruction from Mr. A. Cobham

Lady Heath's introduction to flying

While returning from Prague by plane in May 1925, where she had been attending the Olympic Conference and delivered a paper on women's athletics, Sophie Elliot-Lynn was sitting beside an R.A.F. pilot named Reid. When she expressed a keen interest in flying, Reid promised to help her to learn to fly. She immediately joined London Light Aeroplane Club, becoming its first woman member and had her first flight in August 1925.

The home of the London Aero Club was at Stag Lane, where Geoffrey de Havilland had leased a hangar to the club. This hangar was beside the factory where the de Havilland aircraft were manufactured. It was here, August 19th, 1925 that Sir Philip Sassoon, the Undersecretary of the State for Air, performed the official opening ceremony for the London Aero Club. In his speech, Sir Philip praised the role which the clubs would perform and hoped that their efforts would "tend to wean the aeroplane from its warlike associations and develop it more as an agent for civilisation and peace". After his speech, he took part in the inaugural flight with Captain G.F.M. Sparks, the club's chief instructor. When the inaugural ceremony was complete and Sir Philip had safely landed, a ballot was then taken to determine who would be the first pupil to receive instruction at the London Aero Club. The first name out of the hat was Mr. David Kittel, who immediately gave up his place to Sophie. Sophie thus became the first person to receive flying instruction at the London Aero Club and the first person to receive instruction with the subsidised clubs.

"Six garages were built for aeroplanes at Stag Lane Aerodrome, Edgware, which were rented by people who owned light aeroplanes. In this picture, a Moth aeroplane, with its wings folded back, is being pulled out of the garage by the owner and pilot, Mrs. Elliott-Lynn

Going solo

Lady Heath went solo at Stag Lane on October 18th, 1925. She received her 'A' pilot's licence at Stag Lane Aerodrome in November 1925, while flying a D.H. Moth. Having received her pilot's licence, Lady Heath began to pile up a large number of hours in the air on various types of aircraft, including an S.E, 5a, a war-time single-seater biplane. Although Lady Heath gained her pilot's licence at the London Aero Club in 1925, she found that although she could fly, she could not earn a living and have a career in flying. In order to support herself and to fulfil her ambitions in flying which were many, she had to break through the citadel of male chauvinism, which excluded her and her sex from the developing commercial airlines. She had not as yet married Lord Heath, a marriage which would enable her to embark on her epic flight from Capetown, via Cairo, to London. While making the case for the admission of women to commercial flying, Lady Heath earned her living by taking part in exhibitions and by flying mail between London and Paris.

Gypsy Moth being towed through the streets of a town, wings folded

WOMAN AND FLYING

By

LADY HEATH
AND
STELLA WOLFE MURRAY

ILLUSTRATED

London
John Long, Limited
34, 35 & 36 Paternoster Row

Title page of the book, 'Woman and Flying', by Lady Heath and Stella Wolfe Murray

ATHLETICS FOR WOMEN AND GIRLS

HOW TO BE AN ATHLETE AND WHY

BY

SOPHIE C. ELIOTT-LYNN, A.R.C.Sc.I.
VICE-PRESIDENT WOMEN'S AMATEUR ATHLETIC ASSOCIATION

WITH FOREWORD
BY THE
RT. HON. LORD DESBOROUGH, K.C.V.O.

AND APPRECIATION BY
BRIG.-GENERAL R. J. KENTISH, C.M.G., D.S.O.

LONDON: ROBERT SCOTT
ROXBURGHE HOUSE
PATERNOSTER ROW, E.C.
MCMXXV

Athletics for Women & Girls

Sophie Pierce at the door of her British Transport Unit van circa 1918

Dear Sir,

During the summer of this year I became much interested in the advance of Civil Aviation and decided to leave my position as organiser in the world of business and devote myself to it. Better to fit myself, I decided to learn flying and discovered in doing so that I possessed a natural ability for practical aviation.

In compiling newspaper articles on flying, I found that the majority of women pilots, especially in America, have won their way to recognition by daring feats and "stunts" which, although very indicative of the ability of the ladies in question, are not of real practical value as propaganda for steady everyday flying. I therefore decided that the best procedure would be to fit myself for a 'B' licence and, if possible, show that a woman could do a commercial pilot's work with a modicum of efficiency.

My first difficulty presented itself in the resolutions Nos. 146 and 147 of the 6th sitting of the Commission, in which women are debarred from this profession. I see, however, in No. 147 that the Medical Sub-Commission was directed to continue its study of the matter and it is on this account that I venture to write to you.

I realise that the decisions of the Commission were made after due deliberation and with most laudable intentions, but the very lack of suitable material in the shape of women pilots to examine and test exhaustively, means that the Medical Sub-Commission did not have before them all the data desirable for a final ruling on the subject.

I would be intensely grateful if you would put me in touch with the President of this Medical Sub-Commission personally, or lay my views before him. I hold the Government degree in physiology, have worked for years among women and girls, as I started the Women's Amateur Athletic Association of Great Britain and have been myself a member of every International Womens team since then. In addition I am a member of the Medical Sub-Commission of the last Olympic Congress, being the only woman to attend and give evidence at Prague, in June 1925, on the question of the advisability of women's entry into the world of athletics.

I clearly realise that the decision arrived at by your Sub-Commission were due to the very great differences that occur in the nervous and mental systems of some women at certain periods and it is on an examination of a number of women pilots, extended daily over a number of weeks or months that I base my plea.

Having dealt for some years with hundreds of girls and women of all ages and nationalities, I have seen that when a woman is sufficiently fine and healthy to enter the first class of athletics her periods of nervous difference, or her powers of endurance, are imperceptible, even to the acute measurements of such an instrument as the Reid indicator, which is accepted by our Air Ministry for measurements of the nervous reactions of intending pilots.

I would like to offer myself as material for any set of experiments that the Medical Commission would care for me to undergo. As I am leaving my position as Secretary to this Club and entering the De Havilland works at the beginning of the New Year, I propose to be tested daily on this important instrument over a period of a couple of months. The resultant charts should be of some use in showing the nervous variation of a healthy woman of 28. I understand that the very severe medical tests for a 'B' licence would bring all those that passed it into the class of first-class athletes mentioned above.

I will be very grateful if you let me know as soon as possible your own views on this subject and any other move I might make to forward the matter before it again comes up under the deliberations of the Medical Sub-Commission.

Yours truly,

(Signed) S. C. Elliott-Lynn.

Lady Heath's letter to the International Commission for Air Navigation, dated November 1925

A glimpse into the inner history of its rescinding (i.e. the ban on women flying commercially) may prove of interest and all women - no matter what their nationality - adopting aviation as a career, should be grateful to Lady Heath for the excellent practical pioneer work she put in during her first winter as a professional pilot, as well as for the efficient way in which she approached the authorities, i.e, the International Commission for Air Navigation, and wore down their opposition

Lady Heath's role in having the ban on women's flying commercially rescinded

Stella Wolfe Murray wrote in the book, 'Woman and Flying', which she published jointly with Lady Heath: "A glimpse into the inner history of its rescinding (i.e. the ban on women flying commercially) may prove of interest and all women - no matter what their nationality - adopting aviation as a career, should be grateful to Lady Heath for the excellent practical pioneer work she put in during her first winter as a professional pilot, as well as for the efficient way in which she approached the authorities, i.e., the International Commission for Air Navigation, and wore down their opposition.

For the first three months of 1926, she lived near the aerodrome at Stag Lane and went through the workshops of the de Havilland Company, qualifying for her 'B' licence, which involved a very stiff examination not merely in practical flying by day and by night but also in navigation meteorology, engine-fitting, rigging and the theory of flight. She approached the various governments that were signatories to the Air Convention of 1919 and the members of the International Commission for Air Navigation and had obtained the help of the Scandinavian countries, Czechoslovakia and France. She risked her life stunting and giving exhibition flights, having put all her capital into aviation. She flew newspapers between London and Paris during May 1926 when England was affected by a general strike. The Commission found her rational presentation of the case for the admission of women to commercial flying watertight. Her persistence, courage, charm and beauty won the day and the Commission who had earlier been unanimous in banning women from commercial flying were now equally unanimous in rescinding the ban on women pilots.

Record parachute descent

Lady Heath (then Mrs. Elliott-Lynn) achieved fame as the first woman to make a parachute descent from an aeroplane. She made a 1,500 feet descent from an Avro Avian aeroplane piloted by Captain Lawson, A.F.C., in view of a crowd of thousands of spectators. This was the second attempt. In the first attempt, when she had climbed out of the aircraft at a height of 1,500 feet and while standing on the wing just about to jump, the aircraft developed engine trouble and began to drop rapidly from the sky. She hung on precariously while the plane made an emergency landing in a football ground. This historic jump was made in April 1926, at Hereford, England. In 1926, she was also first in a competition in Paris taking apart and re-assembling a light aeroplane.

WOMAN DROPS 1,500 FEET

Mrs. Eliott Lynn, the aviator, suspended from a parachute, making a 1,500 feet descent from an aeroplane at Hereford.

Saturday April 3rd 1926

JUMP FROM 'PLANE

Mrs. Eliott Lynn Makes Record as Parachutist

Successful at her second attempt, Mrs. Eliott Lynn, at Hereford on Saturday, achieved fame as the first woman to make a parachute descent from an aeroplane.

Jumping from an aeroplane piloted by Captain Lawson, A.F.C., Mrs. Eliott Lynn landed safely in a ploughed field in full view of thousands of spectators.

Describing the adventure afterwards, she said: "The sensation of landing by parachute was about the same as a jump from a six-foot wall. I could have wished, however, that the ploughed field had been a little bit softer."

Her first essay on the previous day almost ended in disaster. When the aeroplane had reached a height of 1,500 feet, she climbed out on to the wings, but just as she was about to jump off, the machine, developing engine trouble, began to drop rapidly.

She clung on precariously, and the machine skirted a hedge by a few inches and landed on a football ground where a match was in progress.

Mrs. Eliott Lynn only started flying in August last.

Mrs. Eliott Lynn

Mrs. Elliott-Lynn, making a record 1,500 feet descent from aeroplane at Hereford

In 1927, with Lady Bailey as her passenger, Lady Heath set a world altitude record. The aviation publication of the day, 'Flight Magazine', had no hesitation in emphasising the magnitude of this achievement: "It is still a common practice for women, as aviators, to be rather disdained. Mrs. Elliott-Lynn has perhaps done more for her sex than any other woman.

May 1927 - Elliott-Lynn sets world altitude record

In 1927, with Lady Bailey as her passenger, Lady Heath set a world altitude record. The aviation publication of the day, 'Flight Magazine', had no hesitation in emphasising the magnitude of this achievement: "It is still a common practice for women, as aviators, to be rather disdained. Mrs. Elliott-Lynn has perhaps done more for her sex than any other woman."

This unqualified praise from an established aviation magazine of the day confirms this writer's opinion that she did more than any other woman in promoting women's rights by participating in all aspects of aviation and other key areas, such as sport, than any other woman.

In 1928, Elliott-Lynn established the world altitude record for light seaplanes. This record was set in a Short Mussel, a braced low-wing monoplane which first flew in 1926, which was fitted with a Cirrus 11 engine at the time. The height reached on the occasion of this record was 13,000 ft. It is believed that this record still stands for light seaplanes. A few months later in October 1928, Elliott-Lynn attempted to beat the new record established by Captain de Havilland in his personal machine, Gypsy Moth, G-AAAA, without success.

July 1927 - Flight of the aerodromes

Nobody had done it before and nobody has done it since - a tour of the aerodromes in a day. Elliott-Lynn made a 13 and a half hour long tour of 79 British aerodromes, covering a distance of 1,300 miles in one day, stopping only for re-fuelling. For this remarkable flight, Elliott-Lynn set off alone before dawn on July 19th from Woodford Aerodrome. She made a complete tour of all the aerodromes and landing grounds in England, south of Manchester, after which she flew to Newcastle. The final landing of her Avian G-EBRS was at 9.27p.m. The flying distance of 1,300 miles would have been remarkable in itself for a machine such as the Avro Avian, even if it was completed in a single flight with just one landing. This flight with repeated take-offs and landings at so many different aerodromes, each with its own particular difficulties, makes this a most notable achievement.

Elliott-Lynn wins the Grosvenor Cup

On July 30th, 1927, Mrs. S. C. Elliott-Lynn, won the Grosvenor Cup, which was held at Nottingham (Hucknall). The length of the race was 15 miles and the race consisted of three heats and a final. Elliott-Lynn piloted a D.H. Moth prototype (60 h.p. Cirrus I). Her speed was 88 and a half m.p.h. This was an historic event in that it was the first time that an open race had been won by a woman in the British Isles.

June - September 1927

During the months of June to September, Mrs. Elliott-Lynn, had a very busy schedule. She won several open air races, lectured to audiences on the subject of aviation at various venues, including Ireland, where she spoke to an audience of some 8,000 people, and in Scotland, where she enthralled an even larger audience in Aberdeen. She also toured central Europe in her new Avro Avian.

Sophie Pierce at the height of her flying fame

"And to the woman were given

Two wings of a great Eagle

That she might fly Into the wilderness"

Revelation: XII. 14.

October 1927 - Mrs. Elliott-Lynn marries Sir James Heath

On October 12th, 1927, Mrs. Elliott-Lynn married Sir James Heath. Her previous husband had died some years earlier. Her new title was Lady Heath.

The greatest solo pioneering flight by an Irish person - Cape Town to London

The greatest solo pioneering flight by an Irish person was the epic flight by Lady Heath from Cape Town to London. In completing this flight, she pioneered not only the first ever solo flight from Cape Town to London, but also the first flight from Cape Town to Cairo, Egypt.

The magnitude of this personal achievement cannot be over emphasised. Here was an individual, without the kind of back-up facilities that accompanied many of the pioneering flights, setting out with little more than her own resourcefulness and the support of her husband, Sir James Heath. The world at large paid little attention to this momentous flight. Lady Heath was always an individual, never part of the establishment. Much of the continent of Africa had not as yet been explored. She had been promised a set of maps for her journey by Flight Lieutenant R. Bentley, who had made the first flight from London to Cape Town. For whatever reason, Lady Heath never got the maps which had been promised. Instead, she had to rely on small-scale route maps and tracings from pages torn-out of an atlas.

Although Lady Heath sent messages and telegrams ahead of her, her flight did not get the amount of publicity it deserved. This was partly due to the inadequacy of the postal services on the African continent which, according to Lady Heath, "constituted the main danger of the trip".

November 1927 - Lady Heath sets out by ship for Cape Town, South Africa

In November 1927, the newly married couple, Sir James and Lady Heath, set out by ship for Cape Town, South Africa, with one of her four aircraft, a new Avro Avian Mark III G-EBUG, 80h.p., Cirrus engine, neatly packed in a crate. This was the journey out to set up her epic flight back to London from Cape Town. No Irish pilot had ever pioneered such a solo flight before or since.

Lady Heath flew the eastern route. Her epic flight began in Cape Town, South Africa on February 12th and ended at Croydon, London, on May 17th, 1928. She set off from Pretoria on February 17th, 1928. She was accompanied on the start of her journey, as far as Warmbaths, which is situated 100 miles approximately north of Johannesburg, by Sir Pierre van Reneveld, a pioneering African pilot. After this she was on her own.

Lady Bailey, friend of Lady Heath, who flew the first solo flight by a woman from London to Cape Town at exactly the same time that Lady Heath flew in the opposite direction

Lady Bailey

In 1928, Lady Bailey, a friend of Lady Heath, flew the first solo flight from London to Cape Town at exactly the same time as Lady Heath flew in the opposite direction.

On her approach towards Bulawayo, while flying over the Matopos Hills having flown six hours from Pretoria along the Limpopo River, Lady Heath was struck by a violent bout of severe sunstroke. The temperature in the cockpit of her Avro Avian was more than 120 degrees fahrenheit.

Her epic journey was fraught with every kind of hazard. She had to fly over deserts, vast unchartered territories, with poor quality maps and the constant danger of being shot down when flying over hostile lands. She was forced for some sections of the journey, reluctantly, to accept an escort because of the very real dangers. While in Nairobi, she was robbed

Only a pilot of the highest calibre and resilience could have managed to make a successful landing in such hazardous terrain with such an attack of severe sunstroke. Lady Heath achieved it without injury and only minor damage to her aircraft. There she lay, unconscious for four hours, until she was rescued. She recovered in a couple of days and continued on her journey from Bulawayo to Livingstone.

Her epic journey was fraught with every kind of hazard. She had to fly over deserts, vast unchartered territories, with poor quality maps and the constant danger of being shot down when flying over hostile lands. She was forced for some sections of the journey, reluctantly, to accept an escort because of the very real dangers. While in Nairobi, she was robbed.

She was forbidden to cross the troubled areas of the Sudan unaccompanied. Lieutenant Bentley, who was also flying the route with his bride on their honeymoon, provided the necessary escort to get over this problem. He was flying a Moth which had been presented to him for the first ever solo flight from London to Cape Town. The Johannesburg 'Star' had made the presentation. The Bentleys parted company with Lady Heath at Khartoum. From Khartoum, she flew on to Wadi Halfa.

The final stage of her flight to Cairo, i.e. Wadi Halfa to Cairo, was the longest (700 miles) and the Nile acted as her compass. When she arrived at the Cairo Aerodrome of Heliopolis, she had completed a distance of 5,132 miles in a time of 72 flying hours.

"I intended staying in Cairo some little time. So, after having sent off a few cables to Messrs. A. V. Roe and Company, the makers of my little machine, to the Aircraft Disposal Company, the makers of the Cirrus engine and so on, I went to bed and slept for 15 hours."

Among others, Lady Heath sent the following cables:

To

Aircraft Disposal Company Ltd.-

"During 70 hours' touring South Africa and first light aeroplane flight Cape to Cairo time-honoured route the magnificent Cirrus in my Avian never missed a beat or dropped a revolution although in Southern Rhodesia experienced tropical deluges and in Sudan thermometer showed 120 Fahrenheit

Heath

The magnificent Cirrus in my Avian never missed a beat or dropped a revolution although in Southern Rhodesia experienced tropical deluges and in Sudan thermometer showed 120 Fahrenheit

To

the Robinhood Engineering Works Ltd. (K.L.G. Plugs)-

"During tour South Africa and flight first light aeroplane my Avian time-honoured route Cape Cairo have never found it necessary to change one of your plugs even in gruelling heat Southern Sudan when thermometer registered 120 Fahrenheit tested here and all found perfect congratulations on your product

Heath

Along the North African coast, she was shot at. A bullet hole was found in one of the wings of her Avro Avian when she made her landing at Tunis

Reference to Lady Heath's log shows that once she had finished touring and giving joyrides, her actual flying days in easy stages from Pretoria to Cairo (5,132 miles via Nairobi), numbered 16, while her actual flying hours for these 5,132 miles numbered 72 hours, five minutes.

Dates	Stages	Mileages	Times Hrs. Mins.
Feb. 25	Pretoria-Bulawayo	400	7.00
Feb. 28	Bulawayo-Livingstone	215	3.10
March 1	Livingstone-Broken Hill	350	5.20
March 4	Broken Hill-N'dola	140	2.25
March 5	N'dola-Abercorn	370	5.35
March 7	Abercorn-Tabora	300	4.45
March 8	Tabora-Mwanza	70	2.30
March 14	Mwanza-Nairobi	320	4.30
March 22	Nairobi-Kisumu-Jinja	360	5.30
March 27	Jinja-Nanasajali and return	100	1.00
March 28	Jinja-Mongalla	350	4.30
March 30	Mongalla-Malakal-Kosti	700	6.35
March 31	Kosti-Khartoum	185	2.30
April 2	Khartoum-Atbara	196	2.15
April 3	Atbara-Wadi Halfa	376	5.30
April 4	Wadi Halfa-Cairo	700	9.00
		5,132 miles	72 hrs. 05mins

'Woman and Flying' by Lady Heath and Stella Wolfe Murray
John Long Ltd. London P. 170-171

When she arrived in Cairo, Lady Heath was prevented from crossing the Mediterranean without an escort because the next stop, Malta, was difficult to find. Lady Heath sent cable to Mussolini requesting assistance. He replied by return: "Have put a seaplane at your disposal." But Lady Heath waited in vain for the seaplane which came down with engine trouble.

Along the North African coast, she was shot at. A bullet hole was found in one of the wings of her Avro Avian when she made her landing at Tunis. Lady Heath was delayed at Sollum Aerodrome, Tunis, due to damage to the fuselage of her Avian caused by the very stony landing strip which she had to negotiate. On May 6th, she made the Mediterranean crossing from Tunis to Naples and was lucky again to have an escort, Flight Lieutenant R. Bentley.

Lady Heath arrives in London at the end of her flight from Cape Town to Croydon, via Cairo, May 17th, 1928. Quadrant Picture Library, Sutton, England

Lady Heath shortly after her landing at Croydon at the end of her flight across the continent of Africa

Her preparation was impeccable. She writes: "I had visited Africa each winter and had made a point of going each time to a different area of the route and studying ground conditions, climatic conditions and getting all the information I could about the actual flying, petrol supplies and so on."

She received the heroine's welcome which she had earned from her unrivalled accomplishments. Having successfully conquered the skies of a hostile African continent alone and the legion of perils associated therewith, Lady Heath had fired the imagination and enthusiasm of the world and paved the way for other great pioneering exploits. Her personal appearance was all important for Lady Heath and she always emerged from her aircraft looking her best, often wearing evening dress, fur coat and high heel shoes, having changed out of her pilot's gear in mid-air. Her landing in Croydon was no exception.

In her book, 'Woman and Flying', Lady Heath said: "It had always been in my mind that I would some day fly over the length of Africa, to me the most fascinating continent of the whole world, for I have lived in Kenya and in Tanganyika and love their wild, vast spaces." Her preparation was impeccable. She writes: "I had visited Africa each winter and had made a point of going each time to a different area of the route and studying ground conditions, climatic conditions and getting all the information I could about the actual flying, petrol supplies and so on. I came to the conclusion that the flight would do more good and be more interesting if I reversed the usual order of things and did my organisation from South Africa. Thus on November 18th, 1927, I sailed with my husband to Capetown with my Avro Avian in a crate, where she was assembled by Col. Henderson of the Henderson Flying School, Brooklands, who was joy riding out there. My ambition was not to be the first woman flying over any area, but to bring my machine safely back to England and prove that the organisation of such a flight could be made as well in the colonies as in England. I attempted no record-breaking flight and intended to do it in easy stages."

It is difficult to overstress the importance of this achievement by Lady Heath. The degree of difficulty is best described by Sir Alan Cobham who flew the same route, although not solo: "To start with, one had no meteorological reports. They could not even telephone up ahead to find out what it was like. So you were flying into the unknown as far as weather was concerned. You might meet low cloud, you might meet a snow storm, you might meet a dust storm but you never knew what was ahead of you." And describing his flight over Africa, Sir Alan Cobham went on to say: "Oh that was a nightmare of the worst kind. One had to conduct a sort of correspondence course on the subject of aviation. For instance, in going to the Cape I wrote to everyone in Africa, I should think. You had to describe what an aeroplane was like. You had to tell exactly how much land you wanted cleared. Tell him that he must run his own car over it at 30 miles an hour. If he did not wreck it, then I could manage it and so on and so forth. I wanted about 800 yards at least in Africa because of the high altitudes, the rarefied atmosphere you see. Every landing was an adventure."

Lady Heath, promoter of aviation

Wherever Lady Heath went she always took the opportunity to promote aviation by the setting up or financing of flying clubs, by the setting up of flying scholarships, by lecturing herself or by organising lectures or instruction. Even when she was about to embark on her flight from Cape Town to London, she took time to help out the clubs. She raised £1,200 while in Africa which went towards the promotion of South African flying clubs and the setting up of flying scholarships in England.

Women's rights

The international standards for licensing was set up in 1919 and the British legislation, which covered these rules, was the Air Navigation Act 1920. The law provided for two different licences. Firstly, there was the P.P.L. or Private Pilot's Licence, also called the 'A' licence, which enabled the holder to fly for pleasure, carrying passengers and goods, but not to charge for the service. The second kind of licence enabled the holder to fly for reward or hire, thus giving professional status. This was called the 'B' licence or commercial qualification.

The International Commission for Air Navigation, the governing body with authority to fix standards, met in 1924 and re-stated the ban excluding women from holding a commercial licence.

Lady Heath, then Mrs Elliott-Lynn, wrote to the International Commission for Air Navigation, making her case for qualification. Her credentials were formidable indeed and could not be disregarded lightly. In her university degree, she had majored in Physiology.

Lady Heath - pilot with the Royal Dutch Air Line

Lady Heath was appointed second pilot with the Royal Dutch Air Line and operated between Amsterdam and London and flew all its expanding European routes.

Lady Heath - the engineer

Lady Heath qualified as an engineer. She was the only woman pilot at the time to have such a qualification. The skills of the engineer served her handsomely on her flight from Cape Town to London. She did not arrive in London by chance but as a result of meticulously servicing her aircraft. When she arrived in Cairo, she explained her routine maintenance of her Avro Avian: "I did the tappet clearances every day, no matter how short the flight was and cleaned the petrol and oil filters. Only once did I fly in the heat of the day and I never flew at less than 7,000 ft. to get the cool air. I ran my engine at 1,700 rpm throughout and did one to three hours routine work daily."

Lady Heath was the only woman who had qualified as a ground engineer at the time. She obtained this qualification in America. Up to this time, women were not regarded as being eligible for this aspect of the aviation business.

Near fatal accident (National Air Races, Cleveland, Ohio, 1929)

August 1929, while on a lecture tour of the United States, Lady Heath entered the National Air Races at Cleveland, Ohio and crashed through a factory roof at a speed of more than 100 miles per hour. She was at death's door and had to have silver plates inserted in her skull. She had suffered brain damage. While in the United States, Lady Heath had stayed at 112 Central Park South. She married G.A.R. Williams in November 1931 and visited Mexico City a month later, where they were received by President Rubio, who placed a military plane at their disposal.

Sophie Pierce in Cork 1933 with her husband Jack Williams and a greyhound presented to her by Jim Clarke, the famous Ballybunion greyhound breeder. Examiner photo.

Lady Heath chose Ireland as the place to spend the remaining years of her aviation career, first at Baldonnel Aerodrome, with the Irish Aero Club. She then moved to Kildonan Finglas, and eventually set up her own aircraft company, Dublin Air Ferries. She also set up several flying clubs, the first of which was the National Irish Junior Aviation Club. From the humble beginnings of the National Irish Junior Aviation Club, the present day governing body, namely The Aviation Council can be directly traced. Following its inaugural meeting at the beginning of May 1933, the first ordinary meeting of the National Irish Junior Aviation Club was held on May 22nd, 1933 at Kildonan Aerodrome. It was modelled on similar organisations which existed in the United States of America. The Junior Club was fostered by Iona National Airways Ltd.

Kildonan was, at the time, the home of Iona National Airways Ltd. and Flying School. The club was the first of its kind in these Islands, with an entry fee of one shilling a year. It started with a membership of 14, including one girl, Miss Olive Edmonds.

The first officers of the club were as follows:

President, Lady Heath; vice-president, Mr. George Weston; secretary, Mr. Denville Bowyer; treasurer, Mr. Jas. Murphy. Captain J. Young, manager Iona National Airways Ltd., was an honourary member. Juvenile members were allowed into the aerodrome free of charge on Saturdays and Sundays. They received free instruction on technical matters, aircraft, engines, parachuting and the theory and rules of flight. Each member had a distinctive pinbadge. Membership of the junior club reached 100 within a very short time. In addition to the officers of the junior club, the following committee members were elected: Messrs. T. Cullen, J. Flanagan, Vincent Eddy, R. Doggett and Owen Quinn.

The National Irish Junior Aviation Club was a unique development in the fostering of flying among young people. It held lectures in the old Moira Hotel at Trinity Street. Lady Heath was the founder and main spirit behind its activities. This club did more than anything else to make young people airminded, It set the foundation for heightened interest in flying in general and in the training of young pilots. Barriers of accessibility to the flying experience were broken down for the first time in the Irish Free State. Finglas had been established in 1931 by Hugh Cahill as Ireland's first civil aerodrome and it was at Kildonan that the National Irish Junior Aviation Club under the expert guidance of Lady Heath flourished.

Although founded in May 1933 and making steady progress during the next few years, the Junior Aviation Club made huge strides in 1937, due not only to the hard work of the committee, but also due to the great interest shown in its welfare by many others, particularly the Right Honourable the Lord Mayor of Dublin, Alfie Byrne; Captain St. John Kearney, Imperial Airways Ltd.; The Irish Aero Club; Mr. P. A. Sheehan, B. L.; Dr. Havelock Charles; and Mr. W. Weldon. Its great success was copper-fastened when Colonel Charles F. Russell accepted the presidency of the club.

NATIONAL IRISH JUNIOR AVIATION CLUB
KILDONAN AERODROME
FINGLAS, CO. DUBLIN

President:
LADY HEATH, A.R.C.Sc.I., F.R.G.S.

Hon. Member:
CAPT. T. YOUNG

First Vice-President:
GEORGE WESTON, ESQ.

Secretary:
DENVILLE BOWYER
5 Fitzroy Avenue, Drumcondra
Dublin

Girls' Section:
MISS EDMONDS
54 Ellesmere Avenue
Dublin

Treasurer:
JAMES MURPHY
96 St. Ignatius Road, Drumcondra
Dublin

Vice-Presidents:
SIR ALAN COBHAM
MRS. AMY JOHNSON-MOLLISON
JAMES MOLLISON, ESQ.
CAPT. KÖHL
CAPT. SAUL
ERIC ARMSTRONG, ESQ.
CAPT. HOSIE
MRS. CODY
MICHAEL DOYLE, ESQ., B.Sc.
COL. C. RUSSELL

What an array of big names in aviation are included here in this official headed paper of The National Irish Junior Club. Not surprisingly the junior club had a girl's section. The club's vice-president was George Weston without whose photographs the record of Kildonan would be very incomplete.

A session of the Junior Aviation Club at Kildonan. Lady Heath conducts classes assisted by Mr. Gerorge Weston

Juvenile aviators: Lady Heath and Dr. Myles Keogh, Deputy Lord Mayor, with members of the Irish National (Junior) Aviation Club at the Mansion House. Evening Mail photo

The following shows the different people who were associated with the development of the National Irish Junior Aviation Club from its infancy, through its various changes of name and personages, together with the logos and letterings that were used by the various titles which it assumed.

J. C. Doyle.

NATIONAL IRISH JUNIOR AVIATION CLUB.

SEASON 1936-1937.

IRISH JUNIOR AVIATION CLUB.

National Irish Aviation Club membership card

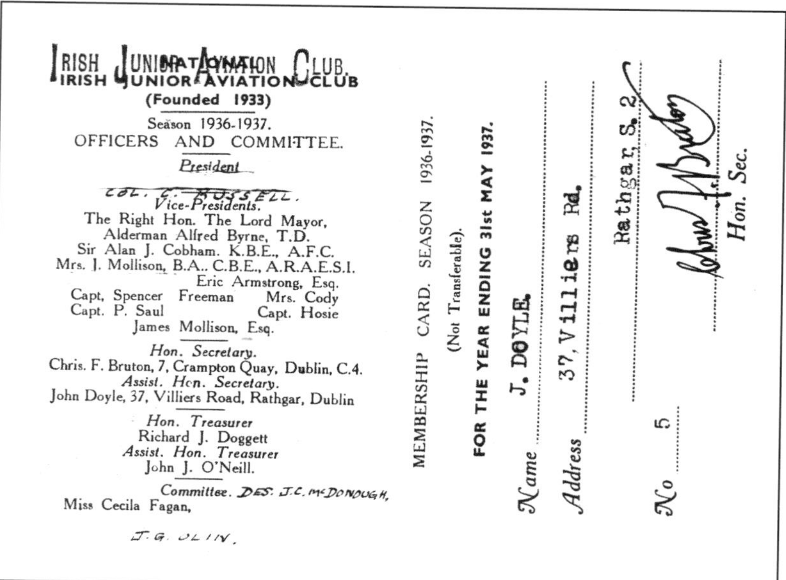

IRISH JUNIOR AVIATION CLUB
(Founded 1933)
Season 1936-1937.
OFFICERS AND COMMITTEE.

President
COL. C. RUSSELL.

Vice-Presidents.
The Right Hon. The Lord Mayor,
Alderman Alfred Byrne, T.D.
Sir Alan J. Cobham. K.B.E., A.F.C.
Mrs. J. Mollison, B.A., C.B.E., A.R.A.E.S.I.
Eric Armstrong, Esq.
Capt. Spencer Freeman Mrs. Cody
Capt. P. Saul Capt. Hosie
James Mollison, Esq.

Hon. Secretary.
Chris. F. Bruton, 7, Crampton Quay, Dublin, C.4.
Assist. Hon. Secretary.
John Doyle, 37, Villiers Road, Rathgar, Dublin

Hon. Treasurer
Richard J. Doggett
Assist. Hon. Treasurer
John J. O'Neill.

Committee. DES. J.C. McDONOUGH,
Miss Cecila Fagan,
J. G. OLIN.

MEMBERSHIP CARD. SEASON 1936-1937.
(Not Transferable).
FOR THE YEAR ENDING 31st MAY 1937.

Name J. DOYLE
Address 37, Villiers Rd. Rathgar, S. 2
No 5

Hon. Sec.

Irish Junior Aviation Club official badge

PRESIDENT:
MARY LADY HEATH, A.R.C.Sc.I., F.R.G.S.
3 UPPER FITZWILLIAM STREET.
DUBLIN

VICE-PRESIDENTS:
THE RT. HON. THE LORD MAYOR,
ALDERMAN ALFRED BYRNE, T.D.
MICHAEL A. DOYLE, ESQ., B.SC. (ENG.), A.F.R.AE.S.
COL. C. RUSSELL
ERIC ARMSTRONG, ESQ.
CAPT. SPENCER FREEMAN
MRS. CODY
MRS. MOLLISON, B.A., C.B.E., A.R.AE.S.I.
JAMES MOLLISON, ESQ.
CAPT. SAUL
CAPT. HOSIE
SIR ALAN J. COBHAM, K.B.E., A.F.C.

National Irish Junior Aviation Club
(AFFILIATED TO IRISH GLIDING ASSOCIATION)

SECRETARY:
CHRIS. BRUTON
7 CRAMPTON QUAY
DUBLIN

TREASURER:
R. J. DOGGETT
28 SMITHFIELD
DUBLIN

Hon Sec.

7th July 1936

7th July 1936

President:
COLONEL CHARLES F. RUSSELL.
Vice-Presidents:
THE RT. HON. THE LORD MAYOR
ALDERMAN ALFRED BYRNE, T.D.
MICHAEL A. DOYLE, ESQ., B.SC., (ENG.) A.F.R.AE.S.
ERIC ARMSTRONG, ESQ.
CAPT. SPENCER FREEMAN.
MRS. MOLLISON, B.A., C.B.E., A.R.AE.S.I.
JAMES MOLLISON, ESQ.
CAPT. SAUL.
SIR ALAN J. COBHAM, K.B.E., A.F.C.

Irish Junior Aviation Club
(FORMERLY NATIONAL IRISH JUNIOR AVIATION CLUB)
AFFILIATED TO THE IRISH AERO CLUB

Honorary Secretary:
CHRIS. F. BRUTON
7 CRAMPTON QUAY
DUBLIN

Honorary Treasurer:
JOHN J. O'NEILL
226 GRIFFITH AVENUE
WHITEHALL, DUBLIN

Hon Secretary.
2th July 1937

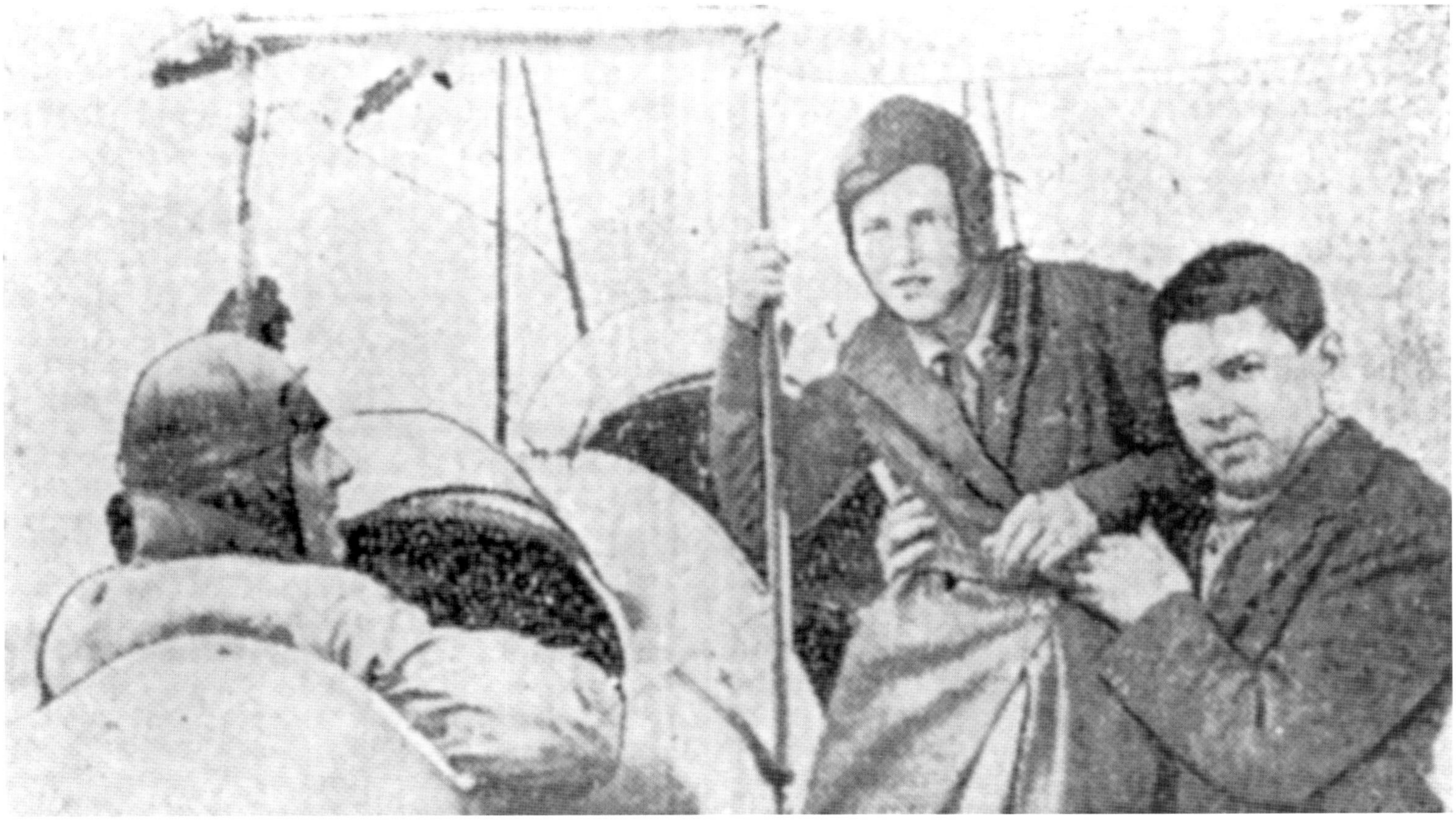

A young lady being assisted into an aircraft for one of the flights which were a feature of the 'Blue Lagoon' pageant held at Dollymount, Dublin on September 23rd, 1931. The pageant was organised by Iona National Airways Ltd. Irish Independent 24.9.31

Just landed : The Master of Sempill's Puss Moth plane arriving at Kildonan Aerodrome, Finglas, Co. Dublin. Photo: Irish Independent

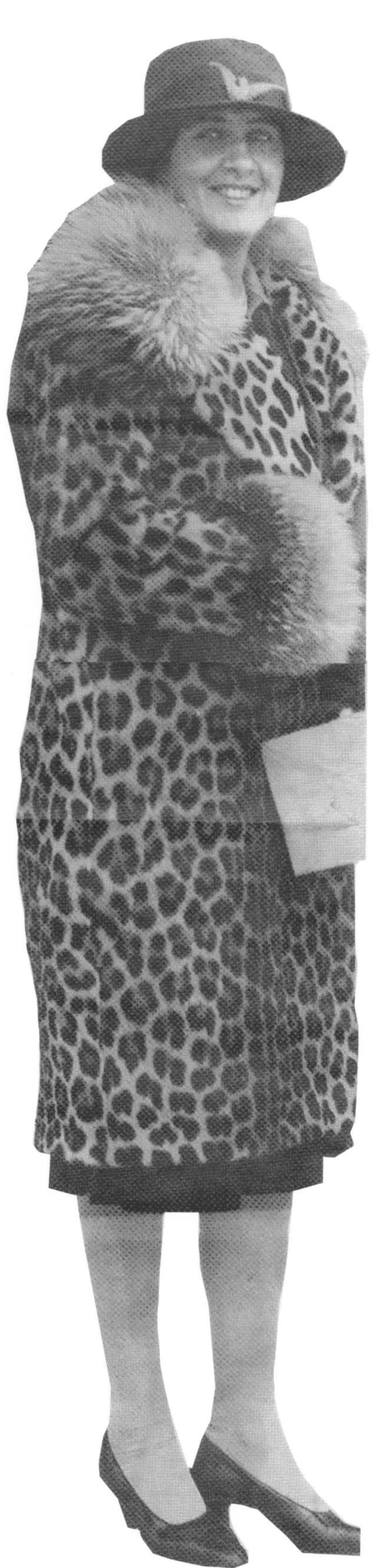

Forgotten Heroine - Lady Mary Heath

By Siobhán Mulcahy

It is 75 years since a Limerick born woman, Sophie Pierce - who later became known as Lady Mary Heath - completed the first solo flight from Cape town to London via Cairo. She also broke the women's seaplane altitude record and light aircraft altitude record, setting a new standard for Amelia Earhart. In the early 1920s, she held the women's world record for high jumping and the British javelin record. Yet she is hardly given a mention in any of the athletics or aviation record books. And apart from a stamp issued four years ago as one of a series in honor of pioneers of Irish aviation, she has never been properly recognized in her country of birth. Ironically, her friend and great rival, Amelia Earhart, features in every textbook on aviation.

1896 - 1939

World Record Breaking Athlete and Aviator

Lady Mary Heath was born on November 10th, 1896 at Knockaderry House, near Newcastle west, Co. Limerick. Her birth name was Sophie Pierce. After attending boarding school in Dublin, she went to Britain to become a dispatch rider shortly after the outbreak of World War 1. The dispatch outfit was attached to the Royal Flying Corps and this is when she first became interested in becoming a pilot. There were no female pilots in Britain at the time.

She worked for a time at Aberdeen University where she developed a passion for athletics, both in competition and in the theory of the sport.

At Aberdeen, she helped to found the British Women's Amateur Athletic Association in 1922, becoming its vice-president. Within a year, she had broken the world high jumping record and held the record for the British women's javelin. She had become a remarkable all-round athlete.

She wrote the well-received reference book, Athletics for Women and Girls, which remained the standard coaching manual in British athletics for several decades. The book was based on papers she presented to the International Olympic Committee in 1925, and the preface is a talk she gave that was also broadcast by the BBC on April 9, 1925.

Sophie was selected as a British representative for meetings of the International Olympic Council (IOC), and was instrumental in the decision to allow women to compete in the Olympic games.

In 1925, with her best years as an athlete behind her, Sophie joined the London Light Aero plane Club. She was its first female member and made her maiden flight in August the same year. She qualified for a private, or 'A' license, but the International Commission for Air Navigation had revoked women's rights to earn a commercial, or B license, in 1924.

Sophie fought the ban and the commission agreed that if she attended flight school and passed the test, she would be granted a commercial license. She succeeded in passing the test, and the commission was forced to rescind its ban on women commercial pilots in 1926.

Sophie therefore became the first woman living in Britain to hold a commercial pilot's license. Immediately, she set up a world altitude record for light planes at over 17,000 feet, and in the same year, she was the first woman in Britain to make a parachute jump. As a professional pilot, she began to take part in flying demonstrations and races in Ireland, Britain and the Continent.

At about the same time, Amelia Earhart had become interested in flying in the US, and the two would compete for flying honors, though mainly on different sides of the Atlantic.

Between February and May 1928, aged 31 years, she completed the first solo flight from Cape Town to London via Cairo. In Cairo the Egyptian crowd had watched in wonder as the tiny, balsawood and canvas Avro Avian came in low over the Cairo rooftops-a tiny far-off dot in the vastness of the empty. Azure sky. The little biplane, its 100hp Armstrong Siddley engine purring softly in the hush of the African dawn, touched down with aplomb on the rutted, packed earth runway.

She also broke the women's seaplane and light aircraft altitude record, setting a new standard for Amelia Earhart, at 23,000 feet. Though Amelia Earhart had become the first woman to cross the Atlantic in 1928, she had not piloted the plane. It would be four years before Lady Mary's rival became the first woman to cross the Atlantic.

Earhart had first become interested in Avro Avian Airplanes in 1928 after her goodwill flight across the Atlantic Ocean to England. While in England, and in great demand by members of the media, she slipped away quietly to meet her rival and fellow aviatrix of whom she had heard so much, Lady Mary Heath. During their meeting, the Irishwoman generously allowed Amelia Earhart to take her first solo test flight in her Avian.

Earhart immediately fell in love with the plane. Lady Mary, who was nearly always strapped for cash, accepted Earhart's offer to buy it. The American shipped it back to the United States, and later that same year, she flew the small, open cockpit biplane across America. Today, this Avro Avian is the only flying Avian in North America. It still carries Amelia Earhart's official registration number, 7083, and Lady Mary's British registration, G-EBUG.

Shortly after her solo record-breaking flight in Africa, Lady Mary went on publicity tours in England and the United States where President Calvin Coolidge received her.

Now in competition with Amelia Earhart on the world stage, she did not always receive the accolades she had once enjoyed. In fact, her rival was now overshadowing her.

She took a job as second pilot to the fledgling KLM Airlines in Amsterdam, and flew on all their European routes. By taking this job, she became the first female commercial pilot in Europe.

In 1929 she again embarked on a long tour of the USA, giving flying demonstrations and lectures. In order to raise funds to continue flying, she co-authored a book called 'Woman and Flying' with Stella

Wolf Murray. By this time, Sophie was known in the US as the Lady-Queen because her second husband had been a 'Lord'. The Jacksonville Journal reported her arrival in the town on January 4th 1929. ®Woman and Flying® by Lady Heath and Stella Wolf Murray, 1929

Her tiny De Havilland Moth appeared as a dot in the far-off sky. Onlookers gaped from the airfield. Perfectly and mundanely, the Moth met the grass. The Queen alighted every inch the British Olympian who had flown the length of darkest Africa.

Lady Mary Heath was tall and imposing, fresh and ruddy and brisk. She was a flyer such as the locals had never seen. She had astonished the world the year before by flying an Avro Avian monoplane from the Cape of Good Hope to Cairo, an amazing jaunt hard on the heels of Charles Lindbergh's solo flight across the Atlantic.

Next day, the story concluded: "in a lonely sky, the Lady-Queen and her Moth again became dots in the distance and were gone."

Lady Mary was seriously injured in August 1929 in a plane crash in Cleveland, Ohio. She returned to Ireland in 1931.

In May 1939, Lady Mary Heath died from injuries received from a fall on a public bus. She was 43 years of age. Her world records were already forgotten and the American, Amelia Earhart, had overtaken her achievements as an aviator.

Lady Heath's Avro Avian G-EBUG

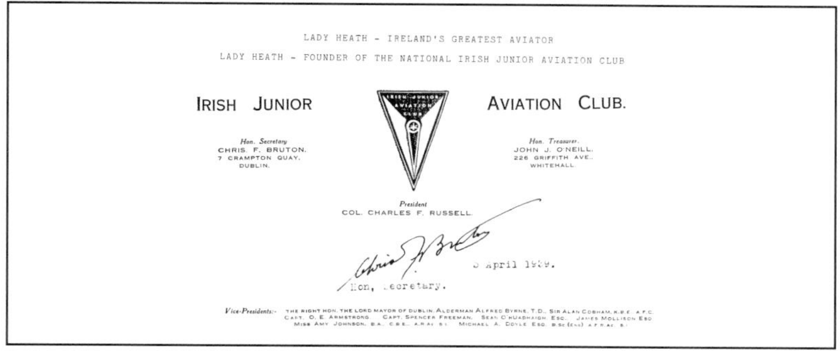

LADY HEATH - IRELAND'S GREATEST AVIATOR

LADY HEATH - FOUNDER OF THE NATIONAL IRISH JUNIOR AVIATION CLUB

IRISH JUNIOR AVIATION CLUB.

Hon. Secretary
CHRIS. F. BRUTON.
7 CRAMPTON QUAY.
DUBLIN.

Hon. Treasurer.
JOHN J. O'NEILL.
226 GRIFFITH AVE.
WHITEHALL.

President
COL. CHARLES F. RUSSELL.

3 April 1939.

Hon. Secretary.

Vice-Presidents:- THE RIGHT HON. THE LORD MAYOR OF DUBLIN. ALDERMAN ALFRED BYRNE, T.D., SIR ALAN COBHAM, K.B.E., A.F.C. CAPT. O. E. ARMSTRONG. CAPT. SPENCER FREEMAN. SEAN O'HUADHAIGH, ESQ. JAMES MOLLISON ESQ. MISS AMY JOHNSON, B.A., C.B.E., A.R.Ae.S.I. MICHAEL A. DOYLE ESQ. B.Sc.(Eng.) A.F.R.Ae.S.I.

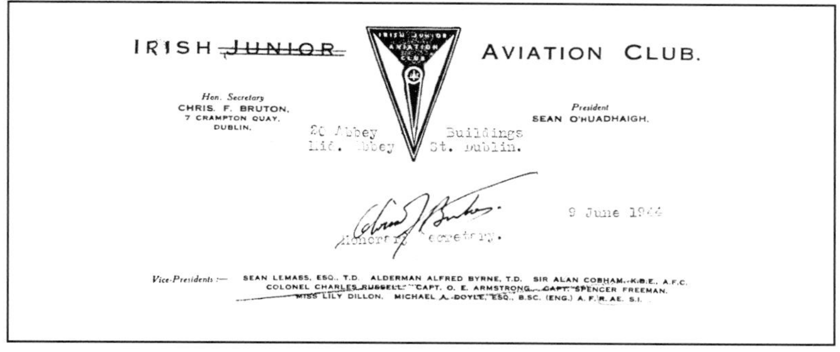

IRISH ~~JUNIOR~~ AVIATION CLUB.

Hon. Secretary
CHRIS. F. BRUTON.
7 CRAMPTON QUAY.
DUBLIN.

President
SEAN O'HUADHAIGH.

20 Abbey Buildings
Mid. Abbey St. Dublin.

9 June 1944

Honorary Secretary.

Vice-Presidents:— SEAN LEMASS, ESQ., T.D. ALDERMAN ALFRED BYRNE, T.D. SIR ALAN COBHAM, K.B.E., A.F.C. COLONEL CHARLES RUSSELL. CAPT. O. E. ARMSTRONG. CAPT. SPENCER FREEMAN. MISS LILY DILLON. MICHAEL A. DOYLE, ESQ., B.SC. (ENG.) A.F.R.AE.S.I.

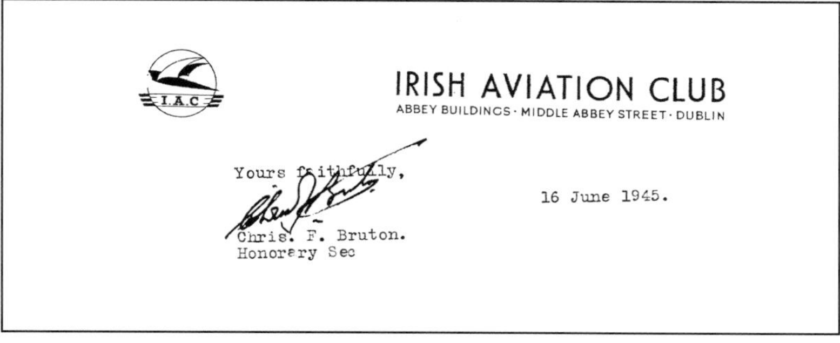

IRISH AVIATION CLUB
ABBEY BUILDINGS · MIDDLE ABBEY STREET · DUBLIN

Yours faithfully,

16 June 1945.

Chris. F. Bruton.
Honorary Sec

CITY OF DUBLIN AERO CLUB
formerly

IRISH AVIATION CLUB
ABBEY BUILDINGS · MIDDLE ABBEY STREET · DUBLIN

Yours faithfully,

27th June 1946

JOHN CARROLL
Hon. Secretary

CITY OF DUBLIN AERO CLUB.

Abbey Buildings,
Middle Abbey Street,
Dublin,
29th July 1947

Honorary Secretary

The above shows the progression whereby the National Irish Junior Aviation Club set up by Lady Heath developed into the City of Dublin Aero Club

Photographic portrait of Lady Heath, sitting in chair

Newspaper clipping, Irish Press, Tuesday 16th July, 1940

ESDAY, JULY 16, 1940. Irish Press News 7

cked
les

Aviation Club Loses 5 Members

Six Dead In Road Crash

car (top picture) and (below) a front view of the badly-damaged 'bus.

IT was learned yesterday that five of the six persons killed in the head-on collision between a private car and a G.N.R. 'bus carrying soldiers, at Rowans, three miles from Balbriggan, Co. Dublin, late on Sunday night, were members of the Irish Junior Aviation Club.

They were returning from a "Scavenger Hunt" at Bettystown. organised by the Club.

A member of the Club told an IRISH PRESS reporter yesterday: "They were all keen, enthusiastic members, and will be a great loss."

The 'bus conductor and 21 of the soldiers, who had been on week-end leave in Dublin, and were being conveyed to Gormanstown, were injured and taken to hospital. Ten of the soldiers were afterwards discharged.

The Dead

The victims of the crash, which occurred during a fog, were:

Thomas J. Mohan, aged 20, of 33 King's Inn Street, Dublin. He was employed as a book-keeper in the Hammond Lane Foundry;

Michael Branagan, 139 Rathgar Rd., son of Mr. Michael Branagan, proprietor of the Powell Press, Parliament Street, Dublin;

John Maher (22), of 36 South Circular Road, an employee of Messrs. A. Guinness, Son & Co., Ltd.;

John Warren (23), of Lansdowne, Temple Gardens, Rathmines, only son of Mr. John Warren, President of the Irish Rugby Football Union, and director of the "Evening Mail" and of Messrs. Drought, printers, Bachelor's Walk, Dublin;

Miss Vera Doggett, 28 Smithfield, and

Miss Nora O'Donoghue, Clarence Mangan Road, South Circular Road.

Miss O'Donoghue was the only occupant of the car not a member of the Aviation Club. Mr. Mohan was secretary and Mr. Maher model secretary, while Mr. Branagan, Mr. Warren and Miss Doggett were committee members of the club.

The Injured

All but one of the injured soldiers were admitted to St. Bricin's Military Hospital. The ten still detained there yesterday were:—

Privates Thomas Alford, Patrick Mahon, Rubert Lawless, Charles O'Regan, Patrick McKevitt, Brian Dolan, Nicholas O'Neill, John Mitchell, Patrick Dwyer, James McCreath.

O'Neill is the most seriously injured. He received a fractured leg.

The other soldier, **James Whelan**, Slane Road, Kimmage, was detained in Jervis Street Hospital. It was learned last evening that he was "getting along nicely."

The driver of the 'bus, **Patrick McGuinness**, Oldbridge, Drogheda, was taken to the Mater Misericordiae Hospital, suffering from head and back injuries. He was stated yesterday to be "as comfortable as could be expected."

Activities of The Irish Junior Aviation Club

October 1937

Capt. St. John Kearney's lecture

On October 7th, Capt. St. John Kearney delivered a lecture on 'Learning to Fly' at the first Ordinary General Meeting of the winter season. The lecture was very successful and was well attended. The lecture was illustrated by a number of slides kindly loaned for the occasion by the Air League of the British Empire. Part II of Learning to Fly is dated for April 21st, 1938.

Second lecture of the Month

As has already been published, there will in future be two meetings every month and the lecture on October 21st was delivered by Mr. Chris Bruton and was entitled 'Elementary Aerodynamics'. As members will appreciate, this was a difficult subject to tackle and every praise goes to the club secretary for the way in which he handled such a technical paper.

New badges

It was announced at the last meeting that new badges were available at the usual price of 6d. Members should note that the badges are still of the original design, the only difference being the omission of the letter 'N' since the word 'National' has been excluded from the name of the club.

Affiliated to Irish Aero Club

The club is now officially affiliated to the Irish Aero Club.

Lectures by members wanted

We want to urge the reading of papers by members as much as possible. Every enthusiastic member should set about preparing such papers. Several dates are still unbooked - February 17th and April 7th, 1938. The scope for titles is unlimited. Examples of the type suitable are 'Famous Record Flights', 'Stages of Aircraft Development in the last 10 Years' etc. These papers need not be very long as it could be arranged to have two or three short lectures delivered at the one meeting if desired.

Title changed

Mr. J. R. Maher, who was to deliver a lecture entitled 'Aircraft Engines' on February 3rd, 1938, has changed his subject to 'Parachutes'.

Irish Gliding Association

IT is not generally known that we have a go-ahead Irish Gliding Association. It was inaugurated at a meeting held in the Dolphin Hotel last September. Major-General Hugo McNeill, A.C.S., representing the Department of Defence, was in the chair.

The Association is representative of all existing clubs and groups interested in Gliding in the Saorstát.

It is hoped that it will receive the approval and encouragement of the Government as a controlling and governing body for all motorless flying in the Saorstát.

The following are the officers :—
President—Mr. Frank Aiken, Minister for Defence.
Chairman—Captain A. Quirke.
Treasurer—Mr. J. Magee.
Secretary—Mr. R. W. O'Sullivan.

The provisional council consists of two members nominated by each club or group until such time as a formal constitution has been adopted. A "Rules Committee" charged with the preparation of a draft constitution, consists of Dr. Loftus, Captain Quirke, Captain Quinn and Mr. Benson.

Technical matters, such as conditions governing pilots' certificates and certificates of air-worthiness for Gliders and Sailplanes, were relegated to a technical Committee consisting of Commandant G. J. Carroll, Captain Quinn, Mr. Benson, Mr. Magee and Mr. O'Sullivan.

The Clubs which form the Association are :—
1st Slaugh (Volunteer) Gliding Club.
Dublin Gliding Club. } Now amalgamated under
National Gliding Club. } the former.
Baldonnel Gliding Club.
Gliding Section, N.I.J.A.C.

While only two primary type Gliders were actually built and in use, several Sailplanes and Primary Gliders are under construction, and many more are projected.

AVIATION, JUNE, 1935.

Subscriptions

The attention of members is drawn to the fact that subscriptions not already paid are now long overdue. The sub. of 5/- may be made in two payments of 2/6 if members so desire.

Flying section notice

Will members interested in the Flying Section please note that entry to Flight I will definitely close on Thursday, November 18th, when the election of the flight captain will take place.

Flying Aces competition

We would like all members to enter for the 'Skybirds' competition. Full particulars may be had from 'The Model Engineers Suppliers', 20 Wicklow Street.

Lord Mayor's Cup

The competition for the Lord Mayor's Cup, which will be for flying models as already announced, will be held early in 1938. All members interested should start preparing their entries for this competition. Why not compete for the 'Skybirds' competition and then enter your model for the Lord Mayor's Cup?

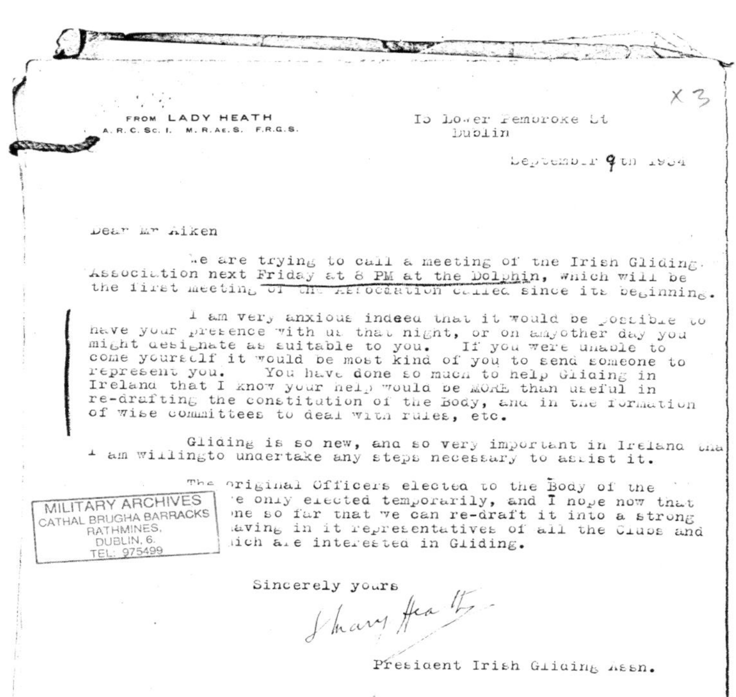

X 3

FROM LADY HEATH
A. R. C. Sc. I. M. R. Ae. S. F.R.G.S.

15 Lower Pembroke St
Dublin

September 9th 1934

Dear Mr Aiken

We are trying to call a meeting of the Irish Gliding Association next Friday at 8 PM at the Dolphin, which will be the first meeting of the Association called since its beginning.

I am very anxious indeed that it would be possible to have your presence with us that night, or on anyother day you might designate as suitable to you. If you were unable to come yourself it would be most kind of you to send someone to represent you. You have done so much to help Gliding in Ireland that I know your help would be MORE than useful in re-drafting the constitution of the Body, and in the formation of wise committees to deal with rules, etc.

Gliding is so new, and so very important in Ireland tha I am willingto undertake any steps necessary to assist it.

The original Officers elected to the Body of the ...e only elected temporarily, and I hope now that ...ne so far that we can re-draft it into a strong ...aving in it representatives of all the Clubs and ...ich are interested in Gliding.

Sincerely yours

Mary Heath

President Irish Gliding Assn.

Irish Gliding Association : letter from Lady Heath to Mr Frank Aiken, Minister for Defence, Dec. 9th 1934

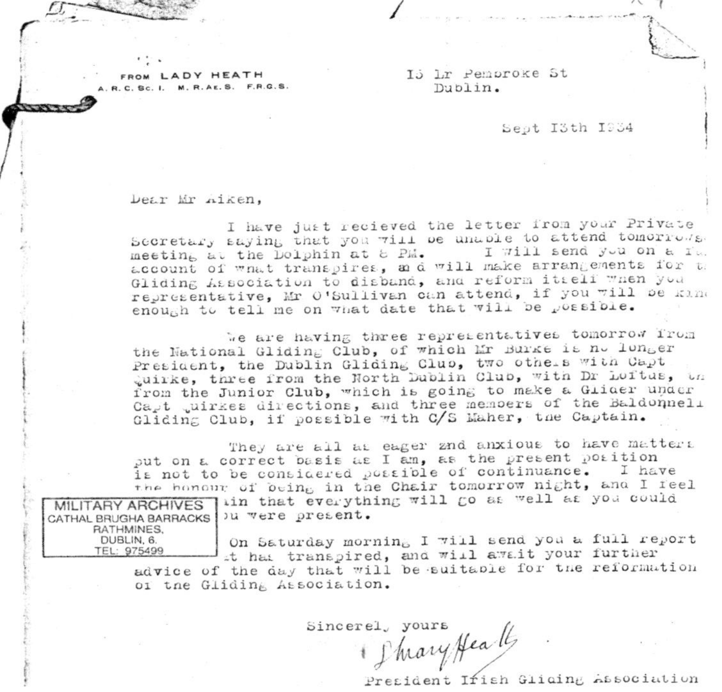

FROM LADY HEATH
A. R. C. Sc. I. M. R. Ae. S. F.R.G.S.

15 Lr Pembroke St
Dublin.

Sept 13th 1934

Dear Mr Aiken,

I have just recieved the letter from your Private Secretary saying that you will be unable to attend tomorrows meeting at the Dolphin at 8 PM. I will send you on a fu... account of what transpires, and will make arrangements for t... Gliding Association to disband, and reform itself when you representative, Mr O'Sullivan can attend, if you will be kin... enough to tell me on what date that will be possible.

We are having three representatives tomorrow from the National Gliding Club, of which Mr Burke is no longer President, the Dublin Gliding Club, two others with Capt Quirke, three from the North Dublin Club, with Dr Loftus, t... from the Junior Club, which is going to make a Glider under Capt Quirkes directions, and three members of the Baldonnell Gliding Club, if possible with C/S Maher, the Captain.

They are all as eager and anxious to have matters put on a correct basis as I am, as the present position is not to be considered possible of continuance. I have the honour of being in the Chair tomorrow night, and I feel ...ain that everything will go as well as you could ...u were present.

On Saturday morning I will send you a full report ...t has transpired, and will await your further advice of the day that will be suitable for the reformation of the Gliding Association.

Sincerely yours

Mary Heath

President Irish Gliding Association

Irish Gliding Association : letter from Lady Heath to Mr Frank Aiken, Minister for Defence, Sept. 13th, 1934

The Irish Gliding Association

Lady Heath was the first president of the Irish Gliding Association. Four letters written by her are to hand and illustrate important aspects of her interest in this aspect of the development of civil aviation in the Irish Free State. In the first letter from her home address at 15 Lower Pembroke Street, she signed herself as president of the newly formed Irish Gliding Association. It was written to Mr. Frank Aiken, the then Minister for Defence of the Irish Free State. The letter demonstrates the deference which she showed for the office and the person of the minister in question, as well as her interest in the development of organisational structures for the development of civil aviation in this country. It also shows tact in the matter of dealing with a multiplicity of different organisations. The first letter is dated the September 9th, 1934. All four letters are addressed to Frank Aiken, Minister for Defence. The second of the four letters gives an account of the different individuals and clubs involved in the sport of gliding. This letter is dated the September 13th, 1934. The third letter is dated September 16th and reports on what was regarded as a very successful meeting held to organise and consolidate the different sub-groups involved in the sport of gliding.

The fourth and final letter appears inconsistent with what had been happening up to that time and Lady Heath is presented with a fait accompli, where the presidency of the new umbrella organisation for gliding has been taken over by Mr. Aiken. Lady Heath, who had been so instrumental in doing much of the initial groundwork in getting the new organisation off the ground, did not apparently get notice of this important meeting. Nevertheless, she is very happy that Mr. Aiken had accepted the presidency and her only concern is that others, particularly the R. Hon the Lord Mayor, Alderman Alfred Byrne TD and Captain Saul, who had consented to be patron and vice-president, should be accommodated in the new structure. This letter is dated the September 30th, 1934. One wonders why there was this lack of communication in the case of a

15 Lr Pembroke St
Dublin.

Sunday Sept 16th 1934

Dear Mr Aiken.

The meeting on Friday went off very well, and I am sending you the minutes, together with a list of the names and addresses of those present. I am sending them to you by Capt Quirke, who is fortunate in being able to see you tomorrow.

Capt Quirke was the very greatest help to us at the meeting, and I think he was as pleased as I was at the way things went.

Dr Loftus had promised to attend with two other members of the North City Volounteer Club, but I was sorry not to have the pleasure of seeing him there..

I hope to hear from you soon as to the date you would like to get the interested people together again for the new wo[rk] you are kind enough to be going to help us with.

If I may venture the remark, I would like to say how very fortunate we are in having the advice and assistance of your good self. I know you are going to help us to put this movement on the solid substantial basis it deverves.

Sincerely yours

Mary Heath

Irish Gliding Association: letter from Lady Heath to Mr Frank Aiken, Minister of Defence, Sept. 16th, 1934

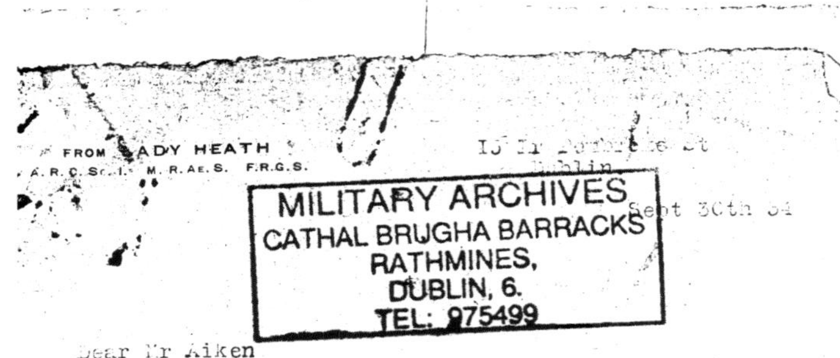

FROM LADY HEATH
A.R.C.Sc.I. M.R.Ae.S. F.R.G.S.

15 Lr Pembroke St
Dublin

Sept 30th 34

Dear Mr Aiken

I am very happy to hear that a new Irish Gliding Association has been formed, and I would like if I may to thank you very heartily for taking the Presidency. It is just what the body needs, and I know it will be a real success from now on.

I do so wish I had had a notice of the meeting as I would absolutely have loved to be present. Even my Junior club did not tell me of it.

Will you think me impertinent to make one or two points of some little importance to me clear to you. The Rt Hon the Lord Mayor, Alderman Alfred Byrne, TD. consented to become Patron of the old Association, and Capt Saul, on my proposal consented to become Vice President. Would it be possible to use these men in any way?. I would be so grateful if you would consent.

Sincerely yours

Mary Heath

Irish Gliding Association: letter from Lady Heath to Mr Frank Aiken, Minister of Defence, Sept. 30th, 1934

The Luftwaffe, whose symbol was a silver seagull worn on the arm, was the secret airforce which was preparing for war. Training as glider pilots was an essential part of their training in Germany. Adolf Hitler, on March 23rd, 1933, had established himself as dictator of Germany by means of the 'Enabling Act', which eliminated Parliament as a political force. All Europe knew his intentions

person of the status of Lady Heath, which on the surface appears to verge on the discourteous. Whether the decision to exclude Lady Heath from the developmental stage in the history of gliding in Ireland was a personal snub, or whether it was motivated by the philosophy to keep things related to flying/gliding in the control of the army, it is not possible to say. The latter interpretation will suffice. However, common courtesy suggests that she should have been properly informed.

It is easier to understand why the military would want to keep strict control over all flying because of what was happening in Europe. The Treaty of Versailles, June 21st, 1919, had placed severe restriction on the development of air power capability on the part of Germany. However, one way around the restrictions was to develop gliding clubs in order to train pilots, while others were trained in Russia. The Luftwaffe, whose symbol was a silver seagull worn on the arm, was the secret airforce which was preparing for war. Training as glider pilots was an essential part of their training in Germany. Adolf Hitler, on March 23rd, 1933 had established himself as dictator of Germany by means of the 'Enabling Act', which eliminated Parliament as a political force. All Europe knew his intentions, which had been spelt out clearly in 'Mein Kampf' which he had written while a prisoner in Landsberg Prison (November 1923-December 1924). The clear message from these writings, which were anti-semitic, was the need as Hitler saw for Germany to acquire living-space, 'Lebenstruam', in eastern Europe. In the quiet oasis of flying at Kildonan, there was little thought of war, but for those whose business was to govern, the storm-clouds of war were already in the offing. The Spanish Civil War, 1936-1939, only copper fastened the inevitability of serious European conflict. Germany had backed the victorious Nationalists.

Single seater gliders were flown at Kildonan, including the 'Gruno Baby' and the 'Scud'.

There appeared to have been a problem of acceptability for Lady Heath. In the early 1930s, she had kept her aircraft at Baldonnel and tried to work with the Irish Aero Club, but soon decided to move to Kildonan. The problem of acceptability appears to have been due to several factors, including the fact that perhaps she married a titled person, Lord Heath; the fact that she was a woman; and the attitudes of the establishment. The Irish Aero Club was founded on status and social acceptability. As an organisation it was male dominated. The Irish Aero Club was the self-appointed arbiter of what was good or bad for civil aviation in the Irish Free State. There were some notable exceptions to the general attitudes of the organisation, however, but in general they failed utterly to recognise the greatness of Lady Heath's achievements. But this did not bother her. She was Ireland's greatest aviator/aviatrix in terms of the number, magnitude, status, uniqueness and individual character of her aeronautical achievements and in the extent of her personal commitment to the promotion of civil aviation in the Irish Free State. But Lady Heath, who had broken down so many barriers to the progress of women in aviation and in other spheres of life, found the entrenched conservatism of the Irish Aero Club more impenetrable. Lady Heath, after long and careful thought, decided to leave the conservative Irish Aero Club for the blue skies and green pastures of Kildonan, Finglas. Its openness, friendliness and unique ambiance was like a breath of fresh air, a relief from the stuffiness of the establishment. At Kildonan, Hugh Cahill, entrepreneur par excellence, had created a unique environment in which innovation and new ideas could be tried and tested.

But Lady Heath, who had broken down so many barriers to the progress of women in aviation and in other spheres of life, found the entrenched conservatism of the Irish Aero Club more impenetrable

Lady Heath's leaving of the Irish Aero Club at Baldonnel was probably due to many factors including the fact that the I.A.C. was not prepared to afford her voice on equal terms with other persons closely associated with the club. The Irish Aero Club also over charged her for routine maintenance and repair of her aircraft and they managed to ignore almost completely her mammoth achievements, while big celebrations were organised by them for lesser achievers. A decision at one of the club's meetings to present a small plaque to Lady Heath appears not to have been acted upon. The club failed to invite her to important functions, to

The Irish Aero Club also over charged her for routine maintenance and repair of her aircraft and they managed to ignore almost completely her mammoth achievements, while big celebrations were organised by them for lesser achievers

which she should not only have been invited, but by any yardstick should have been one of the special guests - in fact arguably pride of place was what she deserved. But it was not only Lady Heath who was exasperated with the Irish Aero Club. Other eminent aviators of the stature of O. E. Armstrong, who later became chief pilot of Aer Lingus, felt the same way and for good reason. It was not unusual for the Irish Aero Club on important occasions to ignore completely the very existence of Kildonan Aerodrome and those associated with it. Things came to a head when, on the very important occasion of National Aviation Day in 1934 which took place in the Phoenix Park and was organised by the Irish Aero Club, neither Kildonan Aerodrome nor any of the individuals associated with it were invited to participate in the displays and air races. On this occasion, even the cool-headed O.E. Armstrong, a world class aviator, a pioneer in Irish civil aviation and a mainstay at Kildonan, had had enough and submitted his resignation to the Irish Aero Club.

Latterly, thankfully, there are people dedicated to honouring the achievements of great Irish aviators of the past. Foremost in this movement has been Mr. Freddie Bond and the 'Trailblazers', a voluntary organisation of aviators of the past.

Lady Heath's scholarship

One of Lady Heath's innovations was the creation of the Lady Heath Scholarship, which was set up to be administered by the Irish Aero Club. This flying scholarship was sponsored in conjunction with the Air League of the British Empire. The scholarship was for women and the first person to receive the award was Miss Shamrock Trench.

The Tramway Aero Club

Lady Heath decided to follow a trend which was starting off all over Britain. Large firms like the British Cable Company and the General Post Office were making flying available to their employees. The British Cable Company was the first to set the trend in this regard. Lady Heath decided to do the same for the Dublin Tramway Company. It was formed in 1937 by the employees of the Dublin United Tramways Company and Lady Heath. The aircraft and instructors of the Dublin Air Ferries Ltd. at Kildonan provided the training facilities. This company owned by Jack Williams and Lady Heath was the third of three companies which operated at different times from Kildonan. The number of members rose to 80. The club existed for about one year. Instruction was available for 30 shillings an hour, which was very reasonable at the time. This was an example of another innovation on the part of Lady Heath. Companies in Britain who set up their flying clubs had in some cases large workforces. The companies subsidised the members so that they could in fact have instruction at a rate even lower than the established clubs associated with the aerodromes. The establishment of these clubs was an incentive to the employees and deemed of value to the prestige of the company and the morale of the workforce. This new departure proved quite a success in the case of Britain. The Dublin United Tramway Company was at the time one of the largest companies in Dublin. When the possibility of setting up a club for this company was discussed at Kildonan, Fr. Furlong, Ireland's first flying priest, offered the use of his aircraft, an Aeronca C3 EI-ABN, ex. G-AKFU, to be used as the training aircraft for the new club. The Aeronca was a small low horse-power aircraft (40 brake horse power - 38 in fact). It was a cabin, high-wing, side by side seater and was extremely low to the ground so that it could easily be damaged if the landing was not a good one.

This aircraft is listed in the Register of Aircraft as having been registered in Fr. Furlong's name on June 16th, 1937. However, May 1936 is regarded by some observers at the time as being a more accurate date for the commencement of the Dublin United Tramway Club and for the utilisation of the Aeronca in connection with the club's activities. Fr. Furlong was its chairman.

DUTC (Dublin United Tram Company) - Balcony Tram (Windjammer) No. 128

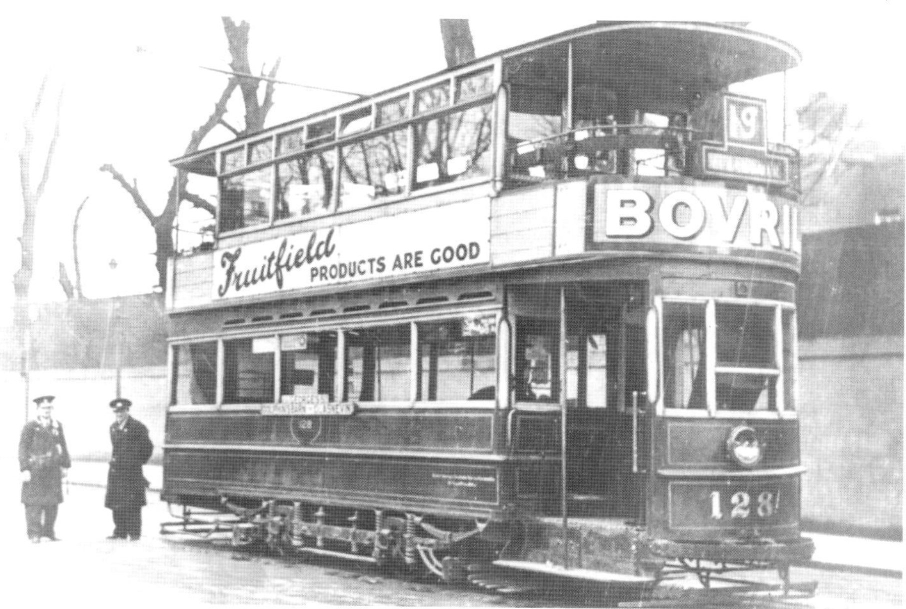

The No.19 Tram which served Finglas. Photo courtesy of The Transport Museum

This tram replaced an older vehicle. It was built as an open topper incorporating inside roof, doors and quarters of an older tram. It was laid down on May 15th, 1919 and left the works on September 20th, 1919. The original truck was transferred to No. 234 while the car was undergoing an overhaul from the 12/4/27 - 25/8/27. It received a Brill truck ex car 142 and was working on route 12 in 1928. It received top cover from car 58 between 16/5/29 and 9/10/29 and was working route 24 on 12/10/29. Numeral blinds fitted in replacement of old route plates 23/10/36. This tram was probably withdrawn in 1939 and scrapped shortly afterwards at either Donnybrook or Dartry

Trams in O' Connell Street, Dublin

Oliver St. John Gogarty

Lady Heath and Oliver St. John Gogarty were firm friends. In September 1928, Lady Heath and Gogarty, who had flown from Renvyle to Tullabawn Strand in the West of Ireland, got stuck on soft sand and were unable to take off again. Lady Heath had to remain for a few days in one of the local cottages until a new propeller with a fuller pitch could be flown down from Dublin, enabling the plane to take off again. James Joyce, one time friend of Gogarty, refers to the incident which he read from a newspaper in a letter to Harriet Weaver. Joyce wrote: "I am glad to see that Buck Mulligan was unhurt." Gogarty who figures in James Joyce's 'Ulysses' as Buck Mulligan, lived in the Martello Tower with Joyce (Stephen Dedalus). Gogarty had invited Joyce to live with him in the tower to enable Joyce to concentrate on his writings.

Oliver St. John Gogarty, aged 21, as a student at Trinity College, Dublin

Gogarty started his flying at the Irish Army Air Corps at Baldonnel Aerodrome, Dublin. His confidence in flying was strengthened by a visit to the Bristol Aircraft Company, where his friend Captain Cyril Unwin, a famous test pilot, had shown him the factory.

On August 16th, 1928, Gogarty proposed the setting up of the Irish Aero Club and became a founder member of this club, which included members of a wide variety of professions including prominent politicians. One of the members who owned his own aircraft was Sir Osmonde Grattan-Esmonde, a member of the Dail and a direct descendant of Henry Grattan.

Although Gogarty was fascinated by flying and had considerable experience with and knowledge of engines, he did not aspire to acquiring the more advanced skills of flying. In fact, he preferred to be co-pilot rather than pilot and had to be flown rather than fly himself in a lot of situations. This is clear from his own comments. On one occasion when considering taking part in an air display at Ards Aerodrome on November 28th, 1934, he wrote to Montgomery Hyde: "I'm rather limited in my stunts but if you see a Moth plane, blue IU, coming from the south, along the west border of Strangford Lough at 4,000 feet, it will be mine. All I can do is to lose height by half a dozen spins, a loop or two and a landing (this last, I hope, shall not be exceptional)."

In 1945 Gogarty described himself as 'One of the first and worst pilots in Ireland'. Gogarty was familiar with Kildonan Aerodrome and often crossed to Bristol with Captain O. E. Armstrong, who spent many years flying at Kildonan before joining Aer Lingus as chief pilot of the new airline. Gogarty, champion athlete, swimmer, surgeon, senator of the Irish Free State, dramatist, poet and aviator, was fascinated by the poetry of motion: "Movement, the ritual and recognition of the Divine nature of our substance, which directs ours bodies towards the All-mover, the PRIMUM MOBILE, whose glory thrills and penetrates the Universe". Gogarty was not just a dreamer; he made very practical use of the skills he perfected. For example, he saved three people from drowning in the Liffey. His view of the inventor was as part of the genius of creativity which makes the poet or artist.

Lady Heath at Tullabawn Strand, unable to take off because of the soft sands, is forced to wait for a replacement propeller for three days, September 1928 J. Cashman

Oliver St. John Gogarty, firm friend of Lady Heath, was also chronicler of the air and poet who recorded in verse the memories of prominent pilots of the time killed in flight. One of his first descriptions of flight appeared in A.E.'s 'Irish Statesman' in the 1920s. A.E. (George Russell) was a friend of Gogarty. The flight in question was one which he made to Bristol in one of Captain Cyril Unwin's aircraft.

"The engine is already running. We are blown by the slipstream as we climb into the cockpit, which is the portal of the blue sky. The seat is so far down that we are up to our neck and feel secure without a belt as with one. But we put the belt on. It steadies the midriff and, like that whiskey mentioned by Hollinshead, it prevents 'the belly from wambling and the stomach from wurching: it puffeth away all ventosities! And here is a 'ventosity', a true air adventure! What if we crash! I notice that the young men around us have no time to dally with the idea of death and, anyway, all one wants to be faced with is good company. It is not dying but flying that we are engaged in now. The roar of the engine increases and increases your assurance. I find that my courage such as it is, is largely a matter of horse-power. If you put your face outside, the little windscreen may blow open or your lips may be blown across your teeth. This is the reason for telephones. Without them it would be impossible for the pilot to speak to the pupil. The men leaning against the wings and the man who leans on the tail, leave go. The wedges are pulled from under the wheels. Our speed increases. It is growing over 60 miles an hour. The seat which slanted back is level now. Our tail is up. Vibration is intermittent. Now there is none at all. We are flying. The air speed rises to 100 miles per hour. Up we go, climbing almost vertically, as few machines can climb. The air speed lessens the more vertical we are. But now another indicator tells us that we are 2,500 feet above the earth, 'the deck' the young men call it. The same young men who christened the cockpit with its array of instruments 'the office' - young men remembering perhaps, the sanctum of some rheumatic uncle, merchant or stockbroker with its barometer, thermometer and clocks. But this 'office' is a magic room - your relations to the sides of which have but little to do with your relations to the world outside. You may be upside down and you would hardly notice it. Presently the floor seems to be surging upwards. Our heads bend forward towards our knees. 'Put your head back,' says the telephone. And on putting it back we see two horizons simultaneously. What phenomenon is this? We are upside down. We are looping the loop. There is a slight vibration again. It is our own airy wake we are in; we have struck our own slipstream. A proof of how perfect the pilot can loop. We are climbing again - 3,000 feet, 3,500 feet now. 'You have control; says the telephone. Good Lord! 'I' have control! Steady! Perhaps it would be as well to begin with a little self-control. Steady now, O son of Daedalus! Let me see! That cross-bar at my heels is the rudder - dual control. This black, rubber-covered, vertical lever is 'the stick' - also dual control. We remember fragments of conversation. 'If you put too much rudder without bank you will get into a flat spin.' 'If you give her too much bank without rudder her nose will come down.' But the machine seems to be flying all right. Unfortunately, the pilot knows that it flies automatically, otherwise he might give me credit...I really must do something to...make it wobble even. That brown canal down there with the waves like those of Botticelli's Birth of Venus is the Bristol Channel. 'Look at your left wing'. Ah, yes, it is dropping. I lean my thumb ever so gently against the tremulous 'stick'. 'You are flying level now'. So I had control even though I didn't do much with it. No silence on earth is equal to it. It falls on the spirit softer than sleep. I can understand the trance that fell on Aucassin, though he was in mid-battle, a trance which made him oblivious of danger, in which he became lost to everything but love. Even from that, at this altitude, there is peace. Here, I may take mine ease in mine ether. This is better than the Immense Void in the Zodiac which the Chinese found so repellent, but in which I thought of sojourning after death for the sake of a little privacy. It lies between the great Splendour and the Fire of the Phoenix, but up here one can 'achieve the Term' and live in Nirvana just as well without the absenteeism of death. 'Si quis piorum animum locus'; I have found it. This must be it, this place for pious souls. Here the spirit rests like younger Julia in her bath on whom Ovid spied. 'She lay at length like an immortal soul In endless bliss in blest Elysium.'

Gogarty was deeply moved by the death of his instructor William Elliott, chief instructor of the Irish Aero Club, and wrote:

"It's not the unreached or unseen;
It's not the 'What might have been';
It's neither this nor that, because
We loved him for the man he was:
A sail top-gallant of the air,
High Admiral of the atmosphere!
Honour his ensign: when he sailed
Or landed, still his flag was nailed.
He worked long-tried and wearied not;
Perfection was the least he taught;
And he could make your spirit stir
By dint of simple character:
Cheerful, trustworthy, clean and bold;
He makes his grave a mine of gold;
And heedless schoolboys may forget
Great names, remembering Elliott."

William Robert Elliott, first permanent chief instructor of the Irish Aero Club. Joined R. A. F. 1919, served Constantinople, 1922-1923.

Gogarty's instructors at Baldonnel were Captain Crosley, Sergeant Elliott and French. Gogarty was a friend of Arthur Russell and wrote the following on the tragic death of his friend.

In memory of my friend, Arthur Russell, Soldier and Statesman

He had the kind and languorous air
Of gentle knights detached from fear;
And he was quiet in his ways.
He who could set the heavens ablaze
And overtake the sinking sun
With speed and soar into his throne.
If modesty clothes bravery.
If gentleness activity:
If earth has ever been the pen
Of heaven-aspiring denizen.
Then Arthur comes into his own
From lowly things released and flown,
And stands for that haut chivalry
Which scorns the world and scales the sky:
So Death, which no brave spirit harms
Let him pass out retaining arms.

10/9/1934, Oliver St. John Gogarty.

Gogarty bridged the gap between the aviator and the poet. His literary achievements got the highest commendations. W. B. Yeats praised his work, to which Gogarty replied:

"There was a kind poet called Yeats

Who put me with those whom he rates-

Don't think it bad of me - In this Academy;

Off which of our heads are the slates?"

Yeats had described Gogarty as one of the great lyrical poets of the day. Gogarty was highly praised for his literary achievements by such eminent people as Professor Mario Rossi, an Italian scholar and A. E.(George Russell). While a prisoner in a house beside the Liffey during the Irish Civil War, Gogarty escaped, plunging into the ice-cold December river liffey under a shower of bullets. As he swam the Liffey he promised it that should it land him in safety, he would present it with two swans, a promise which he later fulfilled.

As a senator he played a significant part in the debates of the day and claimed that Eamon De Valera had done more damage to Ireland than Cromwell. De Valera abolished university representation in the Dail and abolished the Senate between 1934 and 1936.

On one occasion, Gogarty crashed, landing on a sheep at Baldonnel Aerodrome. He stated that sheep should not have been permitted on a properly conducted aerodrome. With regard to the Government's attitude, he stated that the 'Government at the time had neither heart nor vision for aviation. One would think that they had invented and pioneered it now.' (Letter written from New York, Hotel Chatham, December 6th, 1945). Gogarty was born in 1878 and died in New York in 1957.

In 1990, Aer Lingus celebrated its 50th anniversary. Due to Ireland's membership of the European Union, discrimination against women has been greatly lessened and all jobs have been open to both sexes. Grainne Cronin (Mrs. Neil Johnson) was Aer Lingus' first woman pilot and the first woman captain the national airline has had. To many, this is a historic breakthrough. To others, it is indicative of the discrimination which had taken place in the Irish job scene generally for the best part of 50 years. In the context of this discriminatory atmosphere, Grainne's achievements are considerable indeed. Lady Heath had fought for the equality of treatment for women and achieved the historic breakthrough in the 1920s when she became the first woman to receive a commercial licence in Britain. One of the routes in the commuter division had all women crew, which illustrates the kind of progress that this airline has made in the recent past promoting accessibility for women in the air.

Aer Lingus, July 1991, New pilots with Minister for Transport and Communications, Mr. Seamus Brennan (fourth from left)

PEARSE'S ANGELS

Some of the lady flyers who learned to fly at Iona;

Top: Liz Ryan, Centre: Camilla Tsan, Top right: Niamh O' Connor, Bottom Right: Siobhan Coughey and Carol McCluskey

Aer Lingus celebrates its 50th anniversary. In the foreground, an air hostess with the original uniform of the company and in the background, the 'Iolar', the sister craft of the very first aircraft flown by Aer Lingus. Photo courtesy of Aer Lingus

Grainne Cronin

Grainne Cronin, the first Aer Lingus woman pilot and the first woman to command an Aer Lingus aircraft, flew first as an air hostess and started her training as a pilot in September 1977. In 1979 she flew the Boeing 737 fleet as co-pilot and flew as systems pilot on Boeing 747 (Jumbos). She also flew the Shorts 360 Commuters. Grainne's husband, Captain Neil Johnson, was also an Aer Lingus pilot. Grainne got her first flying lessons in her father's Piper Cub aircraft. Her father, Captain Felim Cronin, became a senior pilot with Aer Lingus. He retired in 1986 and to mark the occasion Grainne flew as his co-pilot on his last flight. She was born in County Clare and studied at University College Dublin.

Lillian Bland was Ireland's first woman pilot. She lived at Carmoney near Belfast. In 1910 she constructed her own bi-plane which she named the "Mayfly". This was the first bi-plane constructed in Ireland. she succeeded in getting the aircraft off the ground and it flew at an altitude of 30ft for a short distance at Randalstown.

Lynn Ripplemeyer, first woman captain of Boeing 747 jet 1984

In the final chapter of her book, 'Women of the Air', Judy Lomax states:

"When women pilots cease to become news, other than for outstanding achievements regardless of sex, the battle fought by pioneers such as Lady Heath, Amy Johnson, Amelia Earhart, Jacqueline Cochran and Jacqueline Auriol and by many others whose names have been all but forgotten will have been won."
(Conclusion - Equality at Last? Judy Lomax 'Women of the Air'. p. 201.)

Lady Heath was a trendsetter in a whole lot of spheres of life, leading women into professions from which they had traditionally been excluded. She broke down the barriers of discrimination against women in aviation, including commercial. Her single mindedness and dedication led her to enter other male preserves, including engineering and athletics. Through her efforts, women gained access to Olympic competition. Another characteristic of Lady Heath, which differentiated her from many other pioneers of aviation of the time, was her individuality. Others achieved with the back-up of large retinues, whether technical, professional or advisory. Lady Heath's achievements were entirely her own personal successes and were not dependent on others. This is one of the reasons why her achievements have not got the publicity which they deserved.

Sophie's death

Lady Heath had been ill for some time and went into a nursing home in London in late 1938. She died in May 1939 at St. Leonard's Hospital, Shoreditch, London from injuries received in a fall from a London tramcar. Mary Russell, who wrote a book about women travellers of the world called 'The Blessings of a Good Thick Skirt', described Sophie Pierce's great achievements and christened her 'The Glittering Butterfly' who had dared to fly higher than any other woman. Sophie's love for her native Newcastle stayed with her right to the end. Her last wish was that her remains would be cremated and her ashes be taken by aeroplane and strewn over the Square in Newcastle West. Her wish was acceded to. Today, the Pierce family house is gone and the house of Captain Richbel Curling, agent of the Earl of Devon's Limerick Lands, also a prominent house in the square is gone. The Church of Ireland church with its fine stone walls, another prominent building on the square, are all gone. But the flame of the memory of Sophie Pierce grows and grows and where her ashes fell from the sky, sweet flowers grow.

The Oakwood Arms Hotel, near Shannon Airport, is dedicated to the memory of Sophie Pierce - the following song, written by a local singer Tadgh Horan, is displayed permanently in the hotel.

CERTIFIED COPY OF AN ENTRY OF DEATH GIVEN AT THE GENERAL REGISTER OFFICE, LONDON

Application Number Y104922

REGISTRATION DISTRICT Shoreditch

1939. DEATH in the Sub-district of Shoreditch N.E. in the Metropolitan Borough of Shoreditch

Columns:— 1 No.	1 When and Where died	2 Name and surname	3 Sex	4 Age	5 Occupation	6 Cause of death	7 Signature, description and residence of informant	8 When registered	9 Signature of registrar
237	Ninth May 1939 St Leonard's Hospital	Mary Sophie Catherine Tereoa Williams	Female	45 years	of 25 Princes Square Paddington formerly wife of George Reginald Williams from whom she obtained divorce	Shock from multiple injuries sustained when deceased fell down the stairs of a Tramcar accidental P.M.	Certificate received from R. B. Hervey Wyatt, Coroner for County of London Inquest held 11th May 1939	Eleventh May 1939	Simpson Registrar

CERTIFIED to be a true copy of an entry in the certified copy of a Register of Deaths in the District above mentioned.
Given at the GENERAL REGISTER OFFICE, LONDON, under the Seal of the said Office, the 5th day of February 1990

This certificate is issued in pursuance of the Births and Deaths Registration Act 1953. Section 34 provides that any certified copy of an entry purporting to be sealed or stamped with the seal of the General Register Office shall be received as evidence of the birth or death to which it relates without any further or other proof of the entry, and no certified copy purporting to have been given in the said Office shall be of any force or effect unless it is sealed or stamped as aforesaid.

DX 484753

CAUTION:—It is an offence to falsify a certificate or to make or knowingly use a false certificate or a copy of a false certificate intending it to be accepted as genuine to the prejudice of any person, or to possess a certificate knowing it to be false without lawful authority.

Form A504M Dd 8098433 8640481 20M 11/89 Mcr(738310)

Certificate of Lady Heath's death

Sophie's Dream

Sophie first saw the light in a West Limerick town
As on the eighteen hundreds the curtain was about to come down
She watched the little birds fly as she played in the square
And she promised herself that someday she'd join them there.
II
Sophie was growing her schoolday passed quickly it seems
She saw herself flying up there each night in her dreams
Further and further and higher and higher she flew

Chorus
And this dreamer of dreams became known as the queen of the air
You can be sure that her spirits still flying out there
High above us the jet trails disintegrate into the blue
As if to remind us that Sophie's dream has come true.
III
As the world danced the Charlston young Sophie was learning to fly
The dream of a lifetime came true as she took to the sky
She soared twenty-three thousand feet in her one-engined plane
No woman flew higher before or would fly again.
IV
From Capetown to London is ten thousand miles
The history books beckoned and Sophie took-off with a smile
With a sense of adventure she flew on a wing and a prayer
And the Lady just laughed at the danger awaiting up there.
Chorus
V
It was forty-three years since the day that she first saw the light
When the time it arrived for Sophie to make her last flight
Her loved ones below said a prayer as her ashes fell down
Her last wish was to come back to her little town.
VI
Down the road there's an airport where the big jets take off
and touch down
The Oakwood Arms Hotel stands stately outside Shannon town
It's there you'll find Sophie, her portrait it hangs on the wall
An appropriate place for the dreamer who started it all.
Chorus

Words and Music, Tadhg Horan.

Lady Heath recieves a bouquet of flowers on her arrival at Croydon aerodrome, following her epic flight from Capetown, South Africa May 17th. 1928

Appendices

Appendices

Appendix 1

Kindonan Roll Call - Supplementary

While some of the names mentioned below are included in the text of the book for others it has not been possible to get material for the publication. Yet they and others were part of the golden age of flying at Kildonan. As additional details became available the record can be in time made more complete.

Mr. Oliver Morrogh Ryan

Mr. R. Little

Mr. George Everett

Mr. C. Kirkwood Hackett held the Irish time record by going solo after only three hours and 30 minutes

Mr. J. Thurlowe

Mr. Byrne, apprentice G. E.

Miss Rosenthal

Mr. Lennox

Mr. McCormack

Mr. Crosbie

Mr. George Cooke

Mr. Hill - kept a Miles Hawk at Kildonan Aerodrome

Mr. C. Scott

Mr. A. Barry

Dr. R. Warren Darley

Mr. G. C. Whiteside

Mr. Bateson

Mr. McCaul

Mr. Robert Little

Mr. Hill

Mr. Dalton, who was from Northern Ireland

John C. O'Donnell of Galway

H. W. R. Graham

Mr. Eberell who had a keen interest in gliding

Mr. Hartie - well known in gliding circles

Mr. Joly

Mr. McDermott

Mr. D. Delaney

Mr. E. J. Gleeson

Mr. B. Regan

Miss K. Wilson

Miss N. Wilson

Mr. Claude Wilson

Mr. Peacock, who was deaf and dumb, who had to be trained entirely by signs and he knew no hand language

Finglas in the 1990s

Foynes, Co.Limerick - Landing place for Flying Boats

Notes